Connections I

Connections I

A Cognitive Approach to Intermediate Chinese

Jennifer Li-chia Liu

劉力嘉

Illustrations by Chee Keong Kung

This book is a publication of

Indiana University Press
601 North Morton Street
Bloomington, IN 47404-3797 USA

http://iupress.indiana.edu

Telephone orders   800-842-6796
Fax orders   812-855-7931
Orders by e-mail   iuporder@indiana.edu

The paper used in this publication meets the minimum requirements of
American National Standard for Information Sciences—Permanence of
Paper for Printed Library Materials, ANSI Z39.48-1984.

Manufactured in the United States of America

Cataloging information is available from the Library of Congress

By Jennifer Li-chia Liu
ISBN 0-253-21663-X paperback (Connections I)
ISBN 0-253-21664-8 paperback (Connections I: Workbook)
ISBN 0-253-34385-2 CD-ROM (Connections)

ISBN 978-0-253-21663-2 paperback (Connections I)
ISBN 978-0-253-21664-9 paperback (Connections I: Workbook)
ISBN 978-0-253-34385-7 CD-ROM (Connections)

By Jennifer Li-chia Liu
ISBN 0-253-21665-6 paperback (Connections II)
ISBN 0-253-21666-4 paperback (Connections II: Workbook)

ISBN 978-0-253-21665-6 paperback (Connections II)
ISBN 978-0-253-21666-3 paperback (Connections II: Workbook)

2   3   4   5   6   14   13   12   11   10   09

Contents

目錄

6.	Fashion and Leisure	Talking about hobbies Commenting on songs and pop stars Discussing movies Asking for and giving advice	S千萬別/要/得V 本來/原來…現在/後來… 一來…二來…(三來…) 多(麼)Adj啊 向來(不); 從來不V; 沒V過 (O) (只要)…就好了/就行了/就可以了	世紀偉愛 導演拍片 清楚精彩 失望認靠 象足土目
7.	Dating and Making Friends	Asking someone out Meeting an old friend Talking about appearance and personality Talking about a date	S到底QW(呢) A對B的印象Adj S竟然(不/沒)V V(不)出(O)來; (沒)V出(O)來 …要不然/要不/不然 S 也/就 難怪/怪不得S…	竟遇姑娘 互罵呆聰 惜戴鏡架 印滿咖啡 猜伙排班
8.	Love and Marriage	Expressing surprise Showing disapproval Relating an event Sharing a concern	能V…就V S非(要/得)VO不可 …，再說… A嫌B sth. negative A受到(B的)歧視/影響/歡迎 A為B Adj/VO	洋化背景 幸福保守 將白勸醒 歧觀偏嫌 克困代件
9.	Family and Gender Roles	Indicating wishes Making concessions Asking for and responding to help Summarizing opinions	(每)(當)…(的)時(候) …，總之… 任何O (S) 都V S (等)V₁(了)(以後)再V₂ S好(不)容易才V 為了A, B; B是為了/為的是A	任何夫婦 母顧庭務 職業由運 主幹爭願 需須燒之
10.	Education and Career	Urging someone to do something else Expressing doubts Giving consent Objecting to an idea	S不但V₁O₁，連O₂也V₁ V著玩兒(的) 在 sb. 看來 即使/就算S…，(S) 也… 在 sb. 的N下; 在N上/方面 連A都(不/沒)…，更別說B了	即使游泳 尊敬藝術 處理成績 聯畫立功 試例鋼育

Preface

Connections I and *II* is a complete course designed for students who have finished the equivalent of one year of Chinese in a typical college setting in the U.S. or abroad. This intermediate series is closely coordinated, in terms of vocabulary, characters, grammatical structures, and approach, with its predecessor, *Interactions I and II*. It is intended for learners with diverse interests and backgrounds and varying degrees of exposure to Chinese language and culture. No matter whether one's skills are well developed in some respects but lacking in others or whether one has no other training in the language beyond a first-year course, one will find these two learner-centered textbooks accommodating, motivating, and thought-provoking. In these textbooks one's individual needs and learning styles are facilitated by a balanced and multimodal treatment of the four language skills. Essential information is supplemented with explanatory notes, diagrams, tables, and graphics.

I. Rationale and Instructional Design

A number of convictions underlie the writing of this intermediate Chinese textbook. First, the method of instruction is a cognitive approach. The idea behind this approach is that effective teaching of Chinese must go beyond rote practice and linguistic information, by focusing on students' thought processes in order to promote more active and meaningful learning. Therefore, this book is designed to enable one not only to constructively *interact* with the language, but also to make *connections* with the language by means of mnemonic and allusive aids. For example, whenever possible, vocabulary terms are reintroduced from chapter to chapter. Grammar is explicated not only with linguistic rules but also by naming the semantic purpose of a given sentence pattern. Characters in the vocabulary lists are often listed with those of similar graphs or pronunciation, so that appropriate links between characters are made. Furthermore, a variety of texts such as narrative, dialogue, stories, journal entries, riddles, jokes, news headline and ads are all included to enrich one's learning of the language.

Second, language acquisition is enhanced with texts written from a learner's perspective rather than that of the teacher. In these textbooks, the lesson topics revolve around events relevant to students' lives, such as studying abroad, weekend activities, and so on. The relationships between the four personae created in *Interactions*, a Chinese from mainland China, another from Taiwan, a non-Chinese American, and a Chinese American, are further developed in *Connections*, introducing respective family members and a new series of concerns and situations.

Third, so that one acquires natural, appropriate, and contextualized language rather than contrived textbook idioms, students are exposed not only to language structures but also to the dynamic use of language in varied socio-cultural contexts. "Appropriateness" is valued over what might be considered "standard." Thus, the different forms of Chinese characters (traditional vs. simplified) and usage (mainland China vs. Taiwan) are presented. As to the criteria for the texts, naturalness and frequency of use take precedence over considerations of difficulty. Texts are communication-oriented rather than grammar-centered. Nonetheless, due attention was paid to include most of the common linguistic structures identified in *The Standard Outline of Grammatical Levels for Chinese* 漢語水平等級標準與語法等級大綱 (1996) as appropriate for intermediate learners of Chinese. In addition, as a departure from traditional explications of grammar points, patterns and usage are presented from a functional perspective so that their "semantic value" will be easily registered in the learner's mind. Efforts were made to derive descriptions of the structures that will be comprehensible to students. Because it is a semantic approach, it is bound to be subjective and might seem inexact at some point. Still, while it might not be as plausible to come up with a typology for the semantic aspect of a structure as it is for the syntactic aspect, I believe that it can be very beneficial to learners if the descriptions are precise and consistent.

Fourth, knowledge of culture, both past and present, is inseparable from target language instruction. Therefore, included in each lesson is important cultural information that can help one develop a better understanding of Chinese people and society.

Fifth, timeliness is an important factor in the organization of the lessons. Therefore, a chapter which touches upon Chinese New Year is the first chapter of the winter term coinciding with the actual event. The same goes for the Mid-Autumn and Tomb Sweeping festivals.

Sixth, maximum learning results are achieved not merely by studying hard, but by studying effectively and cleverly. To help one in this regard, these textbooks provide numerous learning cues to help students focus on key information. There are cues to lesson vocabulary listings and indexes facilitating review and preview of vocabulary and grammar. There are also helpful graphics and illustrations to maintain learning interest and provoke class discussions.

II. Organization of the Text
These books consist of twenty lessons, 1 through 10 in **Connections I** and 11 through 20 in **Connections II**. These chapter topics progress from everyday situations to more abstract concerns. In addition, each lesson focuses on a particular theme, discussing current issues as well as important cultural concepts and practices.

Lesson Topics
Lesson 1 introduces usage related to greeting and terms of address through the narration of an American going abroad to study and his first encounter in China. Lesson 2, with a description of the school facilities and the American's peculiar roommate, explains the Chinese way of showing concern. Lesson 3 covers Mid-Autumn Festival, an important Chinese holiday, and the protocol of host and guest. Lesson 4 narrates the American student's weekend activities, focusing on interesting phenomena of Chinese daily life, such as morning exercises and bargaining with street peddlers. Lesson 5 deals with American and Chinese cuisine, introducing many expressions related to food and food preparation. Lesson 6, with its topic, fashion and leisure, describes the confession of a Chinese female who falls in love with her internet friend and her plans for meeting him in

person. While introducing phrases concerning personality and appearance, Lesson 7 tells the story of their date. Lesson 8 highlights critical issues such as racial discrimination and parent-child relationships by way of an argument between a mother and daughter over their views on love and marriage. Lesson 9 discusses gender roles and family matters as understood by a Chinese man and woman. With a portrait of two Chinese students' career choices, Lesson 10 contrasts the typical Chinese and American views on learning and education.

With the start of the spring semester, Lesson 11 discusses the American student's travel plans for Chinese New Year as he is about to leave mainland China. Lesson 12 underlines the problem of traffic and environmental pollution through the narration of the events encountered by the student on his trip around China and his arrival in Taiwan. Lesson 13, with its theme of animals and pets describes how the student settles down in Taipei and introduces expressions for various delicacies, folk beliefs about food and the impetus toward conservation. Lesson 14 describes the experience of the student's job search in Taipei and portrays various aspects of the Chinese fascination with the West. Lesson 15 highlights the concept of face, together with the Chinese way of making friends and doing business over meals. Lesson 16 examines social trends and problems in both mainland China and Taiwan and brings in the Chinese concept of utopia. Lesson 17, centering on philosophy and religion, touches upon Taoism, Confucianism, and other folk beliefs such as *feng shui* and lucky numbers. Lesson 18 talks about various language issues and problems encountered by students of Chinese such as retroflex pronunciation, accents, different scripts, and so on. Lesson 19 has its scene set in a dreamscape "adventure" taken by the American student in a museum, where prominent literary figures and works are introduced. Economics and politics are the focus of Lesson 20 and, as the American student is finishing his studies abroad, he comments on the progress made on both sides of the Taiwan Straits and offers his hopes for the future.

Lesson Structure
Throughout the textbooks, each lesson contains seven sections: (1) Vocabulary, (2) Text, (3) Mini-Dialogue, (4) Stories, (5) Characters, (6) Grammar, (7) Culture Notes, and (8) Songs. After a humorous cover illustration, meant to intrigue learners about the chapter contents, the vocabulary section, with three ways of grouping new words, facilitates preview and review. The text section is composed of one or two e-mail exchanges among the four personae relating details of their lives abroad or expressing their views and observations. It presents provocative issues from different perspectives while exposing students to a longer narrative text. The mini-dialogues provide comprehensible input and the natural use of language in a conversational setting. This section not only captures the essential communicative functions in the text, but also enriches the text by providing an outlet for further comment. It can be used for memorization or as a model for writing one's own skit or performance. The story section provides the source of a certain idiom in ancient texts and encourages one to guess at the idiom's meaning in the context of the lesson. The character section gives stroke-by-stroke analysis and sample use of twenty characters in focus. Students are, nonetheless, encouraged to read and write all of the chapter vocabulary. The grammar section covers the six major sentence patterns in each

lesson and explains target language usage and structure with diagrams, examples, and notes. The section on cultural notes aims to provide students with concise tips on important concepts that will enhance their understanding of the chapter text and enable them to interact with Chinese appropriately. The songs section is intended to refresh students with fun tunes and lyrics that reintroduce lesson vocabulary and patterns.

Appendixes

Two appendixes are included in each book. The first one sketches the differences between traditional and simplified characters. The second appendix supplies a bibliography of sources used in the textbooks and refers one to other important resources.

Indexes

Each book concludes with four useful indexes: (1) lesson vocabulary, (2) lesson characters, (3) sentence patterns, and (4) idioms.

This set of textbooks stems from an ongoing attempt to tackle some of the teaching and learning issues from a fresh perspective and to share the experiences and insights that have come along over the years. I hope these textbooks will motivate more students to take the path of Chinese language studies and inspire more teachers to pioneer the frontier of Chinese language instruction with pedagogical innovations and imagination.

Jennifer Liu
Bloomington, July 2003

Acknowledgments

This textbook series is the result of many years of work and study in the field of Chinese language education. Though the conceptualization and outline of this project came long before, the research on the language data was completed during 1998–1999. This research provided a basis for selecting the core vocabulary and sentence structures appropriate for intermediate level Chinese learners and incorporating the material into these textbooks.

A project of this scope cannot succeed without institutional support and the help of many people. I would like to thank the Department of East Asian Languages and Cultures of Indiana University for funding the cartoon illustrations and the recordings that go with the books. Thanks must also be extended to the students and teachers at IU as well as at Smith College for their willingness to work with the drafts of these books and for their feedback and suggestions.

Special gratitude goes to Brian Baumann for his editorial help and for plowing through the many grammar examples with me to come up with appropriate descriptions for the function of each sentence structure. I appreciate Dawn Ollila's editorial assistance on the English text. Dr. Zhijie Wang and Zhen Chen's feedback on the grammar section is greatly appreciated. I would also like to thank Dr. Rongming Zhang, Dr. Deming An and Dr. Lihui Yang, Yan Li, Denise Gigliot, Hui-Ya Xu, and Tiaoguan Huang for their editorial help on the Chinese text. My heartfelt gratitude also goes to Chee Keong Kung for his excellent artwork and illustrations that have greatly enriched the books. I am also grateful to Ting-yi Ma, Ya-shih Liu and Yu-chen Lee for their original music and lyrics, a wonderful contribution to this project. Thanks to Mei-yun Tyan for her generous technical help, and to Janet Donley for helping me find the necessary equipment and seeing to all the paperwork.

Last but not least, I am grateful to Dr. James Chan for his inspiration during the development of this project, his excellent technical advice, and his valuable comments on book layout and design. I also thank him for the wonderful electronic resources he provided, which made the creation of visuals and modification of clipart images possible. The clip art used is from Corel Gallery by Corel Corporation (1994), ClipArt Library by Softkey International Corporation (1994), and Art Explosion 125,000 by Nova Development Corporation (1996).

Connections I-II is dedicated to my family, James, Eric, and Emily, who have put up with the numerous demands on my time and energy and support me with their characteristic good cheer and understanding. If there are any errors or inadequacies in the books, the author alone is responsible for them.

A Note to Students

Connections I and *II* will provide you with many useful resources and tools. However, you cannot benefit from them unless you actively engage in the learning process. As the subtitle of the books suggests, the cognitive aspect of language learning is being emphasized. The essence of this approach lies in the attempt of student and teacher both to take Chinese class beyond passive reception and rote memorization of presented information and rules. To this end you, as a student, need to actively try to organize, connect, sort, construct, or de-construct knowledge for yourself. You need to be creative with your own study, prioritize learning tasks, and tackle challenges from many different angles and perspectives.

At the intermediate stage, you may feel overwhelmed at times by the numerous new words or characters you will have to study. You may feel frustrated when you can't express yourself fully, despite many hours spent practicing. However, as long as you are willing to continue to venture to explore this language and culture and use it whenever you can (e.g., greeting your classmates, writing a note to your teacher in Chinese, etc.), you will find yourself picking up the language in short order. As long as you are not afraid of making mistakes and are willing to take the initiative to test your own hypotheses, again and again, you will continue to make progress in your study. A lighthearted attitude and a sense of humor will ease many of the frustrations that are part of your everyday life when you study Chinese. Certainly, the language is difficult, but you do not have to make it harder than it needs to be. If you can make things fun and relevant to you, you will surely be able to handle and even enjoy the many challenges that come with your ongoing study of Chinese.

The following are a few tips on how to make the most of these textbooks. The tips follow the different sections appearing in the textbooks and workbooks.

1. Vocabulary

The chapter vocabulary is organized into three lists: order of appearance, grammatical category, and pinyin. Obviously, the first one is good for first-time study and the latter two for the purpose of review and quick reference. New lexical items appearing in the mini-dialogues are noted with asterisks and the useful ones included in the pinyin list. There are about 40 new words in each lesson. Break them down and study an acceptable segment, say 8 or 10 words, each day. Pay attention not only to the new compound itself but also try to recall other terms studied previously that share similar components or characters. This practice will help you build a web of vocabulary in your mind that facilitates memorization and recall. Also, you are encouraged to guess at the meaning of words based on their constituent characters. To this end, the definitions of some words in each chapter are intentionally omitted. If you learn to see the logic of compound formation, you will not be afraid of new terms and will develop skill at guessing the meaning of new words that native speakers have. In addition, study the example sentences provided and see how the new terms are used in context. To create opportunity for you to interact, the example sentences are usually in the form of questions. See if you can understand and answer the questions by yourself.

2. Characters

While you are encouraged to learn to read and write all the characters associated with the new words, twenty characters are selected from each chapter for additional practice or supplemental study. Although the traditional way to practice characters in China is to copy them as many times as possible, you shouldn't fall into the trap of thinking repetition alone will work magic. In fact, it will be much more effective if you can be creative with your learning methods. Break a character down into parts which you understand. Think of other characters that either look like or sound like the one you are focusing on. Compare and contrast the characters you have studied and organize them into meaningful groups. Invent your own stories or mnemonics to go with the characters you have trouble remembering. To help you in this regard, a brief etymology is provided for each character, so is the use of the character in a sample phrase. Hopefully these will help register or anchor the image of the character in your mind. After one year of study, you may have noticed that studying characters has a snowballing effect. The more characters you acquire, the easier it is to remember them.

As with studying vocabulary, you need to adopt a disciplined approach to learning to write characters. If you want to learn twenty characters over five days, you have to study four per day; better still, you need to build a system of review for yourself. In addition, you need to be flexible in arranging your study schedule. Instead of spending three straight hours writing characters or memorizing words, it may be more effective to practice the language for shorter periods two or three times per day, making use of the odd hours when you wait for a bus or a class, when you take an afternoon break, when you retire in the evening, etc.

3. Text and Story

The text is typically a longer narrative. After studying half of the vocabulary, you should try to start reading the text and figure out its overall meaning. You can skip or circle unknown words or characters and guess at the main idea of the passage on the basis of context. Also, try to understand what you have read without translating it word-for-word into your native language. Use titles and illustrations to make inferences, and use dictionaries as a last resort. When you are done skimming the passage, you can read it again more carefully. Paraphrase what you have read and summarize paragraphs in the margin. Underline the phrases you don't understand and bring questions to your teachers. Since the text is mostly composed of e-mail exchanges, anticipate the responses and make predictions about what will come next in the text. It is important to remember that one reads not only for information, but also for fun. To this end, a story is included in each chapter and it tells the source of an ancient Chinese idiom. Learn to read the story and the example sentence first, then guess at the meaning of the idiom by yourself.

4. Mini-Dialogues

While the text and story will build your reading skill, mini-dialogues will enhance your abililty to interact with people in Chinese. When studying the dialogue for comprehension, try to cover up the English translation, and figure out the meaning first by yourself. English is included for you to confirm your understanding of the Chinese text or as a crutch when you have trouble. Another way to study the dialogue is to focus on one line at a time, cover up the rest, and see if you can come up with an appropriate response youself. Then unfold the next line to compare your "creation" with a typical response from a native Chinese. This practice helps you carry on a conversation with yourself. Eventually, you may want to memorize one dialogue or use it as a model, since likely you'll be asked to write your own skits and perform them in class with your classmates from time to time. If you have Chinese friends, you can even try to speak with them as you see fit. When you initiate conversations in Chinese, monitor your own utterances. If you notice errors, correct your own mistakes. Also, ask other people for confirmation that you have spoken correctly or to correct your tones, pronunciation, intonation, usage of words or grammar. Find a different way to express your idea when you can't think of the correct expression, or ask a native speaker to tell you the right word. Speaking Chinese can be a humbling experience, so be lighthearted about any embarrassment you may bring upon yourself.

5. Grammar

There are six grammar points in each chapter. When you study them, remember to adopt an inductive approach. That is, read the example dialogues first and then figure out what the sentence structure is doing, what function they accomplish. Then, check your own understanding with the boxed linguistic rule and English translation. After you have done these, you will find the "grammar drills" in class much more productive. You are encouraged to work on the grammar exercises in the Workbook right after you are exposed to grammar lectures and drills. Timely exercise will help reinforce and consolidate your skills and understanding. Don't put off the exercises till the night before the homework is due. Remember that you study grammar not for its own sake, but for the purpose of communication. So, when you have trouble analyzing the way a pattern works, be tolerant of its ambiguities. The more you study Chinese grammatical structure, the better you will understand the significance of contextual cues, which play an important role in the use of this language.

6. Culture Notes

As you may have already discovered, to be able to study Chinese well, you need to be tolerant of and receptive to differences, be they linguistic or cultural. You may feel disoriented or confused at times, given the differences between your native language and Chinese, and it is more than natural that you resort to your own culture and use it as a frame of reference to understand and interpret Chinese ways. Eventually, however, you will want to see things from a Chinese point of view and obtain an insider's perspective. Therefore, cultural notes are offered to help you gain some background knowledge. Read them at your own leisure and add more notes of your own as you make contact with Chinese people and culture.

7. Listening Comprehension

The listening comprehension section appears only in the Workbook. Yet, it is important enough to be singled out for discussion. When you listen to tapes or to native speakers, try to focus on the overall meaning or theme without worrying about the details or translating what you have heard word-by-word into your native language. If you are concerned with every single detail, your general comprehension will suffer. When you don't understand what you hear, use any clues you can to guess the general meaning and make associations between what you hear and what you already know about the topic. Of course, if you are listening to tapes, you can rewind the recording and listen again to confirm the main points or change your understanding. If you have trouble understanding when you are listening to a native speaker, you can ask him or her to slow down or clarify what was said. The rule of thumb is this: it will prove to be far more productive if you learn to take in chunks of information rather than isolated details.

8. Writing

At the intermediate stage, you should not be concerned only with writing individual characters. Instead, you should attempt to write coherent paragraphs and short essays. As adult learners, you may understand and learn various grammatical structures quickly. Yet, when it comes to applying all the things you have studied in writing, it might be very difficult and time-consuming. Although your writing competence probably won't progress at the same rate as your aural-oral skills, you should not avoid or delay the task of writing. Skills reinforce each other. Therefore, an integrated approach of four language skills is advocated in these textbooks. In fact, you will be encouraged to write an essay from time to time, even if it will be painfully slow at the beginning. Be patient and set a realistic goal for yourself. Plan ahead what you intend to write. If you have trouble writing, just take notes on whatever comes to your mind, without worrying about form or structure. Re-read what you have written before continuing, and make sure that your ideas are linked clearly. When you can't think of the correct expression to write, find a different way to express yourself. Stay on track as you write and revise. Always keep in mind your goals and your audience.

Most likely you will find other strategies as well, as you hone a study method of your own.

Abbreviations

Adj	Adjective	形容詞	xíngróngcí
Adv	Adverb	副詞	fùcí
AuxV	Auxiliary Verb	助動詞	zhùdòngcí
Conj	Conjunction	連詞	liáncí
CV	Co-verb	輔動詞	fǔdòngcí
Inter	Interjection	嘆詞	tàncí
IE	Idiomatic Expression	成語/習慣用語	chéngyǔ/xíguàn yòngyǔ
M	Measure Word	量詞	liàngcí
MA	Movable Adverb	可移副詞	kěyí fùcí
MTA	Movable Time Adverb	可移時間副詞	kěyí shíjiān fùcí
N	Noun	名詞	míngcí
Neg	Negative	否定詞	fǒudìngcí
No	Number	數詞	shùcí
NP	Noun Phrase	名詞詞組	míngcí cízǔ
O	Object	受詞	shòucí
Part	Particle	語助詞	yǔzhùcí
Place	Place Word	地方詞	dìfāngcí
PP	Prepositional Phrase	介詞詞組	jiècícízǔ
Pref	Prefix	詞頭	cítóu
P(rep)	Preposition	介詞	jiècí
Pron	Pronoun	代名詞	dàimíngcí
QW	Question Word	疑問詞	yíwèncí
RE	Resultative Verb Ending	結果動詞補語	jiéguǒ dòngcí bǔyǔ
RV	Resultative Verb	結果動詞	jiéguǒ dòngcí
S	Subject	主詞	zhǔcí
Suf	Suffix	詞尾	cíwěi
SV	Stative Verb	靜態動詞	jìngtài dòngcí
V	Verb	動詞	dòngcí
VO	Verb-Object Compound	動賓複詞	dòngbīn fùcí

<TW> Terms used in Taiwan

<PRC> Terms used in the People's Republic of China

Conventions

◎   This icon marks three subsections of Vocabulary in each lesson
—the first one groups new words by their order of appearance in
the main text (in both traditional and simplified characters), the
second by their grammatical categories (in traditional characters),
and the third by pinyin (in simplified characters).

*   This symbol, at the end of entries in the Vocabulary and
Characters sections, calls the learner's attention to supplementary
lexical items of possible interest for further study.

This icon, indicating the various mini-dialogues, highlights the
major communication functions in each lesson.

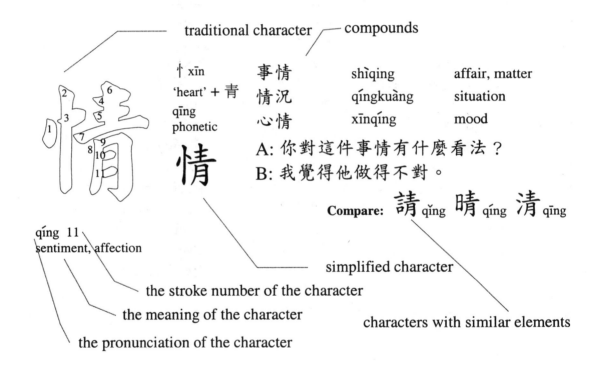

Cast of Characters
人物表Rénwùbiǎo

高德中	Gāo Dézhōng	David Gore
美國人	Měiguórén	American
研究生	Yánjiūshēng	Graduate student
專業：比較文學	Zhuānyè: bǐjiǎo wénxué	Major: Comparative Literature
年紀：二十八歲	Niánjì: èrshíbā suì	Age: 28
性別：男	Xìngbié: nán	Sex: male
個性：穩重、老實	Gèxìng: wěnzhòng, lǎoshí	Personality: practical, sincere
愛好：讀書、看電影	Aìhào: dúshū, kàn diànyǐng	Hobbies: studying, watching movies
父親：高麥克	Fùqīn: Gāo Màikè	Father: Michael Gore
職業：醫生	Zhíyè: yīshēng	Job: doctor
母親：鄧麗莎	Mǔqīn: Dèng Lìshā	Mother: Lisa Downing
職業：報社記者	Zhíyè: bàoshè jìzhě	Job: journalist
大弟：高杰森	Dàdì: Gāo Jiésēn	Elder younger brother: Jason Gore
小弟：高亞倫	Xiǎodì: Gāo Yàlún	Younger brother: Allen Gore

李明	Lǐ Míng	
中國人（大陸）	Zhōngguórén (dàlù)	Chinese (from the mainland)
大學生（大四）	Dàxuéshēng (dà sì)	Undergraduate (senior)
專業：商學	Zhuānyè: shāngxué	Major: Business
年紀：二十三歲	Niánjì: èrshísān suì	Age: 23
性別：男	Xìngbié: nán	Sex: male
個性：外向、好動	Gèxìng: wàixiàng, hàodòng	Personality: outgoing, active
愛好：旅行、拍照、美食	Aìhào: lǚxíng, pāizhào, měishí	Hobbies: travel, photography, fine food
父親：李鐵	Fùqīn: Lǐ Tiě	Father: Tie Li
職業：退休教授	Zhíyè: tuìxiū jiàoshòu	Job: retired professor
母親：周紅	Mǔqīn: Zhōu Hóng	Mother: Hong Zhou
職業：小學教員	Zhíyè: xiǎoxué jiàoyuán	Job: elementary school teacher

林美英	Lín Měiyīng	
華裔美國人	Huáyì Měiguórén	Chinese American
大學生（大三）	Dàxuéshēng (dà sān)	Undergraduate (junior)
專業：音樂	Zhuānyè: yīnyuè	Major: Music
年紀：二十一歲	Niánjì: èrshíyī suì	Age: 21
性別：女	Xìngbié: nǚ	Sex: female
個性：外向、活潑	Gèxìng: wàixiàng, huópō	Personality: outgoing, energetic
愛好：唱歌、跳舞、運動	Aìhào: chànggē, tiàowǔ, yùndòng	Hobbies: singing, dancing, exercising
父親：林偉平	Fùqīn: Lín Wěipíng	Father: Weiping Lin
職業：電腦工程師	Zhíyè: diànnǎo gōngchéngshī	Job: computer engineer
母親：黃樂庭	Mǔqīn: Huáng Lètíng	Mother: Leting Huang
職業：家庭主婦	Zhíyè: jiātíng zhǔfù	Job: housewife
妹妹：林美芳	Mèimei: Lín Měifāng	Younger sister: Meifang Lin

王華	Wáng Huá	
中國人（台灣）	Zhōngguórén (Táiwān)	Chinese (from Taiwan)
大學生（大二）	Dàxuéshēng (dà'èr)	Undergraduate (sophomore)
專業：電腦	Zhuānyè: diànnǎo	Major: Computer Science
年紀：二十歲	Niánjì: èrshí suì	Age: 20
性別：女	Xìngbié: nǚ	Sex: female
個性：内向、文靜	Gèxìng: nèixiàng, wénjìng	Personality: reserved, introspective
愛好：看電視、球賽	Aìhào: kàn diànshì, qiúsài	Hobbies: watching sports on TV
父親：王志強	Fùqīn: Wáng Zhìqiáng	Father: Zhiqiang Wang
職業：進出口公司經理	Zhíyè: jìnchūkǒu gōngsī jīnglǐ	Job: manager of an export-import company
母親：張如蘭	Mǔqīn: Zhāng Rúlán	Mother: Rulan Zhang
職業：旅行社職員	Zhíyè: lǚxíngshè zhíyuán	Job: travel agent
哥哥：王清	Gēge: Wáng Qīng	Elder brother: Qing Wang

Theme First Encounter	**Grammar Focus**
	• 好在⋯(要不然)⋯
Communicative Objectives	• 要不是⋯(早)就⋯
• Greeting people at the airport	• V起來⋯
• Introducing oneself	• 以為⋯原來/其實/哪知道
• Introducing others	• A就是B(的意思)
• Greeting strangers	• A對B感興趣
• Greeting friends	

Focus on Characters
• 感情興趣、敢跑接迎、熟悉海關、面相切搞、利聲突消

那個老外怎麼還沒來？

生詞 Vocabulary

Study the following words for their pronunciation and meaning. When an area is shaded, guess at the meaning of the word based on its constituent characters and then fill in the blank. Read the usage of words and related terms (antonyms, synonyms, compounds sharing the constituent characters, etc.) and try to answer the sample questions in Chinese. Note that proper nouns or incidental terms are not numbered.

◎ By Order of Appearance

1. 老外   lǎowài   N   foreigner   [prefix-foreign]

   →老中、老美

   為什麼中國人在美國還叫美國人老外？

   为什么中国人在美国还叫美国人老外？

2. 敢   gǎn   V   to dare

   你敢吃狗肉嗎？

   你敢吃狗肉吗？

3. 相信   xiāngxìn   V   to believe   [each other-true]

   你相信他做的是對的嗎？

   你相信他做的是对的吗？

4. 出國
 出国   chūguó   VO   [out-country]

   ↔回國

   出國的時候要帶些什麼？

   出国的时候要带些什么？

5. 留學
 留学   liúxué   VO   to study abroad   [stay-study]

   →留學生、留學生活

   你覺得去什麼地方留學最好？

   你觉得去什么地方留学最好？

6. 好在   hǎozài   Adv   fortunately   [good-at]

   好在我昨天學習了，今天老師問了我好幾個問題。

   好在我昨天学习了，今天老师问了我好几个问题。

7. （要）不然
 （要）不然   (yào)bùrán   Conj   otherwise, or else   [if-not-so]

   我得立刻走，要不然就來不及了。

   我得立刻走，要不然就来不及了。

8.	申請 申请	shēnqǐng	V	to apply for	[explain-request]

→申請人、申請信

你申請了哪些學校？

你申请了哪些学校？

9.	護照 护照	hùzhào	N	passport	[protect-permit]

什麼時候你得申請護照？

什么时候你得申请护照？

10.	簽證 签证	qiānzhèng	N	visa	[sign-certificate]

為什麼他們不給你簽證？

为什么他们不给你签证？

11.	辦 办	bàn	V	to do, to handle, to attend to

你辦護照了嗎？

你办护照了吗？

12.	機票 机票	jīpiào	N	plane ticket	[plane-ticket]

→電影票、車票、門票、球票

買一張去台北的來回機票要多少錢？

买一张去台北的来回机票要多少钱？

13.	一切	yíqiè	N	all, everything	[one-close to]

你對這兒的一切都很熟悉嗎？

你对这儿的一切都很熟悉吗？

14.	順利 顺利	shùnlì	SV/ Adv	(to be) smooth, successfully	[along-benefit]

你在那兒工作順利嗎？

你在那儿工作顺利吗？

15.	要不是	yàobushì	Conj	if it were not for, but for	[if-not-be]

要不是他幫我的忙，我就完了。

要不是他帮我的忙，我就完了。

16.	來不及 来不及	láibují	RV	can't do sth. in time	[come-not-reach]

圖書館幾點關門？現在去來得及來不及？

图书馆几点关门？现在去来得及来不及？

Characters with Many Strokes

敢　留　然　護　簽　證　辦　機　票　順

17.	轉機 转机	zhuǎnjī	VO	to change planes	[change-plane]

→轉車、轉學

你是在哪兒轉機的？

你是在哪儿转机的？

18.	搞	gǎo	V	to do	

難搞；搞好；搞不好；搞什麼

你申請學校的事搞好了沒有？

你申请学校的事搞好了没有？

19.	半天	bàntiān	N	a long time, quite a while	[half-day]

我等了你半天，為什麼你現在才來？

我等了你半天，为什么你现在才来？

20.	晚點 晚点	wǎndiǎn	VO	late, behind schedule	[late-point]

<TW>誤點wùdiǎn　　　vs. 遲到

你的飛機晚點了嗎？

你的飞机晚点了吗？

21.	行李	xíngli	N	luggage	[travel-plum]

你一共有幾件行李？

你一共有几件行李？

22.	過 过	guò	V	to pass	

去圖書館我得過幾條街？

去图书馆我得过几条街？

23.	海關 海关	hǎiguān	N	customs	[sea-pass]

你過海關的時候，有沒有什麼問題？

你过海关的时候，有没有什么问题？

24.	出口	chūkǒu	N		[out-opening]

↔入口

請你在出口等我。

请你在出口等我。

25.	突然	tūrán	Adv	suddenly	[abrupt-suffix]

為什麼你得突然回家去？

为什么你得突然回家去？

26.	熟悉	shúxī	Adj/ SV	(to be) familiar	[familiar-know]

對(地方)很熟悉；跟(人)很熟

你對這個地方熟悉嗎？

你对这个地方熟悉吗？

| 27. | 聲音
声音 | shēngyīn | N | sound | [sound-sound] |

→大聲、小聲

你聽得見外面的聲音嗎？

你听得见外面的声音吗？

| 28. | 原來
原来 | yuánlái | Adv | as it turns out |

搞了半天，原來他不是中國人，是日本人，
所以我說什麼，他都聽不懂。

搞了半天，原来他不是中国人，是日本人，
所以我说什么，他都听不懂。

| 29. | 跑 | pǎo | V | to run |

你上午跑到哪兒去了？

你上午跑到哪儿去了？

| 30. | 接 | jiē | V | to pick someone up |

我沒車，你能不能來接我？

我没车，你能不能来接我？

| 31. | 發
发 | fā | V | to issue |

→發作業

你今天給誰發了電子郵件？

你今天给谁发了电子邮件？

| 32. | 封 | fēng | M | measure word for letters |

從開學到現在，你給家裏寫了幾封信？

从开学到现在，你给家里写了几封信？

| 33. | 電子
电子 | diànzǐ | N | electron, electronic | [electricity-sth. small] |

→電子郵件、電子計算機、電子遊戲

| 34. | 郵件
邮件 | yóujiàn | N | postal matter, post, mail | [post-letter] |

| 35. | 上 | shàng | IE | to submit—convention used after the signature in a letter |

Characters with Many Strokes

轉　搞　點　關　熟　悉　聲　發　電　郵

36.	聽到	tīngdào	RV	to hear	[listen-have a result]
	听到			你聽到老師昨天說了什麼？	
				你听到老师昨天说了什么？	
37.	消息	xiāoxi	N	news	
				好消息、壞消息	
				你最近有沒有他的消息？	
				你最近有没有他的消息？	
38.	見面	jiànmiàn	VO	to meet, to see	[see-face]
	见面			你們是第一次見面嗎？	
				你们是第一次见面吗？	
38.	情況	qíngkuàng	N	circumstances, situation	[situation-situation]
	情况				
39.	有趣	yǒuqù	Adj/	(to be) interesting	[have-fun]
			SV	你覺得看什麼電影很有趣？	
				你觉得看什么电影很有趣？	
40.	更	gèng	Adv	even	
				我愛吃美國飯，更愛吃中國飯。	
				我爱吃美国饭，更爱吃中国饭。	
41.	感興趣	gǎn xìngqù	VO	to be interested in	[feel-happy-interesting]
	感兴趣			你對什麼感興趣？	
				你对什么感兴趣？	
42.	學習	xuéxí	V	to study, to learn	[study-practice]
	学习			你喜歡在什麼地方學習？	
				你喜欢在什么地方学习？	
43.	事情	shìqing	N	affair, matter, business	[matter-situation]
				你今天有什麼事情要辦？	
				你今天有什么事情要办？	

Characters with Many Strokes

聽　消　息　情　趣　感　興　習　事

◎ By Grammatical Categories

Nouns/Pronouns/Measure Words

老外	lǎowài	foreigner	郵件	yóujiàn	postal matter, post, mail
護照	hùzhào	passport	消息	xiāoxi	news
簽證	qiānzhèng	visa	事情	shìqing	affair, matter, business
機票	jīpiào	plane ticket	情況	qíngkuàng	circumstances, situation
行李	xíngli	luggage	一切	yíqiè	all, everything
海關	hǎiguān	customs	半天	bàntiān	a long time, quite a while
出口	chūkǒu	exit	封	fēng	measure word for letters
聲音	shēngyīn	sound			
電子	diànzǐ	electron, electronic			

Verbs/Stative Verbs/Adjectives

敢	gǎn	to dare	留學	liúxué	to study abroad
辦	bàn	to do, to handle, to attend to	轉機	zhuǎnjī	to change planes
搞	gǎo	to do	晚點	wǎndiǎn	late, behind schedule
過	guò	to pass	見面	jiànmiàn	to meet, to see
跑	pǎo	to run	感興趣	gǎn xìngqù	to be interested in
接	jiē	to pick someone up	來不及	láibují	can't do sth. in time
發	fā	to issue	聽到	tīngdào	to hear
相信	xiāngxìn	to believe	順利	shùnlì	(to be) smooth, successfully
申請	shēnqǐng	to apply for	熟悉	shúxī	(to be) familiar
學習	xuéxí	to study, to learn	有趣	yǒuqù	(to be) interesting
出國	chūguó	to go abroad			

Adverbs and Others

更	gèng	even	要不是	yàobushì	if it were not for, but for
好在	hǎozài	fortunately	上	shàng	to submit—convention used after the signature in a letter
原來	yuánlái	as it turns out			
突然	tūrán	suddenly			
(要)不然	(yào)bùrán	otherwise, or else			

◎ By Pinyin

Entries with * indicate lexical items used in Mini-Dialogues and of possible interest for supplemental study.

bàn	办	to handle
bàntiān	半天	a long time
chūguó	出国	to go abroad
chūkǒu	出口	exit
diànzǐ	电子	electronic
fā	发	to issue
fēng	封	measure word for letters
gǎn	敢	to dare
gǎn xìngqù	感兴趣	to be interested in
gǎo	搞	to do
gèng	更	even
guò	过	to pass
hǎiguān	海关	customs
hǎozài	好在	fortunately
huānyíng*	欢迎	to welcome
hùzhào	护照	passport
jiànmiàn	见面	to meet, to see
jiàoshòu*	教授	professor
jiē	接	to pick sb. up
jīpiào	机票	plane ticket
láibují	来不及	can't do sth. in time
lǎowài	老外	foreigner
liúxué	留学	to study abroad
pǎo	跑	to run

qiānzhèng	签证	visa
qíngkuàng	情况	circumstances, situation
shàng	上	to submit (a letter)
shēngyīn	声音	sound
shēnqǐng	申请	to apply for
shīfu*	师傅	master worker
shìqing	事情	affair, matter
shúxī	熟悉	familiar
shùnlì	顺利	smooth
tīngdào	听到	to hear
tūrán	突然	suddenly
wǎndiǎn	晚点	late
xiāngxìn	相信	to believe
xiāoxi	消息	news
xíngli	行李	luggage
xuéxí	学习	to study, to learn
(yào)bùrán	（要）不然	otherwise
yàobushì	要不是	if it were not for, but for
yíqiè	一切	all, everything
yóujiàn	邮件	postal matter, mail
yǒuqù	有趣	interesting
yuánlái	原来	as it turns out
zhuǎnjī	转机	to change planes

課文 Text

Use the following questions to guide your reading of the text.

1. 小高出國留學順利嗎？為什麼？
2. 小高到北京機場的時候，有什麼問題？
3. 小高到了北京的時候，誰來接他？

 小李：

真不敢相信我已經到北京了。這一次出國留學，[1]**好在**有你幫忙，從申請護照到辦簽證、買機票，一切都很順利。去機場的那天，[2]**要不是**你送我，**就**來不及了。在芝加哥轉機的時候，搞了半天，所以到北京的飛機晚點了。我拿了行李、過了海關，立刻走到出口。那時突然聽見有人說：「那個老外怎麼還沒來？」好熟悉的聲音啊！[3]**聽起來**很像你，[4]**原來**是你父親。我馬上跑過去，告訴他我[5]**就是**「那個老外」。他接了我，就帶我到學校去。

你開學了嗎？這學期選了幾門課？有空發封電子郵件給我吧！

德中上

小高：

　　很高興這麼快就聽到你的消息了。你跟我父親第一次見面的情況很有趣。在美國你是個「老外」，在中國當然更是個「老外」了。我剛來美國的時候，也6對什麼都很**感興趣**。現在整天學習，沒時間做別的事情了。這學期我選了五門課，有一點兒重，但是我覺得這些課都很有意思。你呢？你喜歡你的學校嗎？

李明上

课文 Text

Use the following questions to guide your reading of the text.

1. 小高出国留学顺利吗？为什么？

2. 小高到北京机场的时候，有什么问题？

3. 小高到了北京的时候，谁来接他？

 小李 ：

真不敢相信我已经到北京了。这一次出国留学，[1]**好在**有你帮忙，从申请护照到办签证、买机票，一切都很顺利。去机场的那天，[2]**要不是**你送我，**就**来不及了。在芝加哥转机的时候，搞了半天，所以到北京的飞机晚点了。我拿了行李、过了海关，立刻走到出口。那时突然听见有人说：“那个老外怎么还没来？”好熟悉的声音啊！[3]**听起来**很像你，[4]**原来**是你父亲。我马上跑过去，告诉他我[5]**就是**“那个老外”。他接了我，就带我到学校去。

你开学了吗？这学期选了几门课？有空发封电子邮件给我吧！

德中上

 小高：

很高兴这么快就听到你的消息了。你跟我父亲第一次见面的情况很有趣。在美国你是个"老外"，在中国当然更是个"老外"了。我刚来美国的时候，也⁶对什么都很感兴趣。现在整天学习，没时间做别的事情了。这学期我选了五门课，有一点儿重，但是我觉得这些课都很有意思。你呢？你喜欢你的学校吗？

李明上

整
zhěng

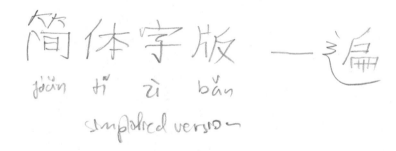

简体字版 一遍
jiǎn tǐ zì bǎn
simplified version

繁体字版
fán
traditional version

练习册
liàn xí cè   workbook

小對話 Mini-Dialogues

Read the supplementary dialogues for a better understanding of the text. See if you can memorize one and perform it in class.

(1) Greeting people at the airport

A: 您好！我是來接您的，歡迎 huānyíng您來中國學習。

您好！我是来接您的，欢迎您来中国学习。

Gao: 您好！謝謝您到機場來接我。

您好！谢谢您到机场来接我。

A: 不用謝。怎麼樣？一路順利嗎？

不用谢。怎么样？一路顺利吗？

Gao: 還好。

还好。

A: 您是第一次來北京嗎？

您是第一次来北京吗？

Gao: 是，我對這個地方不太熟悉。

是，我对这个地方不太熟悉。

A: How do you do! I am here to pick you up. Welcome to China for your study of Chinese.

Gao: How do you do! Thanks for coming to the airport to pick me up.

A: No need to thank me. How is everything? Did you have a nice trip?

Gao: Yes.

A: Is this your first time here in Beijing?

Gao: Yes. I am not familiar with this place.

(2) Introducing oneself

Gao: 我姓高，叫高德中。高矮的高，德國的德，中國的中。是來這兒學習漢語的。您是……

我姓高，叫高德中。高矮的高，德国的德，中国的中。是来这儿学习汉语的。您是……

Li: 我是李明的爸爸，李鐵，從前

我是李明的爸爸，李铁，从前

在北大Běidà 教中國文學。 在北大教中国文学。

Gao: I am Gao Dezhong. Gao as in "height," De as in the character in "Germany," Zhong as in the character in "China." I am here to study Chinese. And you are…?

Li: I am Li Ming's father, Li Tie. I taught Chinese literature at Beijing University.

(3) Introducing others

A: 先讓我介紹一下，他是高德中，從美國來的留學生。這位是劉老師，中文系教授jiàoshòu。

先让我介绍一下，他是高德中，从美国来的留学生。这位是刘老师，中文系教授。

Gao: 您好！很高興認識您。

您好！很高兴认识您。

Liu: 你好！歡迎你來我們學校學習。

你好！欢迎你来我们学校学习。

A: 還有這位，……

还有这位，……

Gao: 不用介紹了，我們原來就認識了。今天上午和李先生也見過面了。

不用介绍了，我们原来就认识了。今天上午和李先生也见过面了。

A: 好！大家都請坐吧！我們坐下談。

好！大家都请坐吧！我们坐下谈。

A: Let me introduce you to each other. He is Gao Dezhong, a student from the U.S. This is Teacher Liu, a professor in the Chinese Department.

Gao: How do you do? It's a pleasure to meet you.

Liu: How do you do? Welcome to our school.

A: And this is…

Gao: There is no need for introduction. We know each other. I met Mr. Li this morning.

A: Great! Let's sit down and talk.

(4) Greeting strangers

A:	您好！	您好！
Gao:	您好！	您好！
A:	您來過中國嗎？	您来过中国吗？
Gao:	沒來過，這是第一次。	没来过，这是第一次。
A:	您叫什麼名字？	您叫什麼名字？
Gao:	高德中。您貴姓？	高德中。您贵姓？
A:	姓趙。	姓赵。
Gao:	趙先生。您在哪兒工作？	赵先生。您在哪儿工作？
A:	留學生宿舍，我是看門的。你就叫我趙師傅shīfu吧！	留学生宿舍，我是看门的。你就叫我赵师傅吧！

A: How do you do!

Gao: How do you do!

A: Have you been to China before?

Gao: No. This is the first time.

A: What's your name?

Gao: Gao Dezhong. What's yours?

A: My surname is Zhao.

Gao: Mr. Zhao, where do you work?

A: At the overseas students' dormitory. I am a doorkeeper. Just call me Master Zhao.

(5) Greeting friends

Gao:	老趙，你早！	老赵，你早！
A:	你早！這幾天沒看到你，最近好嗎？	你早！这几天没看到你，最近好吗？

Gao:　不錯，就是太忙了。你呢？身體好嗎？

A:　　還好。你這麼早到哪兒去呀？

Gao:　到圖書館去，得學習漢語。

不错，就是太忙了。你呢？身体好吗？

还好。你这么早到哪儿去呀？

到图书馆去，得学习汉语。

Gao:　Lao Zhao, good morning!

A:　　Good morning! I haven't seen you lately. How are you doing?

Gao:　Fine, but I am too busy. How about you? Are you well?

A:　　Yes. Where are you going at this early hour?

Gao:　To the library. I have to study Chinese.

小故事 Stories

Read the following tale for your own enjoyment and for your understanding of the highlighted expression that is relevant to the theme of the chapter.

 井底之蛙 jǐng dǐ zhī wā

✿ 我來了中國以後，才知道自己從前真是井底之蛙。

從前有一隻青蛙住在一口井裏。有一天，他在井邊玩兒的時候，突然碰到一隻從海裏來的海龜。青蛙對海龜說：「你看，這個地方真好啊！我高興的時候，可以在井邊玩；我累的時候，可以回到井裏休息。我在這兒生活得非常快樂！誰比得上我呢？」

井	jǐng	well
底	dǐ	bottom
之	zhī	of
青蛙	qīngwā	frog
海龜	hǎiguī	turtle
比得上	bǐdeshàng	can compare with
卡住	kǎzhù	to be stuck
退	tuì	to move back
寬	kuān	wide
世界	shìjiè	world

海龜聽了，就想進井裏看看，可是井太小，左腳還沒有進去，

右腳就卡住了。它只好退了出來，對青蛙說：「你見過海嗎？海又大又寬，住在那樣的地方，才快樂呢！」

青蛙聽了海龜的話，就說：「原來別的地方還有那麼大的世界啊！」

井底之蛙 jǐngdǐ zhī wā

❀ 我来了中国以后，才知道自己从前真是井底之蛙。

从前有一只青蛙住在一口井里。有一天，他在井边玩儿的时候，突然碰到一只从海里来的海龟。青蛙对海龟说："你看，这个地方真好啊！我高兴的时候，可以在井边玩；我累的时候，可以回到井里休息。我在这儿生活得非常快乐！谁比得上我呢？"

井	jǐng	well
底	dǐ	bottom
之	zhī	of
青蛙	qīngwā	frog
海龟	hǎiguī	turtle
比得上	bǐdeshàng	can compare with
卡住	kǎzhù	to be stuck
退	tuì	to move back
宽	kuān	wide
世界	shìjiè	world

海龟听了，就想进井里看看，可是井太小，左脚还没有进去，右脚就卡住了。它只好退了出来，对青蛙说："你见过海吗？海又大又宽，住在那样的地方，才快乐呢！"

青蛙听了海龟的话，就说："原来别的地方还有那么大的世界啊！"

✎ 井底之蛙的意思是＿＿＿＿＿＿＿＿＿＿＿＿＿＿＿＿＿

漢字 Characters

Study the following selected characters for further enrichment of your writing and vocabulary.

心 xīn 'heart'
+ 咸 xián
phonetic

感

gǎn 13
sense, feeling

感興趣	gǎn xìngqù	to be interested in
感覺	gānjué	to feel, feeling
感動	gǎndòng	to move, touch

A: 你為什麼對那部電影感興趣？
B: 聽說很多人看了都覺得很感動。

忄 xīn 'heart'
+ 青 qīng
phonetic

情

qíng 11
sentiment, affection

事情	shìqing	affair, matter
情況	qíngkuàng	situation
心情	xīnqíng	mood

A: 你對這件事情有什麼看法？
B: 我覺得他做得不對。

Compare: 請 qǐng　晴 qíng　清 qīng

舁 yú 'lift up'
+ 同 tóng
'same'—
lifting by joint
effort

兴

xìng, xīng 16
interest, excitement

| 興趣 | xìngqù | interest |
| 高興 | gāoxìng | happy |

A: 你對什麼感興趣？
B: 我對什麼都感興趣。

Compare: 與 yǔ

走 zǒu 'go' +
取 qǔ 'take'
phonetic

趣

qù 15
interest, fun

| 有趣 | yǒuqù | interesting |
| 樂趣 | lèqù* | delight, pleasure |

A: 你覺得學中文有趣嗎？
B: 很有趣。

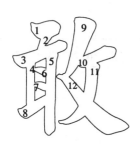

a picture of a bear, not 耳 ěr 'ear' + 攵 (攴 pū) 'beat'

敢

| 不敢當 | bùgǎndāng* | I don't deserve it |
| 勇敢 | yǒnggǎn* | brave, courageous |

A: 你為什麼不敢去見那個教授？
B: 他太嚴了。

Compare: 嚴 yán

gǎn 12
dare, have the courage to

足 zú 'foot' + 包 bāo phonetic

跑

| 跑步 | pǎobù | jog |
| 賽跑 | sàipǎo* | race (on foot) |

A: 你為什麼跑來跑去？
B: 我在找我的行李。

Compare: 足 zú 跳 tiào 跟 gēn

pǎo 12
to run

扌/手 shǒu 'hand' + 妾 qiè 'concubine' phonetic

接

| 接到 | jiēdào | to receive |
| 接著 | jiēzhe* | to catch, next |

A: 你要去飛機場接誰？
B: 接一個美國來的留學生。

Compare: 提 tí 搬 bān 拉 lā

jiē 11
to meet, to receive

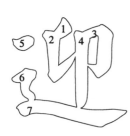

辶 chuò 'go' + 卬 áng phonetic

迎

| 歡迎 | huānyíng* | to welcome, to greet |

A: 歡迎！歡迎！
B: 你太客氣了。

yíng 7
to welcome, to meet

shú, shóu 15
ripe, familiar

丸 a hand offering up a 享 xiǎng 'feast' 灬/火 huǒ 'fire' was added later

熟

熟人	shúrén*	acquaintance, friend
熟睡	shúshuì*	to sleep soundly
面熟	miànshú*	familiar-looking

A: 你看起來很面熟。

B: 可是我從來沒見過你。

Compare: 熱 rè

xī 11
to know well

采 biàn 'discern' + 心 xīn 'heart'

悉

| 熟悉 | shúxī | to know sth./sb. well |

A: 你對這個地方熟悉嗎？

B: 很熟悉，這兒我來過三次了。

Compare: 忘 wàng 念 niàn 怎 zěn

hǎi 10
sea, ocean

氵/水 shuǐ 'water' + 每 měi 'every' phonetic→ every drop of water in the ocean

海

海關	hǎiguān	customs, customhouse
海外	hǎiwài*	overseas, abroad
人山人海	rénshān-rénhǎi*	oceans of people

A: 你過海關的時候，有沒有問題？

B: 沒有，我只有一件行李。

Compare: 洗 xǐ 每 měi 母 mǔ

guān 19
to shut, barrier

門 mén 'door' + 絲 'threads being woven' phonetic

关

關門	guānmén	to close door
關心	guānxīn	to be concerned about
有關	yǒuguān	to have bearing on

A: 現在圖書館關門了沒有？

B: 早就關了。

Compare: 門 mén 開 kāi 送 sòng

From 首 shǒu 'head,' with the face circled

見面	jiànmiàn	to meet, see
裏面	lǐmiàn*	inside, interior
前面	qiánmiàn*	in front, ahead
後面	hòumiàn*	in back, behind

面

A: 你見過他嗎？

B: 沒有，這是我們第一次見面。

miàn 9
face, surface

Compare: 麵 miàn

An 目 eye mù, spying, looking out from behind a 木 mù tree

相信	xiāngxìn	to believe in
相反	xiāngfǎn	opposite, contrary
相同	xiāngtóng*	be alike
互相	hùxiāng	mutually, each other

相

A: 我相信他說的是真的。

B: 我的想法和你相反。

xiāng, xiàng 9
mutual, to look at

Compare: 想 xiǎng　箱 xiāng

刀 dāo 'knife' + 七 qī 'seven' phonetic

一切	yíqiè	all, every, everything
切開	qiēkāi*	to cut open

切

A: 希望你一切都很順利。

B: 謝謝。

qiè, qiē 4
absolutely, ardently, to cut

Compare: 功 gōng

扌 shǒu 'hand' + 高 gāo phonetic

搞好	gǎohǎo*	to do well
搞不好	gǎobuhǎo*	to do/go wrong
難搞	nángǎo*	messy, tricky

搞

A: 你的報告搞好了沒有？

B: 還沒有，這個研究真難搞。

Compare: 高 gāo

gǎo 13
generalized doing,
do/work/manage/etc.

Harvest the 禾 hé 'grain' with a 刂/刀 dāo 'knife' — benefit, profit

利

lì 7
profit, sharp

順利	shùnlì	smooth, successful
有利	yǒulì	to be beneficial
不利	búlì*	unfavorable
利用	lìyòng	to use, to utilize

A: 你常利用週末做什麼？
B: 我常利用週末學寫漢字。

stone-age chimes with 殳 shū 'beat' (a hand holding a mallet) + 耳 ěr 'ear'

声

shēng 17
sound, tone, fame

聲音	shēngyīn	sound, voice
大聲	dàshēng*	loud voice
小聲	xiǎoshēng*	soft sound

A: 你為什麼把雨衣穿上了？
B: 我聽到外面有雨聲。

A 犬 dog suddenly charging into a 穴 hole, to catch a rabbit, with its tail sticking out.

突

tū 9
to stick out, suddenly

| 突然 | tūrán | suddenly, abruptly |

A: 為什麼他突然不見了？
B: 他出去抽煙。

Compare: 空 kōng

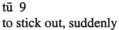

氵/水 shuǐ 'water' + 肖 xiào phonetic

消

xiāo 10
to disappear, to eliminate

| 消息 | xiāoxi | news, tidings |

A: 你最近有小高的消息嗎？
B: 沒有，他還沒給我寫信呢。

語法和用法 Grammar and Usage

Pay attention to the function of the structure and then study the example sentences.

1. Expressing a fortunate condition

好在(S)…,(要不然)…	hǎozài…(yàoburán)…	fortunately…(otherwise)

好在有你幫忙，從申請護照到辦簽證、買機票，一切都很順利。

1. 你事情辦得怎麼樣？　你事情办得怎么样？　How's business?

　　好在有你幫忙，要不然就糟糕了。　好在有你帮忙，要不然就糟糕了。　I am lucky to have your help. Otherwise, it would be a mess.

2. 那天的晚會怎麼樣？　那天的晚会怎么样？　How was the party the other day?

　　好在買了很多的東西，要不然就不夠吃了。　好在买了很多的东西，要不然就不够吃了。　Fortunately we bought enough food; otherwise, there would not have been enough for everyone.

3. 你的機票買了沒有？　你的机票买了没有？　Have you bought your ticket yet?

　　好在上個月就買了，現在買一定很貴。　好在上个月就买了，现在买一定很贵。　Fortunately I bought it last month. If I were to buy it now, it would surely be very expensive.

A general rule of Chinese usage which applies to the pattern above and numerous others that follow is that if the subject is established in the previous context, it may be subsequently dropped. If the subject of two adjoining clauses is the same, either may be dropped. If it does exist in the pattern above, it often occurs behind 好在.

2. Expressing a contingency

要不是S₁… S₂(早)就 S₁要不是… S₂(早)就	yàobushì…(zǎo)jiù…	If it had not been for…, then…

去機場的那天，**要不是**你送我，**就**來不及了。

1.	你為什麼不出國留學呢？	你为什么不出国留学呢？	Why don't you go abroad to study?
	要不是我沒有錢，我早就出國留學了。	要不是我没有钱，我早就出国留学了。	If I hadn't been poor, I would have gone abroad a long time ago.
2.	你不是想跟那個女的見面嗎？	你不是想跟那个女的见面吗？	Don't you want to meet that woman?
	我要不是太忙，早就請她去看電影了。	我要不是太忙，早就请她去看电影了。	If I hadn't been so busy, I would have taken her to see a movie some time ago.
3.	你不是說中文功課太多嗎？怎麼還學呢？	你不是说中文功课太多吗？怎么还学呢？	Didn't you say that Chinese (course) has too much homework? Why are you still taking it?
	要不是中文這麼有趣，我就不學了。	要不是中文这么有趣，我就不学了。	If Chinese hadn't been so interesting, I would have given it up.

This pattern often applies to events in retrospect. The subject is movable, going either before or after 要不是. (早) 就 is an adverb, so it always goes before the verb, not before the subject. If the meaning of the first clause is positive, that of the second clause is negative and vice versa. Don't confuse this pattern with 要是…就 'if… then.'

3. Expressing a sensory reaction

V起來 Adj	…qǐlái…	when, in the doing of V

好熟悉的聲音啊！**聽起來**很像你……

1.	你喜歡這兒嗎？	你喜欢这儿吗？	Do you like this place?
	看起來很漂亮，不知道住起來怎麼樣。	看起来很漂亮，不知道住起来怎么样。	It looks great, but I don't know how it will feel once I live here.

2. 你為什麼買了那輛車子？

你为什么买了那辆车子？

Why did you buy that car?

因為看起來很漂亮，開起來也不錯。

因为看起来很漂亮，开起来也不错。

Because it looks very attractive and drives well too.

3. 那家飯館的菜怎麼樣？

那家饭馆的菜怎么样？

How's the food in that restaurant?

吃起來還不錯。

吃起来还不错。

It tastes good.

In this pattern, 起來 goes after verbs of sense/perception such as 聽、看、聞、吃、住、開. Phrases after the V 起來 are usually adjective or adverbs that describe one's sensory reaction.

4. Expressing the actual reality behind a false assumption

S（以為）…原來…	… (yǐwéi)…yuánlái…	(thought)…it turns out that…
S 以為…其實…	…yǐwéi…qíshí…	thought…actually…
S 以為…哪知道…	…yǐwéi…nǎzhīdào…	thought…who knew that…

聽起來很像你，**原來**是你父親。

1. 你為什麼不問問他出國留學的事？

你为什么不问问他出国留学的事？

Why don't you ask him things about studying abroad?

我以為他是個教授，原來只是個學生。

我以为他是个教授，原来只是个学生。

I thought that he was a professor. It turns out that he is just a student.

2. 你出去做什麼？

你出去做什么？

Why did you go out?

我聽見外面有聲音，出去一看，原來下雨了。

我听见外面有声音，出去一看，原来下雨了。

I heard a noise outside, and I went out to see what was happening. It turned out that it was raining.

3.　你認識他嗎？你叫 | 你认识他吗？你叫 | Do you know him? Why
他，他怎麼不跟你 | 他，他怎么不跟你 | didn't he speak to you
說話？ | 说话？ | when you said hello?

我以為我認識他， | 我以为我认识他， | I thought that I knew him.
原來我看錯 cuò 人 | 原来我看错人了。 | Actually, I had mistaken
了。 | | him for someone else.

4.　中文容易嗎？ | 中文容易吗？ | Is Chinese easy?

我以為中文很容 | 我以为中文很容 | I thought that Chinese
易，其實中文很 | 易，其实中文很 | would be easy. Actually
難！ | 难！ | it's very hard.

5.　我以為他是中國 | 我以为他是中国 | I thought that he was
人，哪知道他連一 | 人，哪知道他连一 | Chinese. Who knew that
句中文也不會說。 | 句中文也不会说。 | he couldn't even say a
 | | single Chinese sentence.

其實他是日本人。 | 其实他是日本人。 | Actually he is a Japanese.

5.　Making a confirmation

A就是B	…jiùshì…	A is B
A就是B的意思	…jiùshì…de yìsi	A means/refers to B

告訴他我**就是**「那個老外」。

1.　站在那兒的人是 | 站在那儿的人是 | Who is that standing
誰？ | 谁？ | there?

他就是那個剛從美 | 他就是那个刚从美 | He is the student who just
國來的學生。 | 国来的学生。 | came from the U.S.

2.　請問，留學生宿舍 | 请问，留学生宿舍 | May I ask where the dorm
在哪兒？ | 在哪儿？ | for foreign students is?

留學生宿舍就是這 | 留学生宿舍就是这 | The dormitory for foreign
間。 | 间。 | students is right here.

3. 你知道什麼是「老   你知道什么是"老   Do you know what a
    外」嗎？   外"吗？   "Lao Wai" is?

    「老外」就是外國   "老外"就是外国   A "Lao Wai" is a
    人的意思。   人的意思。   foreigner.

This pattern is often used to emphasize, explain, or clarify some previously mentioned information. When used to provide a definition, "…的意思" often comes at the end of the sentence.

6. Expressing interest in something

A對B(Adv)感興趣	…duì…gǎn xìngqù	A is interested in B

我剛來美國的時候，也**對**什麼都很**感興趣**。

1. 你對什麼感興趣？   你对什么感兴趣？   What are you interested in?

    我對中國文學、英   我对中国文学、英   I am interested in Chinese
    國文學、美國文學   国文学、美国文学   literature, English literature,
    都感興趣。   都感兴趣。   and American literature.

2. 你為什麼不選那位   你为什么不选那位   Why didn't you take that
    教授的課？   教授的课？   professor's course?

    我對他的課一點兒   我对他的课一点儿   Because I was not interested
    也不感興趣。   也不感兴趣。   in his course at all.

3. 你為什麼借這麼多   你为什么借这么多   Why did you check out
    新書？   新书？   so many new books?

    因為我對新的語言   因为我对新的语言   Because I am very
    研究非常感興趣。   研究非常感兴趣。   interested in new research
                                                on language.

In this pattern, adverbs expressing degree of intensity such as 不、一點兒也不、很、非常、特別、十分、不太 always go before 感興趣. However, when forming a question, the adverb is often dropped. Note that in this pattern, B is **something** in which the subject A is interested; whereas in the pattern A對B (Adv) 有意思 'A is interested in B', B is **someone**.

文化點滴 Culture Notes

1. **Self and Others:** Among all the colloquial terms that Chinese use to denote foreigners (e.g., 洋人 yángrén 'foreigners,' 洋鬼子 yángguǐzi 'foreign devils'), 老外 lǎowài sounds relatively neutral. In fact, a common use of 老 is as a prefix for different ethnic groups such as 老美 lǎoměi, 老英 lǎoyīng, and 老法 lǎofǎ, and this includes Chinese 老中 themselves. Yet, what is worth noticing is that many Chinese, even when residing in foreign countries, still call non-Chinese 老外. This may reveal how Chinese view themselves, always as the people of the "middle kingdom" 中國.

2. **Names:** Chinese people attach great importance to the choice of names. Some considerations parents make when naming their children regard a desired quality, future prospect, or a situation at the time of birth. Formerly, when boys were more valued than girls, parents may have given a girl a name like 招弟 zhāodì 'come-brother' with the hope that next child would be a son. Someone with a name like 台生 táishēng 'Taiwan-born' is likely to have been born in Taiwan. If a fortune-teller judges that a child is lacking in one of the five elements (metal, wood, water, fire, and earth), she/he may find the characters for the child's name that are filled with "water" or "wood" radicals so as to compensate for the claimed deficiency. If one sees a name with hóng 紅 'red,' jūn 軍 'army,' gémìng 革命 'revolution,' bīng 兵 'soldier,' dōng 東 'east,' or tiě 鐵 'iron,' that person is likely to come from mainland China. Also, people in China tend to have more two-character names than those from Taiwan. In Taiwan, names with flower or grass radicals are still common for girls and those such as qiáng 強 'strong,' chéng 成 'success' or zhì 志 'aspiration' are often associated with boys.

3. **Terms of address:** When addressing one's family members, particularly elders, one always use kinship terms such as dàgē 大哥 'big elder brother,' èrdì 二弟 'second younger brother,' sānjiě 三姐 'third elder sister,' sìmèi 四妹 'fourth younger sister.' When addressing people outside of one's family, it's always safe to use professional titles such as lǎoshī 老師 'teacher,' jiàoshòu 教授 'professor,' zhǔrèn 主任 'director,' bùzhǎng 部長 'department head.' To address close friends, one can use a first name or 小/老 plus a family name. Yet, to address strangers or less familiar people on the street, Chinese seem to observe the sìhǎi yì jiā 四海一家 'the whole world is a family' principle, and extend kinship terms generously to outside members. Those who look older than one's father will be addressed as bóbo 伯伯 'uncles,' and those who look younger than one's father will be addressed as shūshu 叔叔 'uncles,' those who appear to be the same age as one's mother will be addressed as āyí 阿姨 'aunts,' and those who appear to be the same age as one's sister will be addressed as jiějie 姐姐 'elder sisters.'

歌兒 Songs

你的消息
Your News

Andante

詞、曲：李毓真

好 久 都 沒有 你的 消息，　聽說 你 已經 出國
Hǎo jiǔ dōu méiyǒu nǐ de xiāoxi.　Tīngshuō nǐ yǐjīng chūguó
It has been a long time since I heard from you.　I heard that you have gone abroad

學 習，　好 突然　我 真 的 不 敢 相　信
xué xí.　Hǎo tūrán　wǒ zhēn de bù gǎn xiāng xìn.
to study.　This is so sudden that I can hardly believe it.

來 不 及　聽聽 你 的 聲　音。　今 天 收
Lái bù jí　tīngting nǐ de shēng yīn.　Jīn tiān shōu
I couldn't even hear you one last time.　Today, I received

到 你 的 電 子 郵件，　讓 我 好 想 再 和 你
dào nǐ de diàn zǐ yóujiàn,　Ràng wǒ hǎo xiǎng zài hé nǐ
your e-mail.　This made me want to see you again.

見　面。　你 的 事 情　我 感 到 非 常 有 趣，
jiàn miàn.　Nǐ de shì qíng wǒ gǎn dào fēi cháng yǒu qù,
　Your stories sound very interesting to me.

很 高 興　聽到 你 一　切 都 順　利
Hěn gāo xìng　tīngdào nǐ yí qiè dōu shùn lì.
I'm glad to hear that everything is going smoothly for you.

第二課

Theme School Life and Roommates

Communicative Objectives
- Talking about school
- Discussing a room
- Commenting on one's roommate
- Expressing surprise

Focus on Characters
- 桌椅整齊、甚至無床、討論歷史、各地極閑、卻居交係

Grammar Focus
- 無論/不管⋯，S都⋯
- ⋯甚至還；⋯甚至連⋯都
- 雖然⋯(但是)S卻
- 這 time span (以)來
- (沒想到)⋯居然
- A跟B(沒)有關係

他怎麼那麼愛管閑事？

生詞 Vocabulary

Study the following words for their pronunciation and meaning. When an area is shaded, guess at the meaning of the word based on its constituent characters and then fill in the blank. Read the usage of words and related terms (antonyms, synonyms, compounds sharing the constituent characters, etc.) and try to answer the sample questions in Chinese. Note that proper nouns or incidental terms are not numbered.

◎ By Order of Appearance

1. 管閒事
   管闲事
   guǎn xiánshì   VO   to meddle, to poke one's nose into another's business   [manage-idle-matter]

   你覺得誰最愛管閒事？
   你觉得谁最爱管闲事？

2. 各   gè   Pron   each

   各人、各地、各國、各班
   中國各地的人都說一樣的話嗎？
   中国各地的人都说一样的话吗？

3. 適應
   适应
   shìyìng   V   to get used to   [suitable-adapt to]

   這裏的生活你適應了嗎？
   这里的生活你适应了吗？

4. 教材   jiàocái   N   teaching materials   [teach-timber]

   這一套教材要多少錢？
   这一套教材要多少钱？

5. 課本
   课本
   kèběn   N   textbook   [lesson-book]

   你一年級的時候用什麼課本？
   你一年级的时候用什么课本？

6. 內容   nèiróng   N   content, substance   [inside-contain]

   你覺得那本課本的內容有意思嗎？
   你觉得那本课本的内容有意思吗？

7. 生詞
   生词
   shēngcí   N   new word, vocabulary item   [unfamiliar-term]

   你一個星期學多少個生詞？
   你一个星期学多少个生词？

8. 句型   jùxíng   N   sentence pattern   [sentence-type]

   昨天你學了哪幾個句型？

昨天你學了哪幾個句型？

| 9. | 有用 | yǒuyòng | Adj | ▓▓▓▓▓▓▓▓▓▓ | [have-use] |

你覺得什麼活動對學中文最有用？

你觉得什么活动对学中文最有用？

| 10. | 常常 | chángcháng | Adv | frequently, often | [constant] |

你常常複習中文嗎？

你常常复习中文吗？

| 11. | 討論
讨论 | tǎolùn | V/N | to discuss, discussion | [discuss-mention] |

學生喜歡討論什麼樣的問題？

学生喜欢讨论什么样的问题？

| 12. | 課文
课文 | kèwén | N | text | [lesson-writing] |

這一課的課文你看了嗎？

这一课的课文你看了吗？

| 13. | 課外
课外 | kèwài | N | ▓▓▓▓▓▓▓▓ | [course-outside] |

你課外時間喜歡做什麼？

你课外时间喜欢做什么？

| 14. | 活動
活动 | huódòng | N/V | activity, to exercise | [life-move] |

大學生課外喜歡做些什麼活動？

大学生课外喜欢做些什么活动？

| 15. | 複習
复习 | fùxí | V | to review | [again-practice] |

你每天花多長時間複習中文？

你每天花多长时间复习中文？

| 16. | 預習
预习 | yùxí | V | to preview (lessons) | [prepare-practice] |

今天的課文你預習了沒有？

今天的课文你预习了没有？

| 17. | 無論
无论 | wúlùn | Conj | regardless of, no matter (how/who/what/etc.) | [not-discuss] |

無論忙不忙，你每天都會做什麼？

无论忙不忙，你每天都会做什么？

Characters with Many Strokes

管　閑　適　應　型　論　複　習　預　無

18.	地方	dìfang	N	place	[place-place]
19.	想像	xiǎngxiàng	V	to imagine, to fancy	[think-image]
	想象				

你能想像他在中國的生活嗎？

你能想象他在中国的生活吗？

| 20. | 床 | chuáng | N | bed | |

你睡單人床dānrénchuáng 'twin-size bed' 還是雙人
床shuāngrénchuáng 'full-size bed'？

你睡单人床还是双人床？

| 21. | 桌子 | zhuōzi | N | table, desk | [table-suffix] |

你的桌子上有些什麼東西？

你的桌子上有些什么东西？

| 22. | 椅子 | yǐzi | N | chair | [chair-suffix] |

你的屋子裏有幾把椅子？

你的屋子里有几把椅子？

| 23. | 甚至 | shènzhì | Conj | even (to the point of), so much so that | [very-to] |

他學了兩年的中文，甚至連自己的名字都不
會寫。

他学了两年的中文，甚至连自己的名字都不
会写。

| 24. | 套 | tào | M | set | |

一套衣服、一套書、一套沙發

你身上這套衣服要多少錢？

你身上这套衣服要多少钱？

| 25. | 沙發 | shāfā | N | sofa | [sand-rise] |
| | 沙发 | | | | |

你的沙發舒服嗎？

你的沙发舒服吗？

| 26. | 乾淨 | gānjìng | Adj/ | clean, neat and tidy | [dry-clean] |
| | 干淨 | | SV | | |

你的同屋是一個愛乾淨的人嗎？

你的同屋是一个爱干净的人吗？

| 27. | 整齊 | zhěngqí | Adj/ | neat, tidy | [arrange-even] |
| | 整齐 | | SV | | |

你的房間整齊嗎？

你的房间整齐吗？

| 28. | 地毯 | dìtǎn | N | carpet, rug | [ground-blanket] |

你的房間裏有地毯嗎？

你的房间里有地毯吗？

| 29. | 空調 | kōngtiáo | N | <PRC> | [air-adjust] |
| | 空调 | | | | |

<TW>冷氣 lěngqì

你覺得這裏的空調夠不夠冷？

你觉得这里的空调够不够冷？

| 30. | 卻 | què | Conj/ | however, but, yet | |
| | 却 | | Adv | 雖然那個老師很嚴，我卻喜歡上他的課。 | |

虽然那个老师很严，我却喜欢上他的课。

| 31. | 極了 | -jíle | Suf | extremely, very | [extreme-particle] |
| | 极了 | | | | |

好極了、美極了

這個校園美極了。

这个校园美极了。

| 32. | 唯一 | wéiyī | Adj | only, sole | [only-one] |

唯一的問題/興趣/孩子

你是你家唯一的孩子嗎？

你是你家唯一的孩子吗？

| 33. | 頭疼 | tóuténg | V/N | | [head-hurt] |
| | 头疼 | | | | |

什麼事情讓你很頭疼？

什么事情让你很头疼？

| 34. | 歷史 | lìshǐ | N | history | [past-history] |
| | 历史 | | | | |

你對中國歷史感興趣嗎？

你对中国历史感兴趣吗？

| 35. | 系 | xì | N | department (in a college) | |

你是哪一個系的學生？

你是哪一个系的学生？

| | 狗拿耗子 | gǒu ná hàozi | IE | to be meddlesome | [dog-catch-mouse] |

Characters with Many Strokes

像　套　發　整　齊　毯　調　極　頭　歷

| 36. | 不管 | bùguǎn | Conj | no matter, regardless of | [not-manage] |

不管有沒有錢，我都想上大學。

不管有没有钱，我都想上大学。

| 37. | 好奇 | hàoqí | Adj/ SV | curious | [like-strange] |

對⋯⋯很好奇

你對什麼很好奇？

你对什么很好奇？

| 38. | 沒想到 | méixiǎng dào | RV | unexpectedly | [not have-think of] |

學中文以前，你沒想到什麼？

学中文以前，你没想到什么？

| 39. | 以來 以来 | -yǐlái | Suf | since | [from a point on-come] |

這三個星期以來，你給家裏打電話了嗎？

这三个星期以来，你给家里打电话了吗？

| 40. | 居然 | jūrán | Adv | unexpectedly, to one's surprise | [claim-so] |

他沒問我，居然就拿了我的書。

他没问我，居然就拿了我的书。

| 41. | 過去 过去 | guòqù | N | past | [pass-go] |

你對他的過去熟悉嗎？

你对他的过去熟悉吗？

| 42. | 交 | jiāo | V | to make (friends), to hand over | |

交朋友、交作業

你現在交了幾個中國朋友？

你现在交了几个中国朋友？

| 43. | 等等 | děngděng | Part | and so on, etc. | [and so on] |

課外的時候，我喜歡看電影、聽音樂、打球等等。

课外的时候，我喜欢看电影、听音乐、打球等等。

Characters with Many Strokes

管　然　等

◎ By Grammatical Categories

Nouns/Pronouns/Measure Words

教材	jiàocái	teaching materials		椅子	yǐzi	chair
課本	kèběn	textbook		沙發	shāfā	sofa
課文	kèwén	text		地毯	dìtǎn	carpet, rug
課外	kèwài	extracurricular		空調	kōngtiáo	air-conditioning
內容	nèiróng	content, substance		歷史	lìshǐ	history
生詞	shēngcí	new word, vocabulary item		系	xì	department (in a college), faculty
句型	jùxíng	sentence pattern		過去	guòqù	past
地方	dìfang	place		活動	huódòng	activity, to exercise
床	chuáng	bed		各	gè	each
桌子	zhuōzi	table, desk		套	tào	set

Verbs/Stative Verbs/Adjectives

交	jiāo	to make (friends), to hand over		管閑事	guǎn xiánshì	to meddle, to poke one's nose into another's business
適應	shìyìng	to get used to		沒想到	méixiǎngdào	unexpectedly
預習	yùxí	to prepare lessons before class		乾淨	gānjìng	clean, neat and tidy
複習	fùxí	to review		整齊	zhěngqí	neat, tidy
討論	tǎolùn	to discuss, discussion		好奇	hàoqí	curious
想像	xiǎngxiàng	to imagine, to fancy		唯一	wéiyī	only, sole
頭疼	tóuténg	headache				
有用	yǒuyòng	useful				

Adverbs and Others

常常	chángcháng	frequently, often		甚至	shènzhì	even (to the point of), so much so that
居然	jūrán	unexpectedly, to one's surprise		卻	què	however, but, yet
無論	wúlùn	no matter (how/who/what/ etc.), regardless of		等等	děngděng	and so on, etc.
				極了	-jíle	extremely, very
不管	bùguǎn	no matter, regardless of		以來	-yǐlái	since

◎ By Pinyin

Entries with * indicate lexical items used in Mini-Dialogues and of possible interest for supplemental study.

bùguǎn	不管	regardless of	méixiǎngdào	没想到	unexpectedly
chángcháng	常常	often	nèiróng	内容	content
chuáng	床	bed	què	却	however, yet
děngděng	等等	and so on, etc.	ruǎn*	软	soft
dìfang	地方	place	shāfā	沙发	sofa
dìtǎn	地毯	carpet, rug	shēngcí	生词	new word
fùxí	复习	to review	shènzhì	甚至	so much so that
gānjìng	干净	clean	shìyìng	适应	to get used to
gè	各	each	tǎolùn	讨论	to discuss, discussion
gōnggòng*	公共	public	tào	套	set
guǎn xiánshì	管闲事	to meddle, to poke one's nose into another's business	tóuténg	头疼	headache
			wéiyī	唯一	only, sole
guòqù	过去	past	wúlùn	无论	no matter
hàoqí	好奇	curious	xiǎngxiàng	想象	to imagine, to fancy
huódòng	活动	activity, to exercise	xì	系	department (in a college)
jiāo	交	to make (friends), to hand over			
jiàocái	教材	teaching materials	-yǐlái	以来	since
-jíle	极了	extremely	yìng*	硬	hard
jūrán	居然	unexpectedly	yǐzi	椅子	chair
jùxíng	句型	sentence pattern	yǒuyòng	有用	useful
kèběn	课本	textbook	yùshì*	浴室	bathroom, shower room
kèwài	课外	extracurricular	yùxí	预习	to prepare lessons before class
kèwén	课文	text	zhěngqí	整齐	neat, tidy
kōngtiáo	空调	air-conditioning	zhuōzi	桌子	table, desk
lìshǐ	历史	history			

課文 Text

Use the following questions to guide your reading of the text.

1. 小高喜歡他的學校嗎？為什麼？

2. 小高的房間怎麼樣？裏面有些什麼東西？

3. 為什麼小高不喜歡他的同屋？

小李：

　　我來北京快三個星期了，各方面都適應得不錯。我很喜歡我們的學校，尤其喜歡我們用的教材，課本不但內容很有趣，而且生詞和句型都很有用。老師常常上午讓我們討論課文，下午就讓我們參加課外活動，晚上讓我們自己複習、預習。我覺得我[1]**無論**聽或說，**都**有了很大的進步。

　　現在我住的地方比我原來想像的好得多。有床、桌子、椅子、書架，[2]**甚至還有**一套小沙發！屋子裏乾淨、整齊，也很漂亮，[3]**雖然**沒有地毯和空調，住起來**卻**舒服極了。現在唯

一讓我頭疼的是我那個念歷史系的同屋，他很喜歡「狗拿耗子——多管閑事」。不管我做什麼他都好奇得很：我一出去他就問我上哪兒去，一回來他就問我剛才做了什麼。[4]**這**兩個星期**來**，他[5]**居然**對我過去的「歷史」也開始感興趣了。他問我在美國有沒有交過女朋友、有沒有工作、一個月賺多少錢等等。這些都是我的事，[6]**跟**他**有**什麼**關係**呢？你說他怎麼那麼愛管閑事？

德中

课文 Text

Use the following questions to guide your reading of the text.

1. 小高喜欢他的学校吗？为什么？

2. 小高的房间怎么样？里面有些什么东西？

3. 为什么小高不喜欢他的同屋？

 小李：

　　我来北京快三个星期了，各方面都适应得不错。我很喜欢我们的学校，尤其喜欢我们用的教材，课本不但内容很有趣，而且生词和句型都很有用。老师常常上午让我们讨论课文，下午就让我们参加课外活动，晚上让我们自己复习、预习。我觉得我[1]**无论**听或说，**都**有了很大的进步。

　　现在我住的地方比我原来想象的好得多。有床、桌子、椅子、书架，[2]**甚至还有**一套小沙发！屋子里干净、整齐，也很漂亮，[3]**虽然**

没有地毯和空调，住起来**却**舒服极了。现在唯一让我头疼的是我那个念历史系的同屋，他实在是喜欢"狗拿耗子——多管闲事。"不管我做什么他都好奇得很：我一出去他就问我上哪儿去，一回来他就问我刚才做了什么。[4]**这**两个星期**来**，他

[5]**居然**对我过去的"历史"也开始感兴趣了。他问我在美国有没有交过女朋友、有没有工作、一个月赚多少钱等等。这些都是我的事，[6]**跟**他**有**什么**关系**呢？你说他怎么那么爱管闲事？

德中

小對話 Mini-Dialogues

Read the supplementary dialogues for a better understanding of the text. See if you can memorize one and perform it in class.

(1) Talking about school

A: 聽說這個學校不錯。

听说这个学校不错。

Gao: 那還用說？這裏的老師、教材和教法都好極了！

那还用说？这里的老师、教材和教法都好极了！

A: 你每天上幾節課呢？

你每天上几节课呢？

Gao: 四節，都在上午，我們練習聽、說、讀、寫。

四节，都在上午，我们练习听、说、读、写。

A: 下午做什麼呢？

下午做什么呢？

Gao: 下午三點半以後是課外活動的時間。

下午三点半以后是课外活动的时间。

A: 晚上呢？

晚上呢？

Gao: 晚飯以後，大家自己去圖書館複習或預習課文。

晚饭以后，大家自己去图书馆复习或预习课文。

A: I heard that this school is great.

Gao: You said it. Our teachers, learning materials, and teaching methods are all superb!

A: How many classes do you have every day?

Gao: Four. They are all in the morning. We practice listening, speaking, reading, and writing.

A: How about afternoons?

Gao: After three o'clock, it is time for extracurricular activities.

A: How about evenings?

Gao: After dinner, we go to the library to review or preview texts.

(2) Discussing a room

A:	你覺得這間屋子怎麼樣？	你觉得这间屋子怎么样？
Gao:	地方小是小，可是什麼都有。	地方小是小，可是什么都有。
A:	你不覺得床有一點兒硬 yìng 嗎？	你不觉得床有一点儿硬吗？
Gao:	床硬一點兒對身體好。	床硬一点儿对身体好。
A:	沙發好像太軟 ruǎn 了。	沙发好象太软了。
Gao:	軟的沙發坐起來舒服。	软的沙发坐起来舒服。

A:　　What do you think of this room?

Gao:　It's small all right, but equipped with everything.

A:　　Don't you think the bed is a bit firm?

Gao:　A firm bed is good for your body.

A:　　The sofa seems to be too soft.

Gao:　A soft sofa is comfortable to sit on.

(3) Commenting on one's roommate

A:	你的同屋怎麼樣？	你的同屋怎么样？
Gao:	他很愛乾淨，東西也放得很整齊。	他很爱干净，东西也放得很整齐。
A:	那不是很好嗎？	那不是很好吗？
Gao:	好什麼好，他的東西都不許別人動。	好什么好，他的东西都不许别人动。
A:	你習慣了以後就好了。	你习惯了以后就好了。
Gao:	可是他又很好奇，整天管別人的閑事。	可是他又很好奇，整天管别人的闲事。
A:	那真是很讓人頭疼。	那真是很让人头疼。

A: How is your roommate?

Gao: He is a real neat-freak and has everything arranged very tidily.

A: Isn't that great?

Gao: What's so good about it? He won't let anyone else touch his stuff.

A: It will be all right after you get used to him.

Gao: But he is also very curious. All day long he is looking into other people's affairs.

A: What a headache!

(4) Expressing surprise

Gao: 天啊！我們的宿舍居然沒有空調。

A: 這有什麼奇怪的？連圖書館都沒有空調。

Gao: 這兒連熱水也沒有。我怎麼洗澡呢？

A: 我們有公共gōnggòng浴室yùshì。

Gao: 那書架呢？我的書放哪兒？

A: 就放在桌子上吧。

Gao: 天啊！我们的宿舍居然没有空调。

A: 这有什么奇怪的？连图书馆都没有空调。

Gao: 这儿连热水也没有。我怎么洗澡呢？

A: 我们有公共浴室。

Gao: 那书架呢？我的书放哪儿？

A: 就放在桌子上吧。

Gao: God! Can you believe there is no air-conditioning in our dormitory?

A: What's so strange about that? Even the library has no air-conditioning.

Gao: And there isn't even hot water here. How will I take a bath?

A: We have public restrooms.

Gao: How about a bookshelf? Where can I put my books?

A: Just put them on the desk.

小故事 Stories

Read the following tale for your own enjoyment and for your understanding of the highlighted expression that is relevant to the theme of the chapter.

 愚公移山 Yúgōng yíshān

❀ 老師說學中文雖然難，可是只要我們有愚公移山的精神，總有一天可以把中文學好。

從前有一個老人名字叫愚公。他九十多歲了，住在一個山腳下。因為他的家門口有一座大山，他出門的時候都要繞很遠的路。他決定要把自己門前的山搬走。

他每天帶著全家人出去工作，把山上的土和石頭，一點兒一點兒地搬到很遠的地方去。附近有一個老人看到了，就對愚公說：「不是我愛管閒事，你已經九十多歲了，怎麼能把山搬走呢？」愚公說：「如果我死了，還有兒子；兒子死了，還有孫子。我們總有一天可以把這座大山搬走。」天上的神聽到他的話，很感動，就把愚公家門口的山搬到別的地方去了。

愚公	Yúgōng	a foolish old man
移	yí	to move
山	shān	mountain
歲	suì	year (of age)
山腳	shānjiǎo	the foot of the mountain
座	zuò	M for 山
繞路	ràolù	to make a detour
遠	yuǎn	far
搬	bān	to move
土	tǔ	soil
石頭	shítou	stone
運走	yùnzǒu	to carry away
丟	diū	to throw
兒子	érzi	son
孫子	sūnzi	grandson
天上	tiānshàng	sky, heaven
神	shén	god
弄	nòng	to fetch, handle

✎ 愚公移山的意思是_____

愚公移山 Yúgōng yíshān

❀　老师说学中文虽然难，可是只要我们有愚公移山的精神，总有一天可以把中文学好。

　　从前有一个老人名字叫愚公。他九十多岁了，住在一个山脚下。因为他的家门口有一座大山，他出门的时候都要绕很远的路。他决定要把自己门前的山搬走。

　　他每天带着全家人出去工作，把山上的土和石头，一点儿一点儿地搬到很远的地方去。附近有一个老人看到了，就对愚公说："不是我爱管闲事，你已经九十多岁了，怎么能把山搬走呢？"愚公说："如果我死了，还有儿子；儿子死了，还有孙子。我们总有一天可以把这座大山搬走。"天上的神听到他的话，很感动，就把愚公家门口的山搬到别的地方去了。

愚公	Yúgōng	a foolish old man
移	yí	to move
山	shān	mountain
岁	suì	year (of age)
山脚	shānjiǎo	the foot of the mountain
座	zuò	M for 山
绕路	ràolù	to make a detour
远	yuǎn	far
搬	bān	to move
土	tǔ	soil
石头	shítou	stone
运走	yùnzǒu	to carry away
丢	diū	to throw
儿子	érzi	son
孙子	sūnzi	grandson
天上	tiānshàng	sky, heaven
神	shén	god
弄	nòng	to fetch, handle

漢字 Characters

Study the following selected characters for further enrichment of your writing and vocabulary.

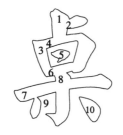

木 mù 'wood'
+ the top of
卓 zhuó 'high'

桌子	zhuōzi	table, desk
書桌	shūzhuō*	(writing) desk
飯桌	fànzhuō*	dining table

A: 你為什麼不喜歡那個房間？
B: 那兒連桌子也沒有。

zhuō 10
desk, table

木 mù 'wood'
+ 奇 qí
phonetic

| 椅子 | yǐzi | chair |
| 輪椅 | lúnyǐ* | wheelchair |

A: 請你把這三把椅子搬出去。
B: 你要我把它們放在哪兒？

Compare: 奇 qí 機 jī 樓 lóu

yǐ 12
chair

敕 chì
'imperial
command' + 正
zhèng 'straight,
correct'

整齊	zhěngqí	in good order
整天	zhěngtiān	the whole day, all day
整夜	zhěngyè*	all night long

A: 我昨天整個晚上都在趕報告。
B: 你整夜沒睡啊！

Compare: 正 zhèng

zhěng 16
tidy, to put in order

a picture of the
even height of
ears in a
cornfield — a
whole, regular
and perfect
harmony

A: 他的房間整齊嗎？
B: 一點兒也不整齊。

qí 14
even, equal in length

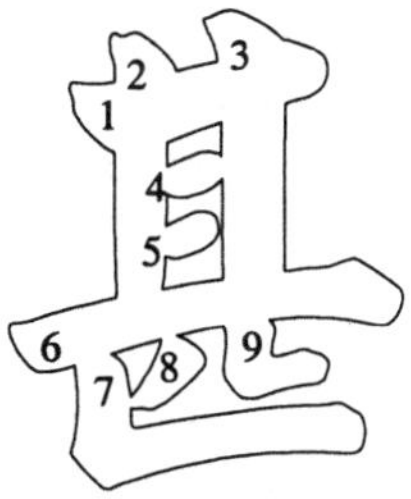

Affection 甘 for the being 匹 that makes the pair (sexual)—superlative, very

甚

甚至	shènzhì	even (to the point of)
甚至於	shènzhìyú*	so much so that
甚/什麼	shénme	what

A: 那家市場怎麼樣？

B: 什麼都賣，甚至連中國的東西也有。

Compare: 什 shén

shèn 9
very, more (than)

Picture of an arrow that has reached its target

至

至於	zhìyú	as for, as to
至少	zhìshǎo*	at (the) least
不至於	búzhìyú*	be unlikely to end up

A: 你忙嗎？不至於連飯都沒吃吧。

B: 忙極了，甚至連水都沒時間喝。

Compare: 到 dào 室 shì 屋 wū

zhì 6
to, until

Picture of a dancer with fancy sleeves or tassels in his or her hands, later borrowed for the word 'without'

无

無論	wúlùn	no matter what/how/etc.
無數	wúshù*	countless
無法	wúfǎ*	unable to, cannot

A: 無論你怎麼說，他都無法了解嗎？

B: 就是，我已經跟他說了無數次了。

Compare: 舞 wǔ

wú 12
without, nothingness

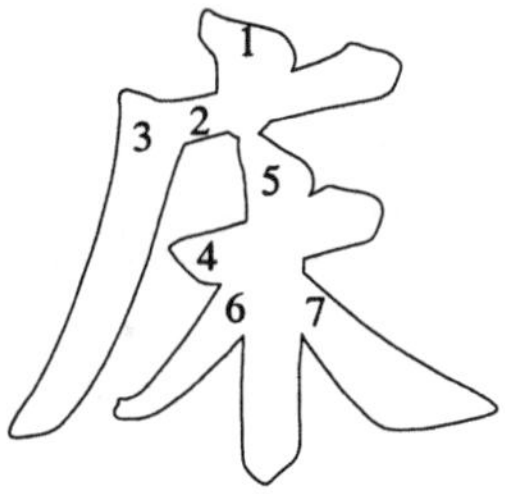

广 guǎng 'roof' + 木 mù 'wood'
Beds are made of wood and located under roofs.

床

起床	qǐchuáng	to get up (from bed)

A: 你每天幾點起床？

B: 八點半。

chuáng 7
bed, bedding

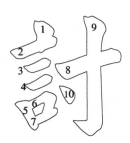

言 yán 'words'
+ 寸 cùn 'inch'

討論	tǎolùn	to discuss

A: 我們今天討論什麼？

B: 討論歷史和語言的關係。

tǎo 10
to discuss

言 yán 'words'
+ 侖 lún
phonetic

不論	búlùn	no matter (how/who/etc.)
結論	jiélùn*	conclusion
論文	lùnwén*	thesis, dissertation
論點	lùndiǎn*	argument, thesis

A: 你覺得他的論文怎麼樣？

B: 論點不錯，可是結論不夠好。

Compare: 語 yǔ 談 tán 許 xǔ

lùn 15
to discuss, to mention

止 zhǐ 'a
foot—to go
through' + 厂
and 秝 a
phonetic
component

歷史	lìshǐ	history, past records
經歷	jīnglì*	experience
學歷	xuélì	record of formal schooling

A: 他的學歷、經歷怎麼樣？

B: 很好，是搞歷史的，去過中國。

Compare: 曆 lì

lì 16
to experience, through

Hand holding a
stylus (pen) and
writing on a □
wooden block

史學	shǐxué*	historiography
史學家	shǐxuéjiā*	historian
史書	shǐshū*	history book

A: 什麼是歷史？

B: 歷史就是過去的事。

shǐ 5
history

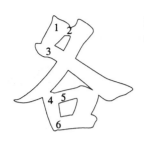

夂 zhǐ 'a foot pointing down over' 口 kǒu 'mouth'

各種	gèzhǒng*	various kinds
各樣	gèyàng*	all sorts/kinds
各地	gèdì*	various places/localities
各位	gèwèi*	you all, everybody

各

A: 你對美國各地都很熟悉嗎？
B: 對！我各種各樣的地方都去過。

Compare: 路 lù 客 kè

gè 6
each, every, different

土 tǔ 'earth' + 也 yě 'also' phonetic

地方	dìfang	place, space
地位	dìwèi	position, status
地球	dìqiú*	the earth/globe
土地	tǔdì*	land, soil

地

A: 這兒誰都認識他嗎？
B: 對，他在這個地方很有社會地位。

Compare: 也 yě 塊 kuài 場 chǎng

dì 6
the earth, land, fields

木 mù 'tree' + 亟 jí phonetic

好極了	hǎojíle	Great!
快極了	kuàijíle	extremely fast
北極	běijí*	North Pole

极

A: 為什麼你什麼都不懂？
B: 那個教授說話說得快極了。

Compare: 級 jí

jí 12
extreme(ly)

Formerly represented by 閒 a door 門 through the crevice of which the 月 moonlight peeps in

閑事	xiánshì	other people's business
閑話	xiánhuà*	gossip
閑人	xiánrén*	idler

A: 誰常常管你的閑事？
B: 我的同屋，他也很愛說別人的閑話。

閑

xián 12
idle, leisure

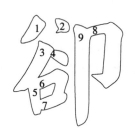

卩 jié 'a person kneeling' + 谷 gǔ phonetic—decline, on the contrary, but

却

A: 你為什麼這麼難過？

B: 我花了很長時間預習，卻考不好。

Compare: 腳 jiǎo

què 9
however, but, yet

尸 shī 'body — depicting a person lying down' + 古 gǔ phonetic

居

居然	jūrán	to one's surprise
定居	dìngjū*	to settle down
同居	tóngjū*	to live together

A: 他今天居然沒來考試？

B: 可不是嗎？我以為他是個好學生。

Compare: 屋 wū

jū 8
to reside, to assert, house

Picture of a person with crossed legs

交

交朋友	jiāo péngyǒu	to make friends
交談	jiāotán*	to converse
外交	wàijiāo*	diplomacy, foreign affairs

A: 你為什麼不跟他交朋友？

B: 因為我們沒法交談。

Compare: 校 xiào　較 jiào　餃 jiǎo

jiāo 6
to hand over, to meet, to deal

亻/ 人 rén 'person' + 系 xì '爪 hand above, now badly contracted, and 糸 silk thread'

系

| 關係 | guānxi | relation, impact |
| 沒關係 | méi guānxi | it doesn't matter |

A: 你用她的電腦，可以嗎？

B: 沒關係，我們倆的關係很好。

Compare: 系 xì　經 jīng　練 liàn

xì 9
to tie, to relate to, system

語法和用法 Grammar and Usage

Pay attention to the function of the structure and then study the example sentences.

1. Expressing invariability

無論/不管A還是B, S都(不/沒) 　　A not A 　　QW…	wúlùn/bùguǎn… háishi…, …dōu (bù/méi)	No matter how/what/ why/when…,

我覺得我**無論**聽或說，**都**有了很大的進步。

1. 你什麼時候在家？
   我來看你。

   你什么时候在家？
   我来看你。

   When will you be home?
   I would like to visit you.

   不管你什麼時候
   來，我都在家。

   不管你什么时候
   来，我都在家。

   No matter when you
   come, I will be home.

2. 我們能不能不聽
   寫？

   我们能不能不听
   写？

   Can we not have a
   dictation?

   無論你們喜歡不喜
   歡，我們都得聽
   寫。

   无论你们喜欢不喜
   欢，我们都得听
   写。

   No matter whether you
   like it or not, we have to
   have a dictation.

3. 你喜歡早上學習還
   是晚上學習？

   你喜欢早上学习还
   是晚上学习？

   Do you like to study in
   the morning or in the
   evening?

   不管早上還是晚上
   學習，我都不喜
   歡。

   不管早上还是晚上
   学习，我都不喜
   欢。

   I don't ever like to study.

4. 我不知道自己考得
   怎麼樣。

   我不知道自己考得
   怎么样。

   I don't know how I did
   on this test.

   無論好不好，你都
   應該繼續努力。

   无论好不好，你都
   应该继续努力。

   No matter whether it turns
   out well or not, you
   should keep working hard.

After 無論/不管 comes one of three forms: alternatives, A not A, or a question word.

Note that "no matter what" in Chinese is 無論怎麼樣, not 無論什麼.

2. Expressing a remarkable extent or degree

…甚至還有N	…shènzhì hái yǒu…	…even has N…
…甚至還要V	…shènzhì hái yào…	…even needs to V…
…甚至(連)NP都V	…shènzhì (lián)…dōu…	…even …

有床、桌子、椅子、書架，**甚至還有**一套小沙發！

1.	你的大學怎麼樣？	你的大学怎么样？	How is your university?
	非常好，甚至每間教室都有電腦。	非常好，甚至每間教室都有电脑。	It's so good; every classroom is equipped with computers.
2.	你的中文課怎麼樣？	你的中文课怎么样？	How is your Chinese class?
	很重，每天要學生字、句型，甚至還要寫日記rìjì。	很重，每天要学生字、句型，甚至还要写日记。	Very heavy. We have to study new words, sentence patterns, and even write a journal entry every day.
3.	那個晚會怎麼樣？	那个晚会怎么样？	How was that evening party?
	很多人參加，甚至連系上的教授都來了。	很多人参加，甚至连系上的教授都来了。	A lot of people showed up; even the department faculty came.

3. Making an argument with a concessive clause

| 雖然S…(但是/可是)(S)卻 | suīrán…(dànshì/kěshì)…què | Although… , …yet |
| S雖然…(但是/可是)(S)卻 | | |

雖然沒有地毯和空調，住起來**卻**舒服極了。

| 1. | 你為什麼不住學校的宿舍呢？ | 你为什么不住学校的宿舍呢？ | Why don't you live in the dorm? |

	宿舍雖然方便，但是卻太貴了。	宿舍虽然方便，但是却太贵了。	Living in the dorm is convenient, but too expensive.
2.	你為什麼不選中國歷史課呢？	你为什么不选中国历史课呢？	Why don't you take Chinese history?
	中國歷史課雖然有意思，功課卻很重。	中国历史课虽然有意思，功课却很重。	The Chinese history course is interesting, but the workload is very heavy.
3.	你不是說中文難嗎？怎麼還學呢？	你不是说中文难吗？怎麼还学呢？	Didn't you say that Chinese is hard? Why do you continue to take it?
	中文雖然難，卻很有用。	中文虽然难，却很有用。	Although Chinese is hard, it is useful.

Note that 卻 as an adverb always precedes the verb, not the subject. It indicates that an action or situation is contrary to what is expected or reasonable.

4. Indicating a period of time from past to present

這time span（以）來	zhè…(yǐ)lái	over the past (days/months, etc.)

這兩個星期**來**，他居然對我過去的「歷史」也開始感興趣了。

1.	你為什麼這麼高興？	你为什么这么高兴？	Why are you so happy?
	這兩個月來，我的中文有很大的進步。	这两个月来，我的中文有很大的进步。	My Chinese has improved a lot over the last two months.
2.	你為什麼好幾次沒來上課？	你为什么好几次没来上课？	Why didn't you come to class several times?
	這兩個星期來，我一直在生病。	这两个星期来，我一直在生病。	I have been sick for the last two weeks.

3. | 為什麼好久沒見到你？ | 为什么好久没见到你？ | Why haven't I seen you for a long time? |
|---|---|---|
| 這一年來，我都在忙著申請學校。 | 这一年来，我都在忙着申请学校。 | This past year I have been busy applying to schools. |

This adverbial time expression indicates a span of time up to the present. 來 is the same as 以來 but sounds more colloquial. Note that if a past event, instead of a period of time, goes before 以來, it means "(ever) since…," as in 自從…以來 (L4, G1).

5. Indicating something contrary to expectation or common sense

(S₁) (沒想到) S₂居然…	… (méi xiǎngdào)…jūrán…	Surprisingly S₂…

這兩個星期來，他**居然**對我過去的「歷史」也開始感興趣了。

1. | 你為什麼這麼不高興？ | 你为什么这么不高兴？ | Why are you so upset? |
|---|---|---|
| 沒想到我的同屋居然要我整理zhěnglǐ他的桌子。 | 没想到我的同屋居然要我整理他的桌子。 | To my surprise, my roommate asked me to clean his desk. |

2. | 他的中文怎麼樣？ | 他的中文怎么样？ | How is his Chinese? |
|---|---|---|
| 不太好，學過一年的中文，居然連「請坐」都不懂。 | 不太好，学过一年的中文，居然连"请坐"都不懂。 | Not too good. He has studied one year of Chinese, but he doesn't even understand the phrase "Sit down, please." |

3. | 你怎麼沒買到書？ | 你怎么没买到书？ | Why didn't you buy the book? |
|---|---|---|
| 沒想到書店居然這麼早關門。 | 没想到书店居然这么早关门。 | Unexpectedly, the bookstore closed early. |

Since 居然 is used to indicate surprise, 沒想到 often goes before it.

6.   Expressing relevancy

A跟B（沒）有關係	gēn…(méi)yǒu guānxi	A is (not) related to B
A跟B 有一點兒關係	gēn…yǒu yìdiǎnr guānxi	A is somewhat related to B
A跟B 沒有什麼關係	gēn…méiyǒu shénme guānxi	A is not really related to B
A跟B一點兒關係也沒有	gēn…yìdiǎnr guānxi yě méi yǒu	A is not related to B at all

這些都是我的事，**跟**他**有**什麼**關係**呢？

1. 你為什麼每天都遲
    到呢？

    你为什么每天都迟
    到呢？

    Why are you late every
    day?

    這跟我的同屋有很
    大的關係。

    这跟我的同屋有很
    大的关系。

    This has a lot to do with
    my roommate.

2. 聽說你認識小李？

    听说你认识小李？

    I heard that you know
    Xiao Li?

    什麼？我跟他一點
    兒關係也沒有。

    什么？我跟他一点
    儿关系也没有。

    What? I have nothing to
    do with him.

3. 你身體不好，怎麼
    還抽煙？

    你身体不好，怎么
    还抽烟？

    Your health is not very
    good. Why do you keep
    smoking?

    抽煙跟身體好不好
    有什麼關係？

    抽烟跟身体好不好
    有什么关系？

    What does smoking
    have to do with my
    health?

Note the various ways to indicate the relationship between A and B. When A and B are
abstract nouns, there is often a causal relationship in which B is often the cause. When
A and B are both people, the relationship is usually personal and the connotation of the
"relationship" is often negative, such as an affair or a (political) scandal.

文化點滴 Culture Notes

1. **Greetings:** When Chinese greet each other, the context (time, place, relationship between addresser and addressee) decides what phrase people will use to say "hi." If you appear to be going out somewhere, people may greet you with the question 你上哪兒去？"Where are you going"; whereas if you look as if you are just returning from somewhere, people may greet you with the question 剛回來啊？"Have you just come back?" Around mealtime, people quite frequently use the phrase 吃飯了沒有？"Have you eaten yet?" Chinese use these questions/phrases as greetings, without any intention of prying into others' business. Thus, these questions do not need to be taken seriously. You can just reply whatever you feel is right or appropriate at the time. One can also detect social changes or concerns embedded in greetings. For example, nowadays young people in Beijing may greet each other with the phrase 你上網了沒有？"Have you logged on yet?"

2. **Privacy:** While it is true that Chinese people do not generally concern themselves with others' business when greeting each other, one still finds it harder to maintain one's "privacy" in China or Taiwan. In one respect, this is due to the fact that China has the largest population in the world. Thus, no matter where one goes, one is bound to "bump" into someone. In addition to this physical proximity (e.g., on the buses and trains), Chinese people tend to have a blurred distinction between public and private matters, and they often ask people all sorts of questions just to show their concern and goodwill.

3. **School facilities:** Although schools in China and Taiwan have greatly improved in recent years, their facilities may not be on par with their Western counterparts. It is common to find dorms with six to eight students staying in the same room and many buildings without air-conditioning. Students from other countries, however, will be placed in much better equipped dorms than those of native Chinese students. In addition to the lack of air-conditioning, one may not find hot water whenever one desires. Usually there is a schedule indicating when hot water for showers will be available.

4. **Enigmatic folk similes:** Enigmatic folk similes, xiēhòuyǔ 歇後語 [arrested-ending-sayings], are a type of popular Chinese folk saying, which often has its second half (final and explanatory) left unsaid. These similes, mostly based on wordplay and punning, are often humorous and satirical. They make use of the full spectrum of traditional Chinese history and culture. The following are a few examples.

Chinese Terms		*Pinyin*	*English*
泥菩薩過江 ——自身難保	泥菩萨过江 ——自身难保	nípúsà guò jiāng —zìshēn nán bǎo	a clay Buddha statue crossing a river—hard put to protect himself, let alone others
貓哭耗子—— 假慈悲	猫哭耗子—— 假慈悲	māo kū hàozi— jiǎ cíbēi	a cat weeping over a mouse—feigning sympathy

沒把的茶壺——光剩嘴	没把的茶壶——光剩嘴	méi bǎ de cháhú—guāng shèng zuǐ	a teapot without a handle—only a mouth
和尚打傘——無法無天	和尚打伞——无法无天	héshàng dǎ sǎn—wú fǎ wú tiān	a monk holding up an umbrella—having neither hair nor (a view of) heaven—having regard for neither law nor heaven
豬八戒照鏡子——裏外不是人	猪八戒照镜子——里外不是人	Zhūbājiè zhào jìngzi—lǐwài bú shì rén	Pigs looking in a mirror—(lit.) a human being neither inside nor outside, (fig.) both sides in the wrong, both sides rejected

歌兒 Songs

胖房東
Chubby Landlord

Andante

詞：劉雅詩　曲：馬定一

1. 我　有　個胖　胖　的　好　房　東。　　常　常　來　去
   Wǒ　yǒu　ge pàng pàng de　hǎo　fáng　dōng,　　chángcháng lái　qù
   I have a chubby landlord who is nice.　　He comes and goes

2. 他　喜　歡　讓　自　己　很　有　用，　　所　以　他　學
   Tā　xǐ　huān ràng　zì　jǐ　hěn　yǒu　yòng,　　suǒ yǐ tā　xué
   He likes to make himself useful,　　so he learns

1. 像　陣　風，　　笑　起　來　像　暖　冬。
   xiàng zhèn　fēng,　　xiào　qǐ　lái　xiàng nuǎn　dōng.
   like a gust of wind.　　When he smiles, he's like warmth in the winter.

2. 習　歷　史，　　參　加　各　種　活　動。
   xí　lì　shǐ,　　cān　jiā　gè　zhǒng huó　dòng,
   history　　and participates in all kinds of activities.

1. 他　會　站　在　椅　子　上　　調　鬧　　鐘，　　甚　至　會　在　地　毯　上
   Tā　huì zhàn zài　yǐ　zi shàng　tiáo nào　zhōng,　　shènzhì huì zài dì tǎn shàng
   He would stand on a chair to tune up the alarm　clock.　　He would even get down on the carpet

2. 雖　然　有　點　胖　胖　的　　像　　熊，　　卻　是　我　最　可　愛　的
   suīrán yǒu diǎn pàngpàng de　xiàng zhī xióng,　　què　shì wǒ zuì kě'ài de
   Though he is a bit chubby like a bear,　　he is my great landlord,

1. 找　小　蟲。
   zhǎo xiǎo chóng.
   to look for little worms.

2. 好　房　東。
   hǎo fáng dōng.
   the cutest person I know.

<table>
<tr><td rowspan="2">第三課</td><td>Theme Holidays and Home Visits

Communicative Objectives
• Making and replying to an invitation
• Entertaining guests
• Presenting and accepting gifts
• Offering and responding to praise/toasts
• Taking leave</td><td>Grammar Focus
• 對…來說
• 並不；並沒(有)
• 既…也/又…
• 根本(就)不/沒…
• 哪兒/哪儿…(呢)？
• 關於…的N</td></tr>
<tr><td colspan="2">Focus on Characters
• 乾淨禮杯、祝親秋愉、誤解便故、圓活命根、並既於反</td></tr>
</table>

誰說美國的月亮更圓？

生詞 Vocabulary

Study the following words for their pronunciation and meaning. When an area is shaded, guess at the meaning of the word based on its constituent characters and then fill in the blank. Read the usage of words and related terms (antonyms, synonyms, compounds sharing the constituent characters, etc.) and try to answer the sample questions in Chinese. Note that proper nouns or incidental terms are not numbered.

◎ By Order of Appearance

1.	月亮	yuèliang	N	moon, moonlight	[moon-bright]

什麼時候的月亮特別圓？

什么时候的月亮特别圆？

2.	圓	yuán	Adj	round, circle	
3.	上次	shàngcì	N		[last-occurrence]

你上次去中國是什麼時候？

你上次去中国是什么时候？

4.	提到	tídào	RV	to mention, to bring up	[refer to-reach]

昨天老師上課的時候，提到什麼？

昨天老师上课的时候，提到什么？

5.	誤會 误会	wùhuì	V/N	to misunderstand, misunderstanding	[miss-understand]

你誤會了我的意思。

你误会了我的意思。

6.	熱情 热情	rèqíng	Adj	enthusiastic	[hot-feeling]

哪兒的人很熱情？

哪儿的人很热情？

7.	親切 亲切	qīnqiè	Adj	cordial, genial	[dear-close]

你覺得這兒的老師親切嗎？

你觉得这儿的老师亲切吗？

8.	禮貌 礼貌	lǐmào	N/ Adj	courtesy, polite	[manners-appearance]

一個有禮貌的人會常說什麼？

一个有礼貌的人会常说什么？

9.	對…來說 对…来说	duì…lái shuō	PP	concerning, about	[to…come-speak]

學中文的時候，對你來說，什麼最難？

学中文的时候，对你来说，什么最难？

10.	自然	zìrán	Adj/	natural, naturally, nature	[self-so]
			Adv/	誰說話不太自然？	
			N	谁说话不太自然？	
11.	並	bìng	Adv	(intensifier used with a negative)	
	并			中文並沒有你想像的那麼難。	
				中文并没有你想象的那么难。	
12.	意思	yìsi	N	meaning, idea	[meaning-think]
				「狗拿耗子」是什麼意思？	
				"狗拿耗子"是什么意思？	
13.	感覺	gǎnjué	N	feeling	[feel-feel]
	感觉			下雨天會給你什麼樣的感覺？	
				下雨天会给你什么样的感觉？	
14.	相反	xiāngfǎn	Adj	opposite, contrary	[mutually-oppose]
				你跟誰的看法總是相反？	
				你跟谁的看法总是相反？	
15.	關心	guānxīn	V/N	▓▓▓▓▓▓▓▓	[close-heart]
	关心			誰對你很關心？你關心誰？	
				谁对你很关心？你关心谁？	
16.	了解	liǎojiě	V/N	to understand	[know clearly-explain]
				你想了解中國的節日嗎？	
				你想了解中国的节日吗？	
17.	實在	shízài	Adv	indeed, really	[solid-exist]
	实在			我實在不喜歡喝酸辣湯。	
				我实在不喜欢喝酸辣汤。	
18.	寂寞	jìmò	Adj	lonely, lonesome	[lonely-lonely]
				你什麼時候會覺得很寂寞？	
				你什麼时候会觉得很寂寞？	
	中秋節 中秋节	Zhōngqiū jié	N	Mid-Autumn Festival	[middle-fall-holiday]

Characters with Many Strokes

圓 誤 熱 禮 貌 關 解 實 寂 寞

19.	既…也	jì…yě	Conj	not only…but also…	
				什麼東西既不好看也不好吃？	
				什么东西既不好看也不好吃？	
20.	辦法	bànfǎ	N	way, means, measure	[do-way]
	办法			你為什麼沒有辦法出國留學？	
				你为什么没有办法出国留学？	
21.	慶祝	qìngzhù	V	to celebrate	[celebrate-wish]
	庆祝			你要怎麼慶祝他的生日？	
				你要怎么庆祝他的生日？	
22.	節日	jiérì	N	festival, holiday	[holiday-day]
	节日			你覺得哪一個節日最有意思？	
				你觉得哪一个节日最有意思？	
23.	要命	yàomìng	Adv	extremely, awfully	[want-life]
				什麼地方熱得要命？	
				什么地方热得要命？	
24.	根本	gēnběn	Adv/ Adj	simply, utterly, basic	[root-origin]
				你根本不會做什麼？	
				你根本不会做什么？	
25.	忙不過來	mángbu guòlái	RV	too busy to deal with	[busy-not-come over]
	忙不过来			你忙得過來嗎？要不要我幫忙？	
				你忙得过来吗？要不要我帮忙？	
26.	心情	xīnqíng	N	state of mind, mood	[heart-feeling]
				你今天心情怎麼樣？	
				你今天心情怎么样？	
27.	過節	guòjié	VO	to celebrate a festival	[observe-holiday]
	过节				
28.	國內	guónèi	N	internal, domestic	[country-inside]
	国内			↔國外	
29.	想家	xiǎngjiā	VO		[think-home]
				你什麼時候特別想家？	
				你什么时候特别想家？	
30.	愉快	yúkuài	Adj	happy, cheerful	[delighted-fast]
				你在這兒生活愉快嗎？	

你在这儿生活愉快吗？

31.	家常便飯 家常便饭	jiācháng biànfàn	NP	home food, simple meal, common occurrence	[home-often-convenient- food]

做什麼事對你來說是家常便飯？

做什么事对你来说是家常便饭？

32.	乾杯 干杯	gānbēi	VO	to drink a toast, bottoms up	[dry-cup]

你昨天跟他乾杯慶祝什麼？

你昨天跟他干杯庆祝什么？

33.	醉	zuì	Adj	drunk, tipsy	

喝醉酒的人不應該做什麼？

喝醉酒的人不应该做什么？

34.	幾乎 几乎	jīhū	Adv	almost, nearly	[some-at]

你幾乎天天都做什麼？

你几乎天天都做什么？

35.	客氣 客气	kèqi	V/ Adj		[guest-spirit]
36.	月餅 月饼	yuèbǐng	N	moon cake	[moon-cake]
37.	美	měi	Adj	beautiful	
38.	關於 关于	guānyú	Prep	about, concerning	[close-at]

你看的那本書是關於什麼的？

你看的那本书是关于什么的？

39.	傳說 传说	chuánshuō	N/V	legend, it is said	[pass on-say]

美國有沒有關於月亮的傳說？

美国有没有關于月亮的传说？

40.	故事	gùshi	N	story, tale	[old-thing]

你小的時候喜歡聽什麼樣的故事？

你小的时候喜欢听什么样的故事？

41.	太空人	tàikōngrén	N		[grand-space-person]
42.	月球	yuèqiú	N	moon	[moon-ball]

Characters with Many Strokes

辦　慶　節　愉　便　乾　醉　幾　餅　傳

◎ By Grammatical Categories

Nouns/Pronouns/Measure Words

中秋節	Zhōngqiū jié	Mid-Autumn Festival
節日	jiérì	festival, holiday
月亮	yuèliang	moon, moonlight
月球	yuèqiú	moon
月餅	yuèbǐng	moon cake
上次	shàngcì	last time
國內	guónèi	internal, domestic
心情	xīnqíng	state of mind, mood
感覺	gǎnjué	feeling

意思	yìsi	meaning, idea
辦法	bànfǎ	way, means, measure
禮貌	lǐmào	courtesy, polite
故事	gùshi	story, tale
傳說	chuánshuō	legend, it is said
太空人	tàikōngrén	astronaut
家常便飯	jiācháng biànfàn	home food, simple meal, common occurrence

Verbs/Stative Verbs/Adjectives

誤會	wùhuì	to misunderstand, misunderstanding
關心	guānxīn	to be concerned about
了解	liǎojiě	to understand
慶祝	qìngzhù	to celebrate
過節	guòjié	to celebrate a festival
想家	xiǎngjiā	to be homesick
乾杯	gānbēi	to drink a toast, bottoms up
提到	tídào	to mention, to bring up
忙不過來	mángbu guòlái	too busy to deal with

圓	yuán	round, circle
美	měi	beautiful
醉	zuì	drunk, tipsy
客氣	kèqi	to be polite
熱情	rèqíng	enthusiastic
親切	qīnqiè	cordial, genial
愉快	yúkuài	happy, cheerful
自然	zìrán	natural, naturally, nature
寂寞	jìmò	lonely, lonesome
相反	xiāngfǎn	opposite, contrary

Adverbs and Others

並	bìng	(intensifier used with a negative)
實在	shízài	indeed, really
要命	yàomìng	extremely, awfully
幾乎	jīhū	almost, nearly
既…也	jì…yě	not only…but also…

根本	gēnběn	simply, utterly, basic, essential
關於	guānyú	about, concerning, with regard to
對…來說	duì…lái shuō	concerning, about

◎ By Pinyin

Entries with * indicate lexical items used in Mini-Dialogues and of possible interest for supplemental study.

àirén*	爱人	spouse	liú*	留	to keep
bànfǎ	办法	way, means	mángbuguò lái	忙不过来	too busy to deal with
bìng	并	(intensifier used with a negative)	měi	美	beautiful
chuánshuō	传说	it is said	qìngzhù	庆祝	to celebrate
duì…lái shuō	对…来说	concerning	qīnqiè	亲切	cordial
fúqi*	福气	happy lot	rèqíng	热情	enthusiastic, warm
gānbēi	干杯	bottoms up	shàngcì	上次	last time
gǎnjué	感觉	feeling	shízài	实在	indeed, really
gēnběn	根本	simply, basic	tàikōngrén	太空人	astronaut
guānxīn	关心	to be concerned about	tídào	提到	to mention
guānyú	关于	about, with regard to	wùhuì	误会	to misunderstand
guòjié	过节	to celebrate a festival	xiāngfǎn	相反	opposite
guónèi	国内	internal, domestic	xiǎngjiā	想家	to be homesick
			xiǎoyìsi*	小意思	small token of kindly feelings
gùshi	故事	story, tale	xīnqíng	心情	mood
jì…yě	既…也	not only…but also…	yàomìng	要命	extremely
jiācháng biànfàn	家常便饭	simple meal	yìsi	意思	meaning
			yúkuài	愉快	happy
jiérì	节日	festival, holiday	yuán	圆	round
jīhū	几乎	almost	yuèbǐng	月饼	moon cake
jìmò	寂寞	lonely	yuèliang	月亮	moon
kèqi	客气	to be polite	yuèqiú	月球	moon
lǎodà*	老大	eldest child (in a family)	zhù*	祝	to wish
lǎojiā*	老家	native place	zìrán	自然	natural, naturally, nature
liǎojiě	了解	to understand	zuì	醉	drunk
lǐmào	礼貌	courtesy, polite			

課文 Text

Use the following questions to guide your reading of the text.

1. 小李覺得小高的同屋兒怎麼樣？

2. 小李想過中秋節嗎？為什麼？

3. 小高是怎麼過中秋節的？他覺得美國的月亮更圓嗎？

 小高：

　　你上次提到的問題很有趣。我想你誤會了你的同屋，我覺得他很熱情、很親切、很有禮貌。他問你的問題，[1]對中國人來說，都很自然，[2]並沒有什麼不好的意思。我剛來美國的時候，感覺和你正好相反。我覺得沒有人關心我、沒有人想了解我做過的事或我去過的地方，這兒的生活實在很寂寞！

　　你知道中秋節快到了嗎？現在應該是回家的時候了，可是我在這兒[3]既沒有時間，也沒有辦法慶祝這個節日。我功課多得要命，[4]根本就忙不過來，[5]哪兒有心情過中秋節呢？從前在國內有人說「美國的月亮更圓」，就是說美國什麼都好的意思。你在中國待了一個多月了，你覺得美國的月亮真的更圓嗎？

李明上

小李：

聽起來你很想家。昨天我去你家過節，玩得很高興，心情愉快極了！說是吃家常便飯，到了一看，才知道你母親準備了很多好菜。你父親一直叫我乾杯，我醉得幾乎走不動了。他們實在很客氣，好在我帶了一盒月餅去，要不然真不好意思。我覺得中國的月亮很美，有很多[6]關於月亮的傳說和故事，比我們太空人見到的月球好多了。誰說美國的月亮更圓！

德中上

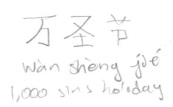

万圣节
wàn shèng jié
1,000 sins holiday

课文 Text

Use the following questions to guide your reading of the text.

1. 小李觉得小高的同屋儿怎么样？

2. 小李想过中秋节吗？为什么？

3. 小高是怎么过中秋节的？他觉得美国的月亮更圆吗？

小高：

　　你上次提到的问题很有趣。我想你误会了你的同屋，我觉得他很热情、很亲切、很有礼貌。他问你的问题，[1]**对**中国人**来说**，都很自然，[2]**并没有**什麽不好的意思。我刚来美国的时候，感觉和你正好相反。我觉得没有人关心我、没有人想了解我做过的事或我去过的地方，这儿的生活实在很寂寞！

　　你知道中秋节快到了吗？现在应该是回家的时候了，可是我在这儿[3]**既**没有时间，**也**没有办法庆祝这个节日。我功课多得要命，[4]**根本就**忙不过来，[5]**哪儿**有心情过中秋节呢？从前在国内有人说"美国的月亮更圆"，就是说美国什么都好的意思。你在中国待了一个多月了，你觉得美国的月亮真的更圆吗？

　　　　　　　　　　　　　　　　　　　　　　　　李明上

小李：

听起来你很想家。昨天我去你家过节，玩得很高兴，心情愉快极了！说是吃家常便饭，到了一看，才知道你母亲准备了很多好菜。你父亲一直叫我干杯，我醉得几乎走不动了。他们实在很客气，好在我带了一盒月饼去，要不然真不好意思。我觉得中国的月亮很美，有很多[6]关于月亮的

传说和故事，比我们太空人见到的月球好多了。谁说美国的月亮更圆！

德中上

小對話 Mini-Dialogues

Read the supplementary dialogues for a better understanding of the text. See if you can memorize one and perform it in class.

(1) Making and replying to an invitation

| Li: | 下個星期我們過中秋，你來我們家一起過節吧！ | 下个星期我们过中秋，你来我们家一起过节吧！ |

| Gao: | 那怎麼好意思呢！太麻煩您了。 | 那怎么好意思呢！太麻烦您了。 |

| Li: | 沒事，家裏就我和我愛人āiren兩個人。如果有空的話，就來吃個便飯吧！都是些家常菜。 | 没事，家里就我和我爱人两个人。如果有空的话，就来吃个便饭吧！都是些家常菜。 |

| Gao: | 您太客氣了，有時間我一定去。 | 您太客气了，有时间我一定去。 |

Li: Next week we will celebrate Mid-Autumn Festival. How about coming to our place?

Gao: That's so kind of you. It is too much trouble.

Li: It's nothing. It is only me and my wife. If you have time, be sure to come and have some homemade dishes.

Gao: You are so kind. I will certainly come if I have time.

(2) Entertaining guests

| Gao: | 李教授在家嗎？ | 李教授在家吗？ |

| Li: | 哎呀！是高德中。歡迎，快請裏邊坐。我來介紹一下，這是我愛人周紅。 | 哎呀！是高德中。欢迎，快请里边坐。我来介绍一下，这是我爱人周红。 |

| Zhou: | 快請坐，你要喝點兒什麼？茶還是汽水兒？ | 快请坐，你要喝点儿什么？茶还是汽水儿？ |

| Gao: | 什麼都可以。 | 什么都可以。 |

Zhou: 你們先聊聊，我去做飯。   你们先聊聊，我去做饭。

Gao: 真不好意思，麻煩您了。   真不好意思，麻烦您了。

Li: 你老家lǎojiā是……？   你老家是……？

Gao: 印地安那州，在美國的中西   印地安那州，在美国的中西
部。   部。

Li: 家裏有幾口人？   家里有几口人？

Gao: 五口：爸爸、媽媽、我是老大   五口：爸爸、妈妈、我是老
lǎodà，下面還有兩個弟弟。   大，下面还有两个弟弟。

Li: 三個兒子，真有福氣fúqi！   三个儿子，真有福气！

Gao: Is Professor Li home?

Li: Ah! It's Gao Dezhong. Welcome,
come on in. Let me introduce you.
This is my wife, Zhou Hong.

Zhou: Please sit down. What do you want
to drink? Tea or soda?

Gao: Anything would be fine.

Zhou: You two chat and I will go in and
cook.

Gao: I've given you too much trouble.

Li: Where is your home?

Gao: Indiana, in the U.S. Midwest.

Li: How many people are there in your family?

Gao: Five: Father, Mother, myself (the eldest child) and two younger brothers.

Li: Three sons! What a blessing!

(3) Presenting and accepting gifts

Gao: 這是我帶來的一盒月餅，請收   这是我带来的一盒月饼，请收
下吧！   下吧！

Li: 你太客氣了！   你太客气了！

Gao: 只是一點兒小意思xiǎoyìsi，希望   只是一点儿小意思，希望你们
你們喜歡。   喜欢。

Li:　　留liú著自己吃吧！　　　　　　留着自己吃吧！

Gao:　This is a box of moon cakes that I brought. Please take it.

Li:　　You are too polite.

Gao:　It is just a little something. I hope you will like it.

Li:　　Keep this for yourself and enjoy it.

(4) Offering and responding to praise/toasts

Li:　　你學了幾年漢語就說得這麼好，真不容易。　　　　　你学了几年汉语就说得这么好，真不容易。

Gao:　哪裏、哪裏。　　　　　　哪里、哪里。

Zhou:　說得就跟中國人一樣。　　说得就跟中国人一样。

Gao:　哪兒的話，還差得遠呢。　哪儿的话，还差得远呢。

Li:　　來，歡迎你到中國留學，乾一杯！　　　　　来，欢迎你到中国留学，干一杯！

Gao:　好，謝謝您請我來過節，乾杯！我不行了，我快醉了。　　好，谢谢您请我来过节，干杯！我不行了，我快醉了。

Li:　　You have only studied a few years of Chinese and speak so well. It's not easy.

Gao:　No! No!

Zhou:　You speak just like a Chinese.

Gao:　No way, I am still far from it.

Li:　　Well, let's celebrate your coming to China to study. Cheers!

Gao:　Cheers! Thanks for inviting me over for the holiday. Bottoms up! I can't take any more. I am getting drunk.

(5) Taking leave

Gao:	時候不早了，我該回去了。	时候不早了，我该回去了。
Li:	忙什麼，再坐一會兒。	忙什么，再坐一会儿。
Gao:	都十點多了，太麻煩你們了，我得走了。	都十点多了，太麻烦你们了，我得走了。
Zhou:	多留一會兒吧！	多留一会儿吧！
Gao:	得走了，謝謝你們對我這麼熱情。今天晚上玩得真高興。	得走了，谢谢你们对我这么热情。今天晚上玩得真高兴。
Li:	你太客氣了，以後常來玩吧！	你太客气了，以后常来玩吧！
Gao:	好，我一定再來。	好，我一定再来。
Li:	慢慢走。	慢慢走。
Gao:	請回吧！再見！	请回吧！再见！
Li	再見！	再见！

Gao: It's getting late. I should go.

Li: Don't hurry off. Stay a bit longer.

Gao: It's already past ten. I am giving you too much trouble. I really should go.

Zhou: Stay a bit longer.

Gao: I have to go. Thanks for being so kind to me. I have had a great evening.

Li: You are too polite. Come visit us often.

Gao: O.K. I will definitely come again.

Li: Watch your step.

Gao: You don't need to wait outside for me. Go on inside. Good-bye.

Li: Good-bye.

小故事 Stories

Read the following tale for your own enjoyment and for your understanding of the highlighted expression that is relevant to the theme of the chapter.

 多多益善 duōduō yì shàn

❀ 他喜歡吃月餅，所以月餅對他來說，是多多益善。

劉邦是漢朝第一個皇帝，韓信是他手下的大將。有一天，他們聊天的時候提到一些將軍，劉邦就問：「你看我可以帶多少軍隊？」韓信說：「十萬人馬。」劉邦又問韓信：「那你呢？」韓信說：「多多益善。」

劉邦聽了不太高興，就問韓信：「要是你這麼厲害，為什麼還是在我的手下呢？」韓信知道皇帝不高興了，就說：「雖然我帶軍隊帶得好，但是您帶將軍帶得好啊！」劉邦聽了，就大笑起來。

益	yì	all the more, increasingly
善	shàn	good
劉邦	Liú Bāng	name of a person
漢朝	Hàncháo	Han dynasty
皇帝	huángdì	emperor
韓信	Hán Xìn	name of a person
手下	shǒuxià	(under the) leadership of
大將	dàjiàng	senior general
將軍	jiāngjūn	general
軍隊	jūnduì	army
萬	wàn	ten thousand
人馬	rénmǎ	forces, troops
厲害	lìhai	sharp, formidable
笑	xiào	to laugh

✎ 多多益善的意思是_____

多多益善 duōduō yì shàn

✿   他喜欢吃月饼，所以月饼对他来说，是多多益善。

刘邦是汉朝第一个皇帝，韩信是他手下的大将。有一天，他们聊天的时候提到一些将军，刘邦就问："你看我可以带多少军队？"韩信说："十万人马。"刘邦又问韩信："那你呢？"韩信说："多多益善。"

刘邦听了不太高兴，就问韩信："要是你这么厉害，为什么还是在我的手下呢？"韩信知道皇帝不高兴了，就说："虽然我带军队带得好，但是您带将军带得好啊！"刘邦听了，就大笑起来。

益	yì	all the more, increasingly
善	shàn	good
刘邦	Liú Bāng	name of a person
汉朝	Hàncháo	Han dynasty
皇帝	huángdì	emperor
韩信	Hán Xìn	name of a person
手下	shǒuxià	(under the) leadership of
大将	dàjiàng	senior general
将军	jiāngjūn	general
军队	jūnduì	army
万	wàn	ten thousand
人马	rénmǎ	forces, troops
厉害	lìhai	sharp, formidable
笑	xiào	to laugh

漢字 Characters

Study the following selected characters for further enrichment of your writing and vocabulary.

日 rì 'sun' +
疒 'jungle' +
乙 —warmth of the sun

干

gān 11
dry, free

乾杯	gānbēi	to drink a toast, Cheers!
乾淨	gānjìng	clean, complete
餅乾	bǐnggān*	biscuit, cracker

A: 這兒不太乾淨。
B: 因為剛才有人在這兒吃餅乾。

Compare: 朝 cháo　幹 gàn

冫 bīng 'ice' +
爭 zhēng phonetic

净

jìng 11
clean, completely, only

| 乾淨 | gānjìng | clean, neat and tidy |
| 不乾不淨 | bùgān-bújìng* | unclean, filthy |

A: 別吃這兒的東西，太不乾淨了。
B: 不乾不淨，吃了沒病。

Compare: 爭 zhēng

礻 shì 'altar' +
曲 over 豆 representing a vase full of flowers, offered as a sacrifice to the gods

礼

lǐ 17
ceremony, courtesy, gift

禮貌	lǐmào	courtesy, politeness
禮物	lǐwù	gift, present
禮拜六	lǐbàiliù	Saturday

A: 下禮拜六我去看他。
B: 記得帶禮物去，才有禮貌。

木 mù 'wood' +
不 bù 'not'
—cups are not made of wood

杯

bēi 8
cup, trophy

乾杯	gānbēi	cheers
茶杯	chábēi*	teacup, tea-glass
杯子	bēizi*	cup, glass

A: 你再喝兩杯吧！
B: 我不能再乾杯了。

Compare: 樓 lóu

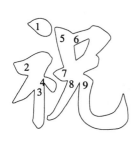

祝 shì 'rites' +
兄 xiōng
'brother'—the
speaker at the
religious
ceremony

祝

zhù 9
to bless, to wish

慶祝	qìngzhù	to celebrate
祝福	zhùfú*	to wish happiness to
祝好	zhùhǎo*	(at end of letter) Best Wishes

A: 祝你們倆生活愉快、學習進步jìnbù。
B: 謝謝你的祝福。

Compare: 兄 xiōng

見 jiàn 'see' +
亲 qīn 'hazel-
nut tree: 辛 +
木' phonetic

亲

qīn 16
relatives, close,
intimate

親切	qīnqiè	cordial, genial, warm
親愛	qīn'ài*	dear, beloved
母親	mǔqīn	mother
父親	fùqīn	father

A: 你喜歡這兒嗎？
B: 喜歡，這兒的人都很親切。

Compare: 新 xīn

禾 hé 'grain,
harvest time' +
火 huǒ 'fire,'
which might
describe the
grain's color, or
burning the
fields after the
harvest

秋

qiū 9
autumn, harvest

中秋節	Zhōngqiūjié	Mid-Autumn Festival
秋天	qiūtiān*	autumn, fall
秋季	qiūjì*	autumn season

A: 你喜歡春天還是秋天？
B: 我喜歡秋天，可以回家過中秋節。

忄 xīn 'heart' +
俞 yú phonetic

愉

yú 12
delighted

| 愉快 | yúkuài | happy, cheerful |

A: 什麼時候你的心情會很愉快？
B: 考完試以後。

Compare: 偷 tōu

言 yán 'words' + 吳 wú phonetic

誤會	wùhuì	to misunderstand
誤點	wùdiǎn*	to be behind schedule
錯誤	cuòwù*	error

A: 這麼重要的會，他居然不來。
B: 你誤會他了，一定是飛機誤點了。

誤

wù　14
to miss, mistake

Cleave with a 刀 dāo knife the 角 jiǎo horn of 牛 niú an ox

了解	liǎojiě	to understand
理解	lǐjiě	to understand
解決	jiějué	to solve, to resolve

A: 那個問題他解決了嗎？
B: 他不了解問題在哪兒，怎麼解決？

解

jiě　13
to separate, to untie, to explain

亻 rén 'person' + 更 gèng 'more'/gēng 'change'

家常便飯	jiācháng biànfàn	home food
隨便	suíbiàn	to do as one pleases
便宜	piányí	cheap
方便	fāngbiàn	convenient, to go to the lavatory

A: 你明天來我這兒吃個家常便飯。
B: 不太方便吧？在外面隨便吃好了。

便

biàn, pián　9
convenient, plain, then

攵 pū 'beat' + 古 gǔ phonetic

| 故事 | bùshi | story, tale, plot |
| 故意 | gùyì* | intentionally, willfully |

A: 她一講故事我就想睡。
B: 你是故意的嗎？

故

Compare: 做 zuò

gù　9
cause, event, old

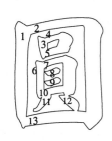

口 wéi 'sound' + 員 yuán 'round money 貝; member' phonetic

圓

yuán 13
round, circle, dollar

| 圓形 | yuánxíng* | circular shape |
| 半圓形 | bànyuánxíng* | semicircular shape |

A: 他好看嗎？
B: 不好看，臉圓圓的、腿短短的。

Compare: 園 yuán

氵 shuǐ 'water' + 舌 shé 'tongue' phonetic—to drink the water of life

活

huó 9
to live, alive, lively, to work

| 活動 | huódòng | activity, to move about |
| 生活 | shēnghuó | life, livelihood |

A: 這兒的生活真沒意思。
B: 你應該多參加課外活動。

Compare: 話 huà

口 kǒu 'mouth' + 令 lìng 'command'—a person kneeling under a roof

命

mìng 8
life, lot, to order

要命	yàomìng	to drive sb. to death
救命	jiùmìng*	to save sb.'s life, Help!
生命	shēngmìng	(physical) life

A: 我生詞還沒有學完，就累得要命。
B: 我也一樣。

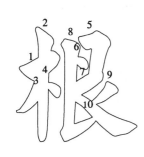

木 mù 'tree' + 艮 gèn phonetic

根

gēn 10
root, origin, cause

| 根本 | gēnběn | essence, basic, simply |
| 根據 | gēnjù | on the basis of |

A: 他剛到這兒，應該很忙吧？
B: 哪裏，他根本不忙。

Compare: 跟 gēn　很 hěn

From 立立 or 从 two people standing together or side by side, with 二 horizontal lines indicating that they are on the same level

並不	bìngbù	not at all, by no means
並非	bìngfēi*	be really not
並且	bìngqiě*	and, besides, moreover

A: 你去過中國，中文一定說得很好吧？
B: 哪裏，我的中文並不好。

Compare: 餅 bǐng 瓶 píng

bìng　8
together, and, actually

并

 'a pot of food— from the bottom of 食' + 兂 'a person, already having eaten, facing away from the food'

| 既然 | jìrán | since, as, now that |

A: 那家飯館的飯既不好吃也不便宜。
B: 既然你不喜歡，就別再去了。

Compare: 概 gài 即 jí

jì　9
since, already, then

既

A sign represents graphically the connection (left side) between 二 two distinct 刀 terms

關於	guānyú	about, with regard to
由於	yóuyú	owing/due/thanks to
於是	yúshì	thereupon, hence

A: 你聽過關於月亮的傳說嗎？
B: 沒聽過，快告訴我吧！

yú　8
in, at, to, from, out of

于

厂 is a line representing the motion of the hand 又 yòu turning over

相反	xiāngfǎn	opposite
反對	fǎnduì	to oppose, be against
反而	fǎn'ér	on the contrary

A: 大家都要去吃中國飯，只有他反對。
B: 他的想法總是和人相反。

Compare: 飯 fàn

反

fǎn　4
to turn over, instead

語法和用法 Grammar and Usage

Pay attention to the function of the structure and then study the example sentences.

1. Highlighting someone's point of view or an area of concern

對sb.來說	duì…láishuō	as for, as to…

他問你的問題，**對**中國人**來說**，都很自然……

1.	你覺得中文難嗎？	你觉得中文难吗？	Do you think Chinese is hard?
	對我來說，聽和說不難，可是讀和寫很難。	对我来说，听和说不难，可是读和写很难。	For me, listening and speaking are easy, but reading and writing are difficult.
2.	這個地方怎麼樣？	这个地方怎么样？	How is this place?
	對孩子來說，活動還不夠。	对孩子来说，活动还不够。	There are not enough activities for children.
3.	這兒的生活你還適應嗎？	这儿的生活你还适应吗？	Are you used to life here?
	對我來說，什麼都好，就是飯館不夠多。	对我来说，什么都好，就是饭馆不够多。	To me, everything is fine except that there are not enough restaurants.

读 dú

够 gòu

What goes after 對 is often a person, and expresses either a point of view (see examples 1 and 3) or an area of concern (see example 2).

2. Making a contrary reply

S並不/並沒(有) V	…bìngbù/bìngméi(yǒu)…	don't (emphatic); actually not

他問你的問題……**並沒有**什麼不好的意思。

1.	她好像對你很有意思。	她好象对你很有意思。	She seems to be interested in you.

	我並不喜歡她。	我并不喜欢她。	I don't like her.
2.	中文的漢字很多，學起來一定很難吧？	中文的汉字很多，学起来一定很难吧？	There are so many Chinese characters. It must be difficult to study Chinese, I suppose?
	並沒有你想像的那麼難。	并没有你想象的那么难。	It's not as difficult as you might imagine.
3.	他是美國人，一定很熟悉美國的歷史吧？	他是美国人，一定很熟悉美国的历史吧？	He is an American. He surely knows American history well.
	美國人並不一定就熟悉美國歷史。	美国人并不一定就熟悉美国历史。	Americans do not necessarily know American history well.

並 is used only with a negative, 不 or 沒. It indicates that reality is different from what one assumes.

3. Expressing contemporaneous qualities or situations

S 既…也…	jì...yě...	not only...but also...
S 既…又…	jì...yòu...	both...and...

可是我在這兒**既**沒有時間，**也**沒有辦法慶祝這個節日。

1.	你為什麼要搬到校外住？	你为什么要搬到校外住？	Why do you want to move off campus?
	因為校外既安靜又便宜。	因为校外既安静又便宜。	Because living off campus is both quiet and inexpensive.
2.	你怎麼不去參加那個晚會？	你怎么不去参加那个晚会？	Why didn't you go to that party?
	我既沒有車也沒有時間，怎麼去？	我既没有车也没有时间，怎么去？	I have neither a car nor the time; how could I go?

3. 你喜歡這本教材嗎？ 你喜欢这本教材吗？ Do you like this teaching material?

   喜歡，內容既有趣、又有用。 喜欢，内容既有趣、又有用。 Yes, the content is not only interesting, but also useful.

Note that what follows 既 and 又/也 have to be either both positive or both negative. It is odd to say 他既不聰明又有錢. "既…又…" often connects two nouns or adjectives; "既…也…" often connects two phrases.

4. Emphasizing a negation

| S 根本 (就) 不/沒… | gēnběn (jiù) bù/méi… | simply not…; not… at all |

我功課多得要命，**根本就**忙**不**過來……

1. 他為什麼不上中文課？ 他为什么不上中文课？ Why doesn't he take Chinese?

   他根本就對中文不感興趣。 他根本就对中文不感兴趣。 He is not interested in Chinese at all.

2. 你為什麼不回家過節？ 你为什么不回家过节？ Why don't you go home for the holiday?

   我根本沒有時間。 我根本没有时间。 I simply do not have the time.

3. 你為什麼不買輛車子呢？ 你为什么不买辆车子呢？ Why don't you buy a car?

   我根本沒錢。 我根本没钱。 I simply do not have the money.

As an adverb, 根本 emphasizes an assertion. It often goes with a negative, 不 or 沒. 就 can be placed after 根本 for extra emphasis.

5. Expressing negation through a rhetorical question

(S) 哪兒/哪裏…（呢）？	nǎr/nǎli…(ne)?	How can it be the case that…? S surely doesn't….

我功課多得要命，根本就忙不過來，**哪兒**有心情過中秋節呢？

1.	你為什麼不買輛車子呢？	你为什么不买辆车子呢？	Why don't you buy a car?
	我只是個學生，哪裏有錢買車呢？	我只是个学生，哪里有钱买车呢？	I am only a student. Where could I get the money to buy a car?
2.	你怎麼不出去玩兒？	你怎么不出去玩儿？	Why don't you go out and have fun?
	我明天有三個考試，哪兒有心情出去玩兒？	我明天有三个考试，哪儿有心情出去玩儿？	I have three tests tomorrow. How could I be in the mood for fun?
3.	你怎麼不和朋友去看電影呢？	你怎么不和朋友去看电影呢？	Why don't you go see a movie with your friends?
	我得趕兩個報告，哪裏有時間去看電影呢？	我得赶两个报告，哪里有时间去看电影呢？	I have to finish two papers. How could I have time to see a movie?

趕
gǎn
rush

報告
bào gào

In this pattern, 哪兒/哪裏 is used as a rhetorical question to express the speaker's negation of something.

6. Focusing on a specific aspect

S V 關於…的N	…guānyú…de…	…about N
S是關於…的	…shì guānyú…de	concerning, in regard to…
關於…, S…	guānyú…, …	Regarding…, S

我覺得中國的月亮很美，有很多**關於**月亮的傳說和故事……

1.	你看，我應不應該去中國留學？	你看，我应不应该去中国留学？	In your view, should I go to China to study?

你應該找王老師談關於留學的問題。	你应该找王老师谈关于留学的问题。	You should talk with Teacher Wang about studying abroad.

2.
你昨天看的書是關於什麼的？	你昨天看的书是关于什么的？	What is the book that you read yesterday about?
我昨天看的書是關於中國歷史的。	我昨天看的书是关于中国历史的。	The book that I read yesterday is about Chinese history.

3.
你對他的事熟悉嗎？	你对他的事熟悉吗？	Are you familiar with his personal affairs?
關於他的事，我沒有什麼話好說。	关于他的事，我没有什么话好说。	Regarding his personal matters, I don't have much to say.

Note the various ways of using 關於 in a sentence. Don't confuse it with 至於 (L14, G1) 'as for (this)' which often refers to a change in topic or raises an additional point.

文化點滴 Culture Notes

1. **Mid-Autumn Festival:** The Mid-Autumn Festival, also known as the Chinese Moon Festival, is on the 15th day of the 8th lunar month (sometime in September of the Western calendar). One of the most important festivals in China, this holiday is celebrated as an occasion for family reunion and for sharing traditional foods such as 月餅 yuèbǐng "moon cakes" together while admiring the full moon at its brightest.  There are many legendary stories about the moon. One says that Chang Er 嫦娥, the wife of a ruler Hou Yi 羿, drank the elixir of life in order to save the people from her husband's tyrannical rule. She found herself floating and flew to the moon, where she till resides today. It is also believed that on the moon there is a man called Wu Kang 吳剛, banished by the immortal. There he works day and night chopping a cassia tree, which magically restores itself after each blow. Another legend says that a rabbit, after offering his own flesh to fairy sages disguised as beggars, was allowed to live in the Moon Palace as yùtù 玉兔 "the Jade Rabbit." The moon cakes are also said to commemorate a legend about how the leaders of the Song dynasty (A.D. 960–1280) attacked and overthrew the Mongolian ruler of the Yuan dynasty (A.D. 1280–1368) on the night of the Moon Festival, to establish the Ming dynasty (A.D. 1368–1644). The rebellion was coordinated with messages outlining the attack placed inside moon cakes.

2. **Hospitality:** Chinese people, in general, are very hospitable. They consider it a great pleasure to entertain guests/friends, particularly from afar. In the beginning of The Analects of Confucius, it is stated 有朋自遠方來，不亦悅乎？Yǒu péng zì yuǎnfāng lái, bú yì yuè hu "Isn't it a great pleasure to have friends coming from afar?" People often reserve the best things in the house for their guests and prepare a big feast for them. Yet, for modesty's sake, the invitation is often understated, described as "a simple meal with homemade dishes."

3. **Politeness:** It is polite for the guest to bring something such as fruit or cookies to the host. Although the host may decline the gift a few times, and will probably not open it in your presence, it doesn't mean that he or she doesn't like it. This is just the Chinese way of being polite. Also, a guest can be expected to be offered all sorts of food and asked to toast 乾杯 gānbēi "bottoms up" many times. It is polite to empty your plate and your cup, though your host will offer more and more, until you just can't take it.

歌兒 Songs

玉兔的家

Jade Rabbit's Home

Adagietto   詞：劉雅詩   曲：馬定一

1. 我 的 家　　在 天 上 的　月 亮，　是 個 既 快 樂 又 有 趣 的 地　　方。
Wǒ de jiā　　zài tiān shàng de　yuè liàng,　shì ge jì kuàilè yòu yǒuqù de dì　　fāng.
My home is the moon in the sky,　　　　　　　a happy and interesting place.

2. 中 秋 節　　都 看 見 人 們 非 常 忙，　慶 祝 過 節 乾杯還要 看 月 亮。
Zhōngqiú jié　　dōu kànjiàn rénmen fēicháng máng, qìngzhù guòjié gānbēi háiyào kàn yuèliàng.
During Mid-Autumn Festival we see people who are very busy, celebrating holidays, offering toasts, and looking at the moon.

1. 親 切 嫦 娥　常 在 我 身 旁，　一 起 關 心 想 家 的 吳　剛。
Qīn qiè Cháng é　cháng zài wǒ shēn páng,　yì qǐ guānxīn xiǎngjiā de Wú Gāng,
Cordial Chang'e is often by my side.　　Together we care for the homesick Wu Gang.

2. 傳 說 故 事　講 得 實 在 棒，　讓 我 心 情 愉 快 寂 寞 忘。
Chuánshuō gù shi jiǎng de shí zài bàng,　ràng wǒ xīnqíng yú kuài jí mò wàng.
Their legends and stories,　well told,　make me feel good and forget loneliness.

1. 上 次　幾 個 太 空 人　來 訪，　我 們 還　一 塊兒 跑 光光。
shàng cì　jǐ ge tàikōng rén　lái fǎng.　Wǒmen hái　yíkuàir pǎoguāngguāng.
Last time several astronauts came to visit.　We all ran away together.

2. 我 喜 歡　我 這 美 麗 的 家，　歡 迎 大 家 有 空 來 拜訪。
Wǒ xǐhuān　wǒ zhè měi lì de jiā.　Huānyíng dà jiā yǒukòng lái bàifǎng.
I like this beautiful home of mine.　Welcome all to visit when you have time.

✍ **My questions:**

第四課

Theme Daily Life

Communicative Objectives
- Describing events in a day
- Asking and giving directions
- Making inquiries
- Bargaining with street vendors

Focus on Characters
- 商院校級、公園跳舞、結合瓜餐、順步騎注、肚渴瓶廣

Grammar Focus
- 自從…以後，S就
- 忙著…；V_2著$O_2V_1O_1$
- Reduplication
- V_1的V_1…V_2的V_2
- 只要…，(S) 就…
- S V也/都 不/沒V 就…

你週末在忙什麼？

生詞 Vocabulary

Study the following words for their pronunciation and meaning. When an area is shaded, guess at the meaning of the word based on its constituent characters and then fill in the blank. Read the usage of words and related terms (antonyms, synonyms, compounds sharing the constituent characters, etc.) and try to answer the sample questions in Chinese. Note that proper nouns or incidental terms are not numbered.

◎ By Order of Appearance

1. 自從   zìcóng   Prep   since   [from-from]
   自从
   自從你學了中文以後，你發現了什麼？
   自从你学了中文以后，你发现了什么？

2. 校園   xiàoyuán   N   [school-garden]
   校园
   你覺得這個學校的校園漂亮嗎？
   你觉得这个学校的校园漂亮吗？

3. 天亮   tiānliàng   N   daybreak, dawn   [sky-bright]
   這兒冬天的時候，幾點天亮？
   这儿冬天的时候，几点天亮？

4. 鬧鐘   nàozhōng   N   alarm clock   [make a noise-clock]
   鬧钟
   鬧鐘響的時候，你起得來嗎？
   闹钟响的时候，你起得来吗？

5. 響   xiǎng   V/N/   to ring, sound, noisy
   响   Adj
   門鈴líng 'bell' 好像在響，是誰來了？
   门铃好象在响，是谁来了？

6. 起床   qǐchuáng   VO   to get up (from bed)   [get up-bed]
   你每天幾點起床？
   你每天几点起床？

7. 早點   zǎodiǎn   N   [early-refreshments]
   早点
   你今天吃了早點沒有？吃了什麼？
   你今天吃了早点没有？吃了什么？

8. 騎   qí   V   to ride
   骑
   你常騎自行車上哪兒去？
   你常骑自行车上哪儿去？

9. 自行車   zìxíngchē   N   bicycle   [self-go-vehicle]

自行车

你會不會騎自行車？什麼時候學會的？

你会不会骑自行车？什么时候学会的？

| 10. | 順著
順着 | shùnzhe | V | to go in the same direction as | [follow-particle] |

順著這條街走，會走到哪兒？

順着这条街走，会走到哪儿？

| | 天安門
天安门 | Tiānānmén | N | Gate of Heavenly Peace,
Tiananmen Square | [heaven-peace-door] |

| 11. | 廣場
广场 | guǎngchǎng | N | public square | [wide-gathering place] |

你去過什麼有名的廣場嗎？

你去过什么有名的广场吗？

| 12. | 方向 | fāngxiàng | N | direction | [place-towards] |

你家在學校的什麼方向？

你家在学校的什么方向？

| 13. | 中間
中间 | zhōngjiān | N | center, middle | [middle-space in between] |

從你家到學校，中間要經過哪些地方？

从你家到学校，中间要经过哪些地方？

| 14. | 經過
经过 | jīngguò | V/N | to pass, to go through | [undergo-pass] |

你去書店，中間會經過什麼地方？

你去书店，中间会经过什么地方？

| 15. | 胡同 | hútòng | N | lane, alley | [foreign-same] |

出去的時候，你喜歡走小胡同還是大街？

出去的时候，你喜欢走小胡同还是大街？

| 16. | 四合院 | sìhéyuàn | N | compound with houses around a courtyard | [four-combine-courtyard] |

你看過四合院嗎？你想住那樣的地方嗎？

你看过四合院吗？你想住那样的地方吗？

| 17. | 公園
公园 | gōngyuán | N | | [public-garden] |

你去過這附近的公園嗎？那兒好玩嗎？

你去过这附近的公园吗？那儿好玩吗？

Characters with Many Strokes

園　鬧　鐘　響　點　騎　順　廣　場　經

18.	男女老少	nán-nǚ-lǎo-shào	NP	men and women, old and young	

美國的男女老少都喜歡什麼活動？

美国的男女老少都喜欢什么活动？

19.	太極拳 太极拳	tàijíquán	N	a kind of shadowboxing	[great-extreme-box (with fists)]

你會打太極拳嗎？一天打多久？

你会打太极拳吗？一天打多久？

20.	氣功 气功	qìgōng	N	qigong system of deep breathing exercises	[energy-achievement]

有機會的話，你想練氣功嗎？為什麼？

有机会的话，你想练气功吗？为什么？

21.	跑步	pǎobù	VO		[run-step]

你喜歡跑步嗎？在公園還是街上跑步？

你喜欢跑步吗？在公园还是街上跑步？

22.	跳舞	tiàowǔ	VO	to dance	[jump-dance]

你喜歡跳舞嗎？你跳什麼舞？

你喜欢跳舞吗？你跳什么舞？

23.	下棋	xiàqí	VO	to play chess	[apply-board game]

你會不會下棋？下什麼樣的棋？

你会不会下棋？下什么样的棋？

24.	注意	zhùyì	V	to pay attention to, to take note of	[concentrate-think]

你在這個地方，常注意到什麼？

你在这个地方，常注意到什么？

25.	商店	shāngdiàn	N	shop, store	[business-shop]

附近有沒有二十四小時都開的商店？

附近有没有二十四小时都开的商店？

26.	比方說 比方说	bǐfāngshuō	IE	for example	[compare-side-say]

你覺得加州好玩嗎？比方說什麼好玩？

你觉得加州好玩吗？比方说什么好玩？

27.	餐廳 餐厅	cāntīng	N	restaurant, dining hall	[eat-hall]

你最喜歡去哪一家餐廳吃飯？為什麼？

你最喜欢去哪一家餐厅吃饭？为什么？

	加州	Jiāzhōu	N	California	[add-prefecture]
28.	牛肉麵 牛肉面	niúròumiàn	N	beef noodles	[ox-meat-noodle]

你吃過牛肉麵嗎？在哪兒吃的？

你吃过牛肉面吗？在哪儿吃的？

29.	有名	yǒumíng	Adj		[have-fame]

這個學校什麼很有名？

这个学校什么很有名？

30.	只要	zhǐyào	Conj	so long as, provided	[only-have]

只要你有錢，就可以做什麼？

只要你有钱，就可以做什么？

31.	高級 高级	gāojí	Adj	high in rank/grade/quality	[tall-level]

你覺得什麼樣的衣服、鞋子比較高級？

你觉得什么样的衣服、鞋子比较高级？

32.	可笑	kěxiào	Adj	funny, ridiculous	[able-laugh]

你覺得什麼事很可笑？

你觉得什么事很可笑？

33.	小販 小贩	xiǎofàn	N	peddler, vendor	[small-buy to resell]

在什麼地方可以看到很多小販？

在什么地方可以看到很多小贩？

	伊麗莎白 伊丽莎白	Yīlìshābái	N	a foreign name, Elizabeth	[she-beautiful-plant-white]
34.	瓜	guā	N	melon	

現在市場上賣西瓜還是南瓜？

现在市场上卖西瓜还是南瓜？

35.	水果	shuǐguǒ	N	fruit	[water-fruit]

你最喜歡吃什麼水果？為什麼？

你最喜欢吃什么水果？为什么？

Characters with Many Strokes

極 拳 舞 棋 餐 廳 麵 級 販

36.	討價還價 讨价还价	tǎojià- huánjià	VP	to bargain, to haggle	[discuss-price-give back-price]

你跟人討價還價的時候都會說些什麼？

你跟人讨价还价的时候都会说些什么？

37.	最後 最后	zuìhòu	Adj	final, last	[most-back]

這是你最後一年學中文嗎？

这是你最后一年学中文吗？

38.	上當 上当	shàngdàng	VO	to be taken in, to be fooled	[submit-pawn]

A上B的當；B讓A上當

你上過誰的當？誰上過你的當？

你上过谁的当？谁上过你的当？

39.	渴	kě	Adj	thirsty	

你口渴的時候，喜歡喝什麼？

你口渴的时候，喜欢喝什么？

40.	瓶	píng	M	bottle	

這兒一瓶汽水賣多少錢？

这儿一瓶汽水卖多少钱？

41.	結果 结果	jiéguǒ	N	result, consequence	[conclude-result]

你昨天看的電影，最後結果怎麼樣？

你昨天看的电影，最后结果怎么样？

42.	拉肚子	lādùzi	VO	to have diarrhea	[pull-stomach-suffix]

你喝牛奶會拉肚子嗎？

你喝牛奶会拉肚子吗？

43.	慘 惨	cǎn	Adj/ Adv	miserable, disastrously	

你什麼時候會有「很慘」的感覺？

你什么时候会有"很惨"的感觉？

44.	問好 问好	wènhǎo	V	to say hello to; to send one's regards to	[ask-good]

請你替我向你父母問好。

请你替我向你父母问好。

Characters with Many Strokes

價　當　渴　瓶　慘

◎By Grammatical Categories

Nouns/Pronouns/Measure Words

瓶	píng	bottle
瓜	guā	melon
早點	zǎodiǎn	breakfast
水果	shuǐguǒ	fruit
牛肉麵	niúròumiàn	beef noodles
自行車	zìxíngchē	bicycle
鬧鐘	nàozhōng	alarm clock
公園	gōngyuán	park
校園	xiàoyuán	campus
餐廳	cāntīng	restaurant, dining hall
商店	shāngdiàn	shop, store
廣場	guǎngchǎng	public square
胡同	hútòng	lane, alley
四合院	sìhéyuàn	compound with houses around a courtyard
氣功	qìgōng	*qigong* system of deep breathing exercises
太極拳	tàijíquán	a kind of shadowboxing
天亮	tiānliàng	daybreak, dawn
方向	fāngxiàng	direction
中間	zhōngjiān	center, middle
結果	jiéguǒ	result, consequence
小販	xiǎofàn	peddler, vendor
男女老少	nán-nǚ-lǎo-shào	men and women, old and young

Verbs/Stative Verbs/Adjectives

騎	qí	to ride
響	xiǎng	to ring, sound, noisy
順著	shùnzhe	to go along, to go in the same direction as
經過	jīngguò	to pass, to go through
問好	wènhǎo	to say hello to, to send one's regards to
注意	zhùyì	to pay attention to, to take note of
起床	qǐchuáng	to get up (from bed)
跑步	pǎobù	to jog
跳舞	tiàowǔ	to dance
下棋	xiàqí	to play chess
上當	shàngdàng	to be taken in
拉肚子	lādùzi	to have diarrhea
討價還價	tǎojià-huánjià	to bargain, to haggle
渴	kě	thirsty
慘	cǎn	miserable, tragic
高級	gāojí	high in rank/grade/quality
可笑	kěxiào	funny, ridiculous
有名	yǒumíng	famous
最後	zuìhòu	final, last

Adverbs and Others

自從	zìcóng	since
只要	zhǐyào	so long as, provided
比方說	bǐfāngshuō	for example

◎ By Pinyin

Entries with * indicate lexical items used in Mini-Dialogues and of possible interest for supplemental study.

bǐfāngshuō	比方说	for example
cāntīng	餐厅	restaurant
cǎn	惨	miserable
fāngxiàng	方向	direction
gāojí	高级	high in rank
gōngyuán	公园	park
guā	瓜	melon
guǎi*	拐	to turn
guǎngchǎng	广场	public square
hútòng	胡同	lane
jiéguǒ	结果	result
jīn*	斤	half a kilogram
jīngguò	经过	to pass
kě	渴	thirsty
kěxiào	可笑	funny
lādùzi	拉肚子	to have diarrhea
liùniǎo*	遛鸟	to take a bird on a stroll
nán-nǔ-lǎo-shào	男女老少	men & women, old and young
nàozhōng	闹钟	alarm clock
niúròumiàn	牛肉面	beef noodles
pǎobù	跑步	to jog
píng	瓶	bottle
qí	骑	to ride
qǐchuáng	起床	to get up (from bed)
qìgōng	气功	deep breathing exercises
shàngdàng	上当	to be taken in
shāngdiàn	商店	shop
shuǐguǒ	水果	fruit
shùnzhe	顺着	to go along
sìhéyuàn	四合院	compound with houses around a courtyard
tàijíquán	太极拳	a kind of shadowboxing
tǎojià-huánjià	讨价还价	to bargain
tiānliàng	天亮	daybreak
tiàowǔ	跳舞	to dance
wènhǎo	问好	to say hello to
xiǎng	响	to ring
xiǎofàn	小贩	peddler
xiàoyuán	校园	campus
xiàqí	下棋	to play chess
yǒumíng	有名	famous
zǎodiǎn	早点	breakfast
zhǐyào	只要	so long as
zhōngjiān	中间	center, middle
zhùyì	注意	to pay attention to
zìcóng	自从	since
zìxíngchē	自行车	bicycle
zuìhòu	最后	final

課文 Text

Use the following questions to guide your reading of the text.

1. 小高為什麼一直沒給美英發電子郵件？

2. 小高去天安門廣場的路上，經過哪裏？看到了什麼？

3. 小高覺得他的週末過得怎麼樣？為什麼？

美英：

[1]**自從**我到中國**以後**，就一直[2]**忙著**學習，沒給你發電子郵件，希望你不要生氣。平常我都待在學校裏學習，上個週末才有時間到校園外面走走。想聽聽我在北京的「故事」嗎？

星期天天剛亮，鬧鐘一響，我就起床了。吃了早點就騎上自行車，順著大街往天安門廣場的方向去，中間經過了很多小胡同，看到不少四合院，還經過一個公園。沒想到這麼早已經有很多人在鍛鍊了。[3]**男男女女、老老少少**，[4]**打太極拳的**打太極拳，練氣功**的**練氣功，還有人在跑步、跳舞、或下棋。

路上我注意到很多商店的名字裏都有英文，比方說有個餐廳叫「加州牛肉麵」。加州最有名的是牛肉麵嗎？好像東西的名字裏[5]**只要**有英文**就**高級些。最可笑的是，有個小販一直叫我買她的「伊麗莎白瓜」。你知道那是什麼水果嗎？我跟她討價還價，搞了半天，最後發現自己還是上當了。那時我又累又渴，[6]**想也沒想就**在路上買了一瓶水來喝，結果一回學校就拉肚子了。真慘！這就是我的「故事」。你怎麼樣？你週末在忙什麼？請替我向王華問好。

德中

课文 Text

Use the following questions to guide your reading of the text.

1. 小高为什么一直没给美英发电子邮件？

2. 小高去天安门广场的路上，经过哪里？看到了什么？

3. 小高觉得他的周末过得怎么样？为什么？

 美英：

　　¹自从我到中国以后，就一直²忙着学习，没给你发电子邮件，希望你不要生气。平常我都待在学校里学习，上个周末才有时间到校园外面走走。想听听我在北京的"故事"吗？

　　星期天天刚亮，闹钟一响，我就起床了。吃了早点就骑上自行车，顺着大街往天安门广场的方向去，中间经过了很多小胡同，看到不少四合院，还经过一个公园。没想到这么早已经有很多人在锻炼了。³男男女女、老老少少，⁴打太极拳的打太极拳，练气功的练气功，还有人在跑步、跳舞、或下棋。

　　路上我注意到很多商店的名字里都有英文，比方说有个餐厅叫"加州牛肉面"。加州最有名的是牛肉面吗？好像东西的名字里⁵只要有英文就高级些。最可笑的是，有个小贩一直叫我买她的"伊丽莎白瓜"。你知道那是什么水果吗？我跟她讨价还价，搞了半天，最后发现自己还是上当了。那时我又累又渴，⁶想也没想就在路上买了一瓶水来喝，结果一回学校就拉肚子了。真惨！这就是我的"故事"。你怎么样？你周末在忙什么？请替我向王华问好。

　　　　　　　　　　　　　　　　　　　　　德中

小對話 Mini-Dialogues

Read the supplementary dialogues for a better understanding of the text. See if you can memorize one and perform it in class.

(1) Describing events in a day

A: 你現在生活得怎麼樣？　　　　　你现在生活得怎么样？

Gao: 很不錯。我每天早上都六點半　　　很不错。我每天早上都六点半
　　　起床，然後跑步、吃早點、學　　　起床，然后跑步、吃早点、学
　　　習漢語。一直搞到晚上十點才　　　习汉语。一直搞到晚上十点才
　　　睡覺。　　　　　　　　　　　　睡觉。

A: 有空兒出去看看嗎？　　　　　　有空儿出去看看吗？

Gao: 還沒有。我週末的時候可能有　　　还没有。我周末的时候可能有
　　　機會出去。　　　　　　　　　　机会出去。

A: 你想去哪兒？　　　　　　　　　你想去哪儿？

Gao: 我想去看看天安門廣場或逛逛　　　我想去看看天安门广场或逛逛
　　　王府井Wángfǔjǐng、西單Xīdān。　　　王府井、西单。

A: What is your life like now?

Gao: Pretty good. Every day I get up at six-thirty. Then I go jogging, have breakfast, and study Chinese. I don't go to bed till ten o'clock.

A: Do you have time to go look around?

Gao: No, but I may have an opportunity to go out this weekend.

A: Where would you like to go?

Gao: I would like to go see Tiananmen Square or go shopping at Wangfujing or Xidan.

(2) Asking and giving directions

Gao: 請問，到天安門廣場怎麼走？　　　请问，到天安门广场怎么走？

A: 順著這條路，一直往東走，到 | 顺着这条路，一直往东走，到
了第二個路口，右拐guǎi就到 | 了第二个路口，右拐就到了。
了。

Gao: 謝謝你！ | 谢谢你！

Gao: May I ask how to get to Tiananmen Square?

A: Follow this road and keep heading east. When you come to the second intersection, turn right and you will be there.

Gao: Thanks!

(3) Making and responding to inquiries

Gao: 老師傅，您在做什麼？ | 老师傅，您在做什么？

A: 我在遛鳥liùniǎo。 | 我在遛鸟。

Gao: 我在美國只看過人遛狗，還沒 | 我在美国只看过人遛狗，还没
有看過遛鳥的。 | 有看过遛鸟的。

A: 不管遛什麼都一樣，大家都得 | 不管遛什么都一样，大家都得
出來活動活動。 | 出来活动活动。

Gao: 您說得對。所以我也出來走 | 您说得对。所以我也出来走
走。沒想到公園早上這 | 走。没想到公园早上这
麼熱鬧。 | 么热闹。

A: 我得去跟我的老朋友 | 我得去跟我的老朋友
下棋了，再見！ | 下棋了，再见！

Gao: Excuse me, what are you doing?

A: I am taking my birds for a walk.

Gao: In America, I have only seen people taking dogs for a walk, not birds.

A: No matter what you take out for walk, it's the same. Everyone needs some exercise.

Gao: That's right. That's why I came out for a walk. It had never occurred to me that the park in the morning could be so full of life.

A: Well, I have to play chess with my old friends. Good-bye!

 **(4) Bargaining with street vendors**

A: 你看，我的伊麗莎白瓜多漂亮啊！

Gao: 一斤jīn多少錢？

A: 一斤六塊錢，兩斤十塊錢。您想買點兒嗎？

Gao: 我一個人吃不了那麼多。

A: 這放著不會壞的。你看，兩斤差一點，我再給你拿三個，兩斤多了，十五塊好了。

Gao: 十二塊怎麼樣？

A: 不行，十三塊，你要就買。

Gao: 好吧，十三塊給你。

A: 拿好。慢走，下次再來啊！

Gao: 真倒霉，原來最後那三個是壞的。

你看，我的伊丽莎白瓜多漂亮啊！

一斤多少钱？

一斤六块钱，两斤十块钱。您想买点儿吗？

我一个人吃不了那么多。

这放着不会坏的。你看，两斤差一点，我再给你拿三个，两斤多了，十五块好了。

十二块怎么样？

不行，十三块，你要就买。

好吧，十三块给你。

拿好。慢走，下次再来啊！

真倒霉，原来最后那三个是坏的。

A: See, how pretty are my "Elizabeth melons"!

Gao: How much per *jin*?

A: Six dollars per *jin* or two *jin* for ten dollars. Do you want to buy some?

Gao: I can't eat that many by myself.

A: They won't go bad for a few days. See, it's about two *jin*. Let me give you three more. Now it's over two *jin*. How about 15 dollars?

Gao: How about 12 dollars?

A: No. 13 dollars. Buy them if you want.

Gao: All right, here is 13 dollars.

A: Hold onto this. Take your time. Come back again.

Gao: Oh, no! The last three melons she gave me were bad.

小故事 Stories

Read the following tale for your own enjoyment and for your understanding of the highlighted expression that is relevant to the theme of the chapter.

 瞎子摸象 xiāzi mō xiàng

❀ 我對中國人的生活習慣不太了解，我只去過北京，還是瞎子摸象。

瞎子	xiāzi	blind person
摸	mō	to feel, to stroke
象	xiàng	elephant
牆	qiáng	wall
尾巴	wěiba	tail
繩子	shéngzi	rope
耳朵	ěrduō	ear
扇子	shànzi	fan
鼻子	bízi	nose
蛇	shé	snake
腿	tuǐ	leg
柱子	zhùzi	post, pillar
吵	chǎo	to quarrel

從前有幾個瞎子在聊天，一個人突然問：「大象是什麼樣子呢？」因為沒有人看過，所以他們就請人帶他們去「摸」象。

一個人摸到大象的肚子，就說大象的樣子像一面牆；另外一個人摸到象的尾巴，他說：「不對，大象長得像繩子。」一個摸到象耳朵的人說：「不！象跟一把扇子一樣。」還有一個人摸到象的鼻子，他說：「不可能，象長得就像蛇。」最後一個人摸了象的腿，就說：「你們全錯了！大象長得像柱子一樣。」這些瞎子說的說、吵的吵，大家都不聽別人的，以為只有自己是對的。

✐ 瞎子摸象的意思是＿＿＿＿＿＿＿＿＿＿＿＿＿＿＿＿

瞎子摸象 xiāzi mō xiàng

❀ 我对中国人的生活习惯不太了解，我只去过北京，还是瞎子摸象。

从前有几个瞎子在聊天，一个人突然问："大象是什么样子呢？"因为没有人看过，所以他们就请人带他们去"摸"象。

一个人摸到大象的肚子，就说大象的样子象一面墙；另外一个人摸到象的尾巴，他说："不对，大象长得象绳子。"一个摸到象耳朵的人说："不！象跟一把扇子一样。"还有一个人摸到象的鼻子，他说："不可能，象长得就象蛇。"最后一个人摸了象的腿，就说："你们全错了！大象长得象柱子一样。"这些瞎子说的说、吵的吵，大家都不听别人的，以为只有自己是对的。

瞎子	xiāzi	blind person
摸	mō	to feel, to stroke
象	xiàng	elephant
墙	qiáng	wall
尾巴	wěiba	tail
绳子	shéngzi	rope
耳朵	ěrduō	ear
扇子	shànzi	fan
鼻子	bízi	nose
蛇	shé	snake
腿	tuǐ	leg
柱子	zhùzi	post, pillar
吵	chǎo	to quarrel

漢字 Characters

Study the following selected characters for further enrichment of your writing and vocabulary.

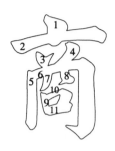
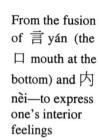

From the fusion of 言 yán (the 口 mouth at the bottom) and 內 nèi—to express one's interior feelings

商店	shāngdiàn	shop, store
商人	shāngrén*	businessman
商量	shāngliang	to consult, to talk over

A: 我應該去哪家商店買這些東西？
B: 你找老王商量商量。

Compare: 適 shì

商

shāng 11
to discuss, business

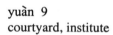

阝 fù 'hill' + 完 wán phonetic

四合院	sìhéyuàn	quadrangle
院子	yuànzi*	courtyard, compound
學院	xuéyuàn*	college, academy
醫院	yīyuàn*	hospital

A: 你家有院子嗎？
B: 有，有前院也有後院。

院

yuàn 9
courtyard, institute

木 mù 'wood' + 交 jiāo phonetic—school houses are made of wood

校園	xiàoyuán	campus
學校	xuéxiào	school
母校	mǔxiào*	alma mater
校長	xiàozhǎng*	principal, president

A: 那個學校的校園大不大？
B: 大極了。

校

xiào, jiào 10
school, to proofread

糸 sī 'silk' + 及 jí phonetic—the grading of silk according to its quality

高級	gāojí	high in rank/ quality
超級	chāojí	super
中級	zhōngjí*	middle rank/level
一年級	yī niánjí*	first grade, first year

A: 那家超級市場賣的東西怎麼樣？
B: 都很高級。

級

jí 9
grade, level

the right 八
division of 厶
'private things'

公

公司　　gōngsī*　　company
辦公室　bàngōngshì*　office
公路　　gōnglù*　　highway, road

A: 那家公司在哪兒？
B: 就在公路旁邊。

Compare: 分 fēn

gong 4
public, common

口 wéi
'surround—
garden fence' +
袁 yuán
phonetic

園

公園　　gōngyuán　　park, garden
花園　　huāyuán　　flower garden
果園　　guǒyuán*　　orchard
動物園　dòngwùyuán*　zoo

A: 你覺得這兒的公園怎麼樣？
B: 不知道，我還沒出過校園呢。

Compare: 圓 yuán

yuán 13
garden, place for
public recreation

足 zú 'foot' +
兆 zhào
phonetic

跳

跳舞　　tiàowǔ　　to dance
跳房子　tiào fángzi*　hopscotch
跳高　　tiàogāo*　　high jump

A: 你喜歡跳舞嗎？你跳些什麼舞？
B: 我什麼舞都跳。

Compare: 跑 pǎo 路 lù

tiào 13
to jump, to skip (over)

Picture of a
dancer holding
some ornaments
by the hands—
舛 chuǎn two big
feet were added
later

舞

舞會　　wǔhuì　　dance (party), ball
舞迷　　wǔmí　　dance enthusiast

A: 我們今天晚上有個舞會，你來嗎？
B: 舞迷怎麼能不來？

wǔ 14
to dance, to brandish

糸 sī 'thread' +
吉 jí 'good luck' phonetic

結

jié 12
to tie, knot

結果	jiéguǒ	result, outcome
結婚	jiéhūn	to get married
結論	jiélùn*	conclusion

A: 我想他們倆結婚一定沒有好結果。
B: 別太早下結論。

Compare: 給 gěi

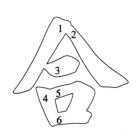

Picture of the lid of an opening

合

hé 6
to close, to join, whole

四合院	sìhéyuàn	quadrangle
合適	héshì	suitable
合作	hézuò	to cooperate
合唱	héchàng	to sing in a chorus

A: 那個四合院住了幾家人？
B: 住了三家人。

Compare: 給 gěi 拿 ná 盒 hé 會 huì

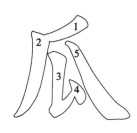

The outer strokes are vines, and the inner part 厶 is a melon.

瓜

guā 5
melon, gourd

西瓜	xīguā*	watermelon
南瓜	nánguā	pumpkin
木瓜	mùguā*	papaya
黃瓜	huángguā*	cucumber

A: 你喜歡吃什麼瓜？
B: 西瓜、木瓜、黃瓜我都喜歡。

歹 dǎi 'broken bone' + 又 yòu 'hand' + 食 shí 'food'

餐

cān 16
to eat, meal

餐廳	cāntīng	restaurant
快餐	kuàican	fast food, quick meal
晚餐	wǎncān*	supper, dinner
西餐	xīcān*	Western-style food
自助餐	zìzhùcān*	buffet, cafeteria

A: 那家餐廳的自助餐很不錯。
B: 對，去那兒吃晚餐最好。

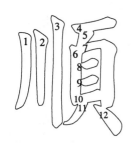

頁 yè 'head' +
川 chuan
phonetic

順著	shùnzhe	to go along
順利	shùnlì	smooth, without a hitch
順路	shùnlù*	on the way

順

A: 順著這條街就能走到公園嗎？

B: 對，到圖書館也順路。

shùn 12
along, to obey, to
follow

The top is 止
zhǐ and the
bottom was
originally 止
backwards—
Picture of one
right foot and
one left foot

跑步	pǎobù	to jog
進步	jìnbù	progress, to improve
散步	sànbù	to take a walk

A: 你每天都散步嗎？

B: 對，我不但散步而且也跑步。

步

Compare: 歲 suì

bù 7
step, to pace off

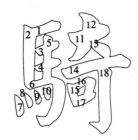

馬 mǎ 'horse'
+ 奇 qí
phonetic

| 騎馬 | qímǎ* | to ride a horse |

A: 這校園太大，走得累死人了！

B: 你為什麼不騎自行車呢？

騎

qí 18
to ride/sit astride

氵 shuǐ 'water'
+ 主 zhǔ
phonetic

注意	zhùyì	to pay attention to
注意到	zhùyìdào*	to notice
注意力	zhùyìlì*	attention

注

A: 你注意到了嗎？那個學生不太好。

B: 是啊！他不注意聽老師說的話。

Compare: 住 zhù

zhù 8
to pour, to concentrate,
notes

月 ròu 'flesh' +
土 tǔ phonetic

肚

拉肚子	lā dùzi	to have diarrhea
大肚子	dàdùzi*	pregnant woman, pot belly
一肚子	yídùzi*	a bellyful

A: 我喝了一肚子的涼水。

B: 小心點，一會兒會拉肚子的。

Compare: 臉 liǎn　腿 tuǐ

dù 7
stomach, belly

氵 shuǐ 'water'
+ 曷 hé
phonetic

渴

| 口渴 | kǒukě* | thirsty |
| 解渴 | jiěkě* | to quench one's thirst |

A: 我太渴了，所以買瓶汽水來喝。

B: 汽水根本不解渴。

Compare: 喝 hē

kě 12
thirsty

瓦 wǎ
'earthenware' +
并 bìng
phonetic

瓶

瓶子	píngzi	bottle
熱水瓶	rèshuǐpíng*	thermos bottle
花瓶	huāpíng*	flower vase

A: 瓶子裏有水嗎？我想泡 pào 'make' 茶。

B: 沒有水了，你用我的熱水瓶吧！

píng 10
bottle, vase

广 yǎn 'half of
a hut, a shed, a
shop' + 黃
huáng phonetic

广

廣場	guǎngchǎng	public square
廣告	guǎnggào*	advertisement
廣播	guǎngbō	to broadcast, to air

A: 你去過天安門廣場嗎？

B: 沒去過，只在廣告上看過。

Compare: 應 yīng　廠 chǎng

guǎng 14
wide, to expand

語法和用法 Grammar and Usage

Pay attention to the function of the structure and then study the example sentences.

1. Expressing a specific time in the past

自從S_1VO以後, (S_1)/S_2就	zìcóng…yǐhòu, …jiù…	ever since…, (S_1)/S_2…

自從我到中國**以後**，**就**一直忙著學習，沒給你發電子郵件，希望你不要生氣。

1.	你有他的消息嗎？	你有他的消息吗？	Have you heard his news?
	沒有，自從他轉學以後，我們就沒有通信。	没有，自从他转学以后，我们就没有通信。	No. Since he transferred to another school, we haven't corresponded with each other.
2.	她人還在這兒嗎？	她人还在这儿吗？	Is she still here?
	不在，自從畢業以後，她就去了芝加哥。	不在，自从毕业以后，她就去了芝加哥。	No. Since she graduated from here, she moved to Chicago.
3.	你什麼時候開始學中文的？學了多久？	你什么时候开始学中文的？学了多久？	When did you start studying Chinese? How long have you been studying?
	自從我上了大學以後，就一直在學中文。	自从我上了大学以后，就一直在学中文。	Ever since I started college, I have been studying Chinese.

As a general rule of thumb, when the subjects in the two clauses are the same, one of them can be omitted, as in examples 2 and 3. When the subjects are different, they need to be stated clearly, as in example 1. A past event often goes after 自從, which expresses a time phrase preceding the main clause of a sentence. It often goes with 以後 or 以來. Whereas 以後 indicates a period since the past event which may or may not have ended before the present, 以來 indicates a period since the past event that continues to the present.

2. Expressing an ongoing activity or concurrent actions

S 忙著V(O)	...mángzhe...	S is busy V-ing
S V_2著O_2 V_1O_1	...zhe...	S does V_1 O_1 while doing V_2 O_2 (an accompanying action)

自從我到中國以後，就一直**忙著**學習……

1. | 你最近在忙什麼？ | 你最近在忙什么？ | What have you been busy doing lately? |
|---|---|---|
| 快考試了，我忙著學習。 | 快考试了，我忙着学习。 | I'm going to have a test. I have been busy studying. |

2. | 你這幾天在忙些什麼？ | 你这几天在忙些什么？ | What have you been busy doing for the past few days? |
|---|---|---|
| 我忙著辦簽證到中國去。 | 我忙着办签证到中国去。 | I have been busy applying for a visa to go to China. |

3. | 你喜歡怎麼學習？ | 你喜欢怎么学习？ | How do you like to study? |
|---|---|---|
| 我喜歡聽著音樂學習。 | 我喜欢听着音乐学习。 | I like to study while listening to music. |

4. | 你爸爸早上喜歡做什麼？ | 你爸爸早上喜欢做什么？ | What does your father like to do in the morning? |
|---|---|---|
| 他喜歡喝著咖啡看報。 | 他喜欢喝着咖啡看报。 | He likes to read the newspaper while drinking coffee. |

Note that in the pattern "V_2著O_2 V_1O_1," V_1 O_1 is the main action, while V_2 O_2 is subordinate.

3. Using reduplication

Reduplication of N: A→AA; AB→AABB	pluralizer
Reduplication of Adj: A→AA; AB→AABB	intensifier
Reduplication of V: A→AA; AB→ABAB	to do something briefly or casually

男男女女、**老老少少**，打太極拳的打太極拳，練氣功的練氣功……

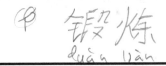 锻炼
duàn liàn   exercise

1. 咱們買個西瓜 xīguā 來吃吧！　　咱们买个西瓜来吃吧！　　Let's buy a watermelon.

   這兒大大小小的瓜這麼多，買哪一個好啊？　　这儿大大小小的瓜这么多，买哪一个好啊？　　There are so many here, big and small; which one shall we get?

2. 現在北京人喜歡做什麼？　　现在北京人喜欢做什么？　　What do people in Beijing like to do nowadays?

   男男女女、老老少少都在學電腦。　　男男女女、老老少少都在学电脑。　　Everyone is studying computers.

3. 你不在家休息休息，穿得漂漂亮亮的，要上哪兒去？　　你不在家休息休息，穿得漂漂亮亮的，要上哪儿去？　　You are not staying home resting, dressed up so nicely. Where are you going?

   我要跟男朋友出去玩玩。　　我要跟男朋友出去玩玩。　　I am going out with my boyfriend.

Note that various functions can be expressed through reduplication. Also, there are different ways of reduplication (AABB; ABAB) when two syllables are involved.

4. Using parallel actions to describe a situation

| $V_1(O_1)$ 的（人）$V_1(O_1)$, $V_2(O_2)$ 的（人）$V_2(O_2)$ | …de(rén)…, …de(rén)… | the ones who do V_1 did V_1, the ones who do V_2 did V_2 some do…, others do… |

男男女女、老老少少，打太極拳的打太極拳，練氣功的練氣功……

1. 你上課的時候，學生專心嗎？　　你上课的时候，学生专心吗？　　Were your students paying attention when you lectured?

   他們聽的聽，寫的寫，都很注意我說的話。　　他们听的听，写的写，都很注意我说的话。　　Yes, some listened and others took notes. They were all very attentive.

2. 昨天的晚會好玩嗎？　　昨天的晚会好玩吗？　　Was the party fun last night?

不錯，我們唱歌的唱歌，跳舞的跳舞，搞到一點才回家。	不错，我们唱歌的唱歌，跳舞的跳舞，搞到一点才回家。	Yes. Some of us sang and others danced. We didn't go home until one o'clock.
3. 你怎麼慶祝你的生日？	你怎么庆祝你的生日？	How did you celebrate your birthday?
我請了很多朋友來家裏。大家吃的吃，喝的喝，都很高興。	我请了很多朋友来家里。大家吃的吃，喝的喝，都很高兴。	I invited many friends to come to my place. Some of them ate and others drank. We all had fun.

This pattern is used to list various things that different people do in one situation. It's the same as 有的 V₁(O₁) , 有的 V₂(O₂). Though 人 is omitted after 的, V₁ 的 is a noun phrase.

5. Expressing a necessary condition

只要 S…, (S) 就…	zhǐyào…, … jiù…	as long as…, then;
S 只要…, (S) 就…		provided that…

好像東西的名字裏**只要**有英文**就**高級些。

1. 我在北京的時候，住學校外面方便嗎？	我在北京的时候，住学校外面方便吗？	When I go to Beijing, will it be convenient to live off campus?
只要你會騎自行車就很方便。	只要你会骑自行车就很方便。	As long as you can ride a bike, it will be convenient.
2. 我得每週跟我的教授見面嗎？	我得每周跟我的教授见面吗？	Do I have to meet with my professor every week?
不必。你只要一個月去見他一次就行了。	不必。你只要一个月去见他一次就行了。	No. As long as you visit him once a month, it will be all right.

3.

聽說在那個地方吃東西很容易拉肚子。	听说在那个地方吃东西很容易拉肚子。	I heard that people had diarrhea when they ate there.
只要你注意、別喝不乾淨的水，就沒有問題。	只要你注意、別喝不干净的水，就沒有问题。	As long as you make sure the water you drink is clean, you will have no problem.

Note that 就 as an adverb always goes after the subject. Be sure to distinguish this pattern with 只有 S..., (S) 才 (L13, G1) 'only; only if.'

6. Expressing negligence

S (O) V 也/都不 V 就…	…yě/dōu bù…jiù…	S…without V-ing
S (O) V 也/都沒 V 就…	…yě/dōu méi…jiù…	

那時我又累又渴，**想也沒想就**在路上買了一瓶水來喝……

1.

你為什麼這麼生氣？	你为什么这么生气？	Why were you so mad?
那個學生跟我說也沒說就走了。	那个学生跟我说也没说就走了。	That student left without telling me.

2.

他知道那個公園在哪兒嗎？	他知道那个公园在哪儿吗？	Does he know where the park is?
不知道，可是他問也不問就一直往前走。	不知道，可是他问也不问就一直往前走。	No. Yet he keeps on walking without asking other people.

3.

今天的課文，他看了嗎？	今天的课文，他看了吗？	Did he read today's text?
沒有，他課文看也沒看就來上課了。	沒有，他课文看也沒看就来上课了。	No. He came to class without reading the text.

Compare this pattern with the strong negation using 一點兒也/都不/沒.

文化點滴 Culture Notes

1. **Morning exercises:** The one thing that newcomers to the Chinese society will notice is how busy people are in the morning doing exercises. Chinese people, especially the elderly, like to get up very early in the morning and go to a park or nearby practice field to do various kinds of exercises. In addition to traditional practices such as *taijiquan* and *qigong*, they also do ballroom dance 交誼舞 jiāoyíwǔ or folk dance 土風舞 tǔfēngwǔ. Some people may practice with their wooden swords 舞劍 wǔjiàn; others take their birds out for a walk 遛鳥 liùniǎo. While you may not see people do extraordinary feats of Chinese martial arts 功夫, such as breaking concrete slabs with their heads or "flying" long distances through the air, as shown in movies, you will surely enjoy these morning calisthenics.

2. **Qigong:** *Qigong*, along with acupuncture, massage, and herbal medicine, are the pillars of traditional Chinese medicine. It is a method by which one discovers, develops, nurtures, and applies the body's vital energy. It is believed that the practice of *qigong* can initiate an automatic self-healing process and manage stress, which in turns relieves one of disease. Those who have practiced deep breathing techniques claim to be able to visualize the entire process of metabolism and circulation within themselves. If you sit up, relax your body, take a deep breath, and rest your mind for just a moment, you are already doing *qigong*.

3. **Tai Chi:** Tai Chi has been practiced in China for centuries as a martial art. It is a movement and breathing system that exercizes all the joints and major muscle groups while improving the circulation of internal energy within the body. It is practiced very slowly and gently and involves the entire body, emphasizing the continuity of movement without a break or pause.

4. **Traditional buildings:** quadrangles 四合院 sìhéyuàn are traditional residences, a building complex formed by four houses around a quadrangular courtyard. These are still very common in Beijing. Surrounding the Forbidden City 故宮 gùgōng, the royal palace, these quadrangles were interconnected by many *hutong* 胡同, an ancient city alley or lane, arranged in an orderly fashion off of the main roads. The size of the quadrangles varied according to the residents' social status. To the east and west of the palace are the stately quadrangles, where imperial kinsmen and aristocrats resided. To the far north and south of the palace are the simple and crude quadrangles, where merchants and ordinary people lived. During the period of the Republic of China (1911–1948), quadrangles previously owned by one family became a compound occupied by many households. In recent years, many quadrangles have been pulled down and replaced with modern buildings.

5. **English letters in Chinese compounds:** Although it sounds funny, with the Western influence one finds more and more English used in Chinese terms. The following are a few examples:

Chinese Terms		*Place Used*	*English*
K書	K书	Taiwan	to study hard
A錢	A钱	Taiwan	to embezzle public funds
AA制	AA制	Mainland China	to go dutch
T恤衫	T恤衫	Taiwan	T-shirts
很Q	很Q	Taiwan	very chewy (refers only to cooked rice or things made of glutinous rice)

歌兒 Songs

北京老師傅
Old Beijing Master

Allegretto

詞：劉雅詩　曲：馬定一

1. 北　京老　師傅　呀，　　北京老　師傅，　　天　亮了起床，就　　溜鳥
   Běi jīng láo shīfu　ya,　　Běi jīng láo　shīfu,　　tiānliàngle qǐchuáng, jiù　　liùniǎo
   Old Beijing Master, oh,　　Old Beijing Master,　　at daybreak you get up and go out

2. 美　國小　伙子　呀，　　美國小　伙子，　　跟　我　打拳跳舞，注意
   Měi guó xiǎo huǒzi　ya,　　Měiguó xiǎo huǒ zi,　　gēn wǒ　dǎ quán tiàowǔ　zhùyì
   Young American,　　oh, young American,　you practice taiji and dance with me, paying attention

1. 上　大　路。　　騎　著自行車　　呀，　　經　過許　多屋。
   shàng dà　lù.　　Qí zhe zì xíng chē　ya,　　jīng guò xǔ duō wū,
   on the street taking your birds for a stroll. Riding your bike, oh,　you pass so many households.

2. 每　一　步。　　搞　不清方向　　呀，　　結果撞到樹。
   měi yī　bù.　　Gǎo buqīng fāngxiàng ya,　　jié guǒ zhuàngdào shù.
   to my every move.　You lose your way, oh,　you bump into a tree.

1. 順著胡同走　呀，　跟小販打招呼。　　最後來到了公園　　，
   shùnzhe hútong zǒu ya,　gēn xiǎofàn dǎ　zhāo hu.　　Zuì hòu lái dàole gōngyuán lǐ,
   Going along the alleys, oh,　you greet the street vendors.　At last you reach the park.

2. 只要身體好　呀，　學習　不怕苦。　　買瓜上了當真要命，
   Zhǐ yào shēntǐ hǎo　ya,　xué xí　bú pà kǔ.　　Mǎi guā shàngledàng zhēnyàomìng,
   As long as you have good health, you can bear hardship when studying.　It's awful to be tricked when
   you buy melons.

1. 先　打太極拳　再　跳交　際　舞。
   Xiān dǎ tài jí quán zài tiào jiāo jì wǔ.
   First you practice Taiji and then do ballroom dance.

2. 討　價還　價　還　得下　功　夫。
   Tǎo jià huán jià hái děi xià gōng fu.
   You need to learn more about bargaining.

第五課

Theme Food and Health

Communicative Objectives
- Commenting on American food
- Commenting on Chinese food
- Dining out
- Explaining how to make a dish

Grammar Focus
- 要不是…就是…再不然
- 除非…否則/要不然…
- 像…這樣/那樣…的 N
- 不但沒/不…反而…
- 不得不 V；不能不 V；不會不 V
- S才/剛…就…

Focus on Characters
- 酸甜苦辣、健康食物、蛋條香飽、怪城濟民、否則講般

酸甜苦辣全都嚐過了嗎？

生詞 Vocabulary

Study the following words for their pronunciation and meaning. When an area is shaded, guess at the meaning of the word based on its constituent characters and then fill in the blank. Read the usage of words and related terms (antonyms, synonyms, compounds sharing the constituent characters, etc.) and try to answer the sample questions in Chinese. Note that proper nouns or incidental terms are not numbered.

◎ By Order of Appearance

1.	酸甜苦辣	suān-tián-kǔ-là	N	all flavors, joys and sorrows of life	[sour-sweet-bitter-hot]

你能不能說說你學中文的酸甜苦辣？

你能不能说说你学中文的酸甜苦辣？

2.　嚐　　cháng　　V　　to taste
　　尝

你嚐過麻婆豆腐嗎？

你尝过麻婆豆腐吗？

3.　藥　　yào　　N　　medicine, drug
　　药

這種藥一天要吃幾次？吃的時候有什麼要注意的嗎？

这种药一天要吃几次？吃的时候有什么要注意的吗？

4.　健康　　jiànkāng　　N　　health　　[healthy-healthy]

要想身體健康應該做什麼？

要想身体健康应该做什么？

5.　想念　　xiǎngniàn　　V　　to miss, to remember with longing　　[think-think of]

你現在特別想念什麼人？什麼東西？

你现在特别想念什么人？什么东西？

　　麻婆豆腐　　mápó dòufu　　N　　Mapo tofu, name of a dish　　[numb-old lady-beancurd]

6.　香　　xiāng　　Adj　　fragrant

→香水

什麼東西很香？

什么东西很香？

7.　老實說　　lǎoshíshuō　　IE　　to tell the truth　　[always-true-say]
　　老实说

老實說，我並不喜歡吃她做的飯。

老实说，我并不喜欢吃她做的饭。

| 8. | 挑剔 | tiāotì | Adj/ | nitpicky, to nitpick | [select-weed out] |
| | | | V | | |

你吃東西挑剔嗎？有什麼東西不吃嗎？

你吃东西挑剔吗？有什么东西不吃吗？

| 9. | 食物 | shíwù | N | food | [eat-thing] |

你不吃什麼食物？

你不吃什么食物？

| 10. | 不行 | bùxíng | V | to be no good, won't work | [not-go] |

你覺得誰做的飯不行？

你觉得谁做的饭不行？

| 11. | 乾
干 | gān | Adj | dry | |

你吃過牛肉乾嗎？喜歡吃嗎？

你吃过牛肉干吗？喜欢吃吗？

| 12. | 炸 | zhá | V | to deep-fry | |

你喜歡吃誰做的炸雞？

你喜欢吃谁做的炸鸡？

| 13. | 薯條兒
薯条儿 | shǔtiáor | N | french fries | [potato-strip] |

cp. 土豆片 tǔdòupiàn 'chips'

我們在哪兒可以吃到薯條兒？

我们在哪儿可以吃到薯条儿？

| 14. | 油 | yóu | Adj/
N | oily, grease, oil | |

什麼東西對你來說太油？

什么东西对你来说太油？

| 15. | 蛋糕 | dàngāo | N | cake | [egg-cake] |

你平常最喜歡吃哪一種蛋糕？

你平常最喜欢吃哪一种蛋糕？

| 16. | 膩
腻 | nì | Adj | greasy, oily, tired of | |

吃膩了/聽膩了/看膩了……

你吃了什麼會覺得很膩？

你吃了什么会觉得很腻？

Characters with Many Strokes

酸　辣　嚐　藥　健　康　剔　薯　糕　膩

| 17. | 點心 | diǎnxīn | N | | [little-heart] |
| | 点心 | | | | |

你會做什麼點心？跟誰學的？

你会做什么点心？跟谁学的？

| 18. | 一般 | yìbān | Adj | ordinary, general | [one-kind] |

中國飯館一般都會有什麼好吃的菜？

中国饭馆一般都会有什么好吃的菜？

| 19. | 所謂 | suǒwèi | Adj | so-called | [so-call] |
| | 所谓 | | | | |

所謂的「吃苦」是什麼意思？

所谓的"吃苦"是什么意思？

| 20. | 炒 | chǎo | V | to stir-fry, to sauté | |

你青菜喜歡生吃還是喜歡吃炒過的？

你青菜喜欢生吃还是喜欢吃炒过的？

| 21. | 生 | shēng | Adj | raw, green, uncooked | |

牛排 niúpái 'steak' 你喜歡吃生一點兒的，還是
熟一點兒的？

牛排你喜欢吃生一点儿的，还是熟一点儿
的？

| 22. | 老 | lǎo | Adj | tough, overdone | |

你覺得這個蛋太老了嗎？

你觉得这个蛋太老了吗？

| 23. | 鹹 | xián | Adj | salty | |
| | 咸 | | | | |

什麼東西很鹹？你喜歡吃鹹的東西，還是
甜的東西？

什么东西很咸？你喜欢吃咸的东西，还是
甜的东西？

| 24. | 除非 | chúfēi | Conj | only if, only when | [except-not] |

我不想去，除非你跟我一起去。

我不想去，除非你跟我一起去。

| 25. | 中國城 | Zhōngguó | N | | [China-city] |
| | 中国城 | chéng | | | |

你去過中國城嗎？哪兒的中國城？

你去过中国城吗？哪儿的中国城？

| 26. | 否則 | fǒuzé | Conj | otherwise, if not, or else | [no-then] |
| | 否则 | | | | |

除非你拼命學習，否則你一定考不好。

除非你拼命学习，否则你一定考不好。

27.	飽 饱	bǎo	Adj	full	
				你一餐要吃幾碗飯才飽？	
				你一餐要吃几碗饭才饱？	
28.	講究 讲究	jiǎngjiu	V	to be particular about, to pay attention to	[speak-study carefully]
				你講究吃的還是穿的？	
				你讲究吃的还是穿的？	
29.	移民	yímín	N/V	e/immigrant, to e/immigrate	[move-people]
				什麼地方有很多中國來的移民？	
				什么地方有很多中国来的移民？	
30.	日子	rìzi	N	day, days, life	[sun-suffix]
				你住過什麼地方？你覺得在那兒的日子怎麼樣？	
				你住过什么地方？你觉得在那儿的日子怎么样？	
31.	不但	búdàn	Conj	not only	
				誰不但不吃肉，而且連蛋都不吃？	
				谁不但不吃肉，而且连蛋都不吃？	
32.	反而	fǎn'ér	Adv	on the contrary, instead	
				為什麼你沒學習反而考得很好？	
				为什么你没学习反而考得很好？	
33.	瘦	shòu	Adj	thin, lean, skinny	
				怎麼樣可以瘦一點兒？	
				怎么样可以瘦一点儿？	
34.	胖	pàng	Adj	fat, plump	
				吃什麼東西容易發胖？	
				吃什么东西容易发胖？	
35.	不得不	bùdé bù	IE	cannot but, have to	[not-get-not]
				為什麼你說你不得不跟他見面？	
				为什么你说你不得不跟他见面？	

Characters with Many Strokes

謂　鹹　城　飽　講　移　瘦　胖

| 36. | 拼命 | pīnmìng | VO | | [risk life-life] |

什麼時候你會拼命學習？

什么时候你会拼命学习？

| 37. | 有的是 | yǒudeshì | IE | to have plenty of, there is no lack of | [have-particle-be] |

這個地方有的是什麼？

这个地方有的是什么？

| 38. | 羨慕 | xiànmù | V | to envy, to admire | [envy-esteem] |
| | 羡慕 | | | | |

你羨慕那些能去中國留學的人嗎？

你羡慕那些能去中国留学的人吗？

| 39. | 怪不得 | guàibude | Conj | no wonder, so that's why | [strange-not-need] |

他吃壞了肚子，怪不得這麼難受。

他吃坏了肚子，怪不得这么难受。

| 40. | 享受 | xiǎngshòu | V/N | to enjoy, enjoyment | [enjoy-receive] |

你覺得吃什麼、看什麼是一種享受？

你觉得吃什么、看什么是一种享受？

| 41. | 經濟 | jīngjì | Adj/ | economical, economy | [manage-aid] |
| | 经济 | | N | | |

你覺得在哪兒買東西比較經濟？

你觉得在哪儿买东西比较经济？

| 42. | 吃苦 | chīkǔ | VO | | [eat-bitterness] |

你在哪兒吃了很多苦？

你在哪儿吃了很多苦？

| 43. | 開心 | kāixīn | V/ | to feel happy, happy | [open-heart] |
| | 开心 | | Adj | | |

你今天為什麼這麼開心？

你今天为什么这么开心？

Characters with Many Strokes

羨　慕　享　經　濟

◎ By Grammatical Categories

Nouns/Pronouns/Measure Words

酸甜苦辣	suān-tián-kǔ-là	all flavors, joys and sorrows of life	點心	diǎnxīn	pastry
健康	jiànkāng	health	中國城	Zhōngguó chéng	Chinatown
食物	shíwù	food	日子	rìzi	day, days, life
薯條	shǔtiáor	french fries	藥	yào	medicine, drug
蛋糕	dàngāo	cake	移民	yímín	e/immigrant, to e/immigrate

Verbs/Stative Verbs/Adjectives

嚐	cháng	to taste	鹹	xián	salty
炒	chǎo	to stir-fry, to sauté	油	yóu	oily, grease, oil
炸	zhá	to deep-fry	膩	nì	greasy, oily, tired of
想念	xiǎngniàn	to miss, to remember with longing	乾	gān	dry
			生	shēng	raw, green, uncooked
講究	jiǎngjiu	to be particular about, to pay attention to	老	lǎo	tough, overdone
羨慕	xiànmù	to envy, to admire	飽	bǎo	full
享受	xiǎngshòu	to enjoy, enjoyment	胖	pàng	fat, plump
開心	kāixīn	to feel happy	瘦	shòu	thin, lean, skinny
不行	bùxíng	to be no good, won't work	經濟	jīngjì	economical, economy
拼命	pīnmìng	to make a do-or-die effort	挑剔	tiāotì	nitpicky, to nitpick
吃苦	chīkǔ	to bear hardship	一般	yìbān	ordinary, general
香	xiāng	fragrant	所謂	suǒwèi	so-called

Adverbs and Others

反而	fǎn'ér	on the contrary, instead	老實說	lǎoshíshuō	to tell the truth
除非	chúfēi	only if, only when	不得不	bùdé bù	cannot but, have to
否則	fǒuzé	otherwise, if not, or else	有的是	yǒudeshì	to have plenty of, there is no lack of
不但	búdàn	not only			
怪不得	guàibude	no wonder, so that's why			

◎ By Pinyin

Entries with * indicate lexical items used in Mini-Dialogues and of possible interest for supplemental study.

bǎo	饱	full	lǎoshíshuō	老实说	to tell the truth
búdàn	不但	not only	nì	腻	greasy, tired of
bùdé bù	不得不	cannot but	pàng	胖	fat, plump
bùxíng	不行	to be no good	pīnmìng	拼命	to make a do-or-die effort
càidān*	菜单	menu	rìzi	日子	day, days
cháng	尝	to taste	shēng	生	raw, green
chǎo	炒	to stir-fry	shíwù	食物	food
chī dòufu*	吃豆腐	to eat beancurd, to flirt with	shòu	瘦	thin, lean, skinny
chīkǔ	吃苦	to bear hardship	shǔtiáor	薯条儿	french fries
chīsù*	吃素	to be a vegetarian	suān-tián-kǔ-là	酸甜苦辣	all flavors
chúfēi	除非	only if	suǒwèi	所谓	so-called
dàngāo	蛋糕	cake	tiāotì	挑剔	nitpicky, to nitpick
diǎn*	点	to order (dishes)	xián	咸	salty
diǎnxīn	点心	pastry	xiāng	香	fragrant
fǎn'ér	反而	on the contrary	xiǎngniàn	想念	to miss
fāpàng*	发胖	to gain weight	xiǎngshòu	享受	to enjoy, enjoyment
fǒuzé	否则	otherwise	xiànmù	羡慕	to envy
gān	干	dry	yán*	盐	salt
guàibude	怪不得	no wonder	yào	药	medicine
guōzi*	锅子	wok, pan	yìbān	一般	ordinary
huǒtuǐ*	火腿	ham	yímín	移民	e/immigrant
jiǎngjiu	讲究	be particular about	yíngyǎng*	营养	nutrition
jiàngyóu*	酱油	soy sauce	yóu	油	oily, oil
jiànkāng	健康	health, healthy	yǒudeshì	有的是	to have plenty of
jīdàn*	鸡蛋	hen's egg	zhá	炸	to deep-fry
jīngjì	经济	economical	Zhōngguó chéng	中国城	Chinatown
kāixīn	开心	to feel happy			
lǎo	老	tough, overdone			

課文 Text

Use the following questions to guide your reading of the text.

1. 小李覺得美國的食物怎麼樣？

2. 小李覺得什麼很奇怪？

3. 小高為什麼說自己「酸甜苦辣」全都嚐過了？

小高：

聽說你肚子不太舒服，現在好了嗎？有沒有吃藥？要多注意身體，健康是最重要的。

我最近很想家，特別想念我媽媽做的麻婆豆腐，那味兒又香又辣，好吃極了。老實說，我這個人並不挑剔，可是我覺得美國

的食物就是不行：漢堡包太乾、炸薯條兒太油、蛋糕太膩、點心又太甜。一般所謂的中國飯也不地道，炒的菜[1]**要不是**太生，就是太老，再不然就是太鹹。[2]**除非**上中國城去，否則不管怎麼吃都吃不飽。[3]**像**我**這樣**不講究吃**的**人在這兒住半年都受不了，真不知道那些中國來的移民是怎麼過日子的？最奇怪的是，我在這兒雖然吃得少，[4]**不但沒**瘦，**反而**越來越胖了。現在[5]**不得不**學美國人，拼命減肥。你在中國有的是機會，現在酸甜苦辣全都嚐過了嗎？真羨慕你，每天幫我多吃兩口吧！

小李

小李：

　　我在中國吃的真的很好，怪不得人說「吃在中國」。我在這兒天天享受餃子和酸辣湯，又好吃又經濟。你看，我學中文吃了很多苦，但是也很開心，⁶**才**來兩個月，**就**把中國的「酸甜苦辣」全都嚐了。

　　　　　　　　　　　　　　　　　　　　　　　　　　　　小高

课文 Text

Use the following questions to guide your reading of the text.

1. 小李觉得美国的食物怎么样？

2. 小李觉得什么很奇怪？

3. 小高为什么说自己"酸甜苦辣"全都尝过了？

小高：

听说你肚子不太舒服，现在好了吗？有没有吃药？要多注意身体，健康是最重要的。

我最近很想家，特别想念我妈妈做的麻婆豆腐，那味儿又香又辣，好吃极了。老实说，我这个人并不挑剔，可是我觉得美国的食物就是不行：汉堡包太干、炸薯条儿太油、蛋糕太腻、点心又太甜。一般所谓的中国饭也不地道，炒的菜[1]**要不是**太生，**就是**太老，**再不然就是**太咸。[2]**除非**上中国城去，**否则**不管怎么吃都吃不饱。[3]**象我这样**不讲究吃**的**人在这儿住半年都受不了，真不知道那些中国来的移民是怎么过日子的？最奇怪的是，我在这儿虽然吃得少，[4]**不但没瘦，反而**越来越胖了。现在[5]**不得不**学美国人，拼命减肥。

你在中国有的是机会，现在酸甜苦辣全

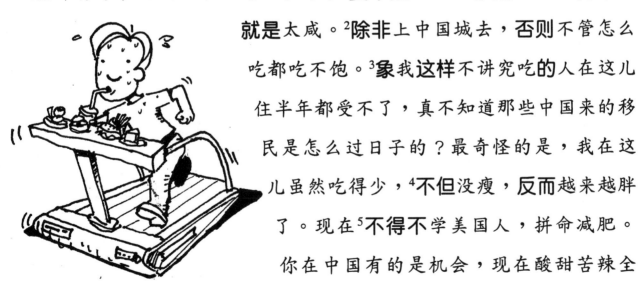

都尝过了吗？真羡慕你，每天帮我多吃两口吧！

小李

小李：

　　我在中国吃的真的很好，怪不得人说"吃在中国"。我在这儿天天享受饺子和酸辣汤，又好吃又经济。你看，我学中文吃了很多苦，但是也很开心，⁶**才**来两个月，**就**把中国的"酸甜苦辣"全都尝了。

小高

小對話 Mini-Dialogues

Read the supplementary dialogues for a better understanding of the text. See if you can memorize one and perform it in class .

(1) Commenting on American food

A: 你吃了早點嗎？今天早上有牛油麵包、雞蛋 jīdàn 火腿 huǒtuǐ、和咖啡。

你吃了早点吗？今天早上有牛油面包、鸡蛋火腿、和咖啡。

Li: 沒吃。那麵包太硬、雞蛋太老、火腿太鹹、咖啡又太苦，像藥一樣。我實在吃膩了這些美國食物。

没吃。那面包太硬、鸡蛋太老、火腿太咸、咖啡又太苦，象药一样。我实在吃腻了这些美国食物。

A: 你太挑剔了！美國飯很有營養 yíngyǎng，有什麼不好？

你太挑剔了！美国饭很有营养，有什么不好？

Li: 嗯，太有營養了！自從來了美國以後，我一直發胖 fāpàng 。現在我決定吃素 chīsù 減肥。

嗯，太有营养了！自从来了美国以后，我一直发胖。现在我决定吃素减肥。

A: Have you had breakfast? This morning there were butter, bread, eggs, ham, and coffee.

Li: No. The bread was too hard, the eggs were overdone, the ham was too salty, and the coffee was too bitter. It tasted like medicine. I am really sick of American food.

A: You are nitpicking. American food is very nutritious. What's so bad about it?

Li: Er, it's too nutritious. Since coming to the U.S., I've been gaining weight. Now I have decided to be a vegetarian and go on a diet.

(2) Commenting on Chinese food

A: 你喜歡吃什麼樣的中國菜？

你喜欢吃什么样的中国菜？

Gao: 我喜歡吃辣的，在美國的時候常叫宮保雞丁和麻婆豆腐。

我喜欢吃辣的，在美国的时候常叫宫保鸡丁和麻婆豆腐。

A: 那你應該試試四川菜、湖南菜。別的口味的菜也不錯，比方說廣東菜。

那你应该试试四川菜、湖南菜。别的口味的菜也不错，比方说广东菜。

Gao: 我聽我的老師說過：「廣東人除了椅子以外，四條腿的東西都吃。」

我听我的老师说过："广东人除了椅子以外，四条腿的东西都吃。"

A: 中國各地的菜都有不同的口味，有人說南甜、北鹹、東辣、西酸。

中国各地的菜都有不同的口味，有人说南甜、北咸、东辣、西酸。

Gao: I came to China this time not only to study Chinese but also to enjoy all the delicious food.

A: What kind of Chinese food do you like?

Gao: I like spicy food. When I was in the U.S., I often ordered Gongbao chicken and Mapo tofu.

A: Then you should try Sichuan or Hunan dishes. Other kinds of dishes are good as well, such as Cantonese food.

Gao: I heard my teacher say, "People in Canton eat everything with four legs except chairs."

A: In China, the dishes of every region have their own taste. Some say, "the dishes in the south taste sweet, in the north salty, in the east hot, and in the west sour."

👤👤 (3) Dining out

A: 先生，想吃點兒什麼？這是菜單_{càidān}。

先生，想吃点儿什么？这是菜单。

Gao: 這些菜名我多半兒都看不懂，不知道點_{diǎn}什麼好？這兒有什麼好菜？

这些菜名我多半儿都看不懂，不知道点什么好？这儿有什么好菜？

A: 那麼，點一隻烤鴨、一個炒生菜、一個蛋花湯，怎麼樣？

那么，点一只烤鸭、一个炒生菜、一个蛋花汤，怎么样？

Gao: 好，就這些吧！……（吃飯）   好，就这些吧！……（吃饭）

A: 菜夠了嗎？還要點兒什麼？   菜够了吗？还要点儿什么？

Gao: 不要了，我吃不下了。你們的   不要了，我吃不下了。你们的
        菜色香味都好極了！   菜色香味都好极了！

A: Sir, what would you like to eat? This is
        our menu.

Gao: I don't understand most of these names,
        and I don't know what to order. What's
        good here?

A: How about roast duck, a dish of fried
        lettuce, and an egg-drop soup?

Gao: Fine. I will have that. … (eating)

A: Have you had enough? Would you like
        some more?

Gao: No. I can't eat any more. The look, smell, and taste of your food are all great!

(4) Explaining how to make a dish

Li: 王華，你會做麻婆豆腐嗎？我   王华，你会做麻婆豆腐吗？我
        最愛吃豆腐chī dòufu。   最爱吃豆腐。

Wang: 小心我打你！   小心我打你！

Li: 我不是那個意思。   我不是那个意思。

Wang: 什麼意思？   什么意思？

Li: 我想學學做飯，宿舍的飯實在   我想学学做饭，宿舍的饭实在
        太難吃了！   太难吃了！

Wang: 好吧！我就教你做蛋炒飯，又   好吧！我就教你做蛋炒饭，又
        好吃又好做。你先倒一點兒油   好吃又好做。你先倒一点儿油
        在鍋guō裏，油熱了以後就把蛋   在锅里，油热了以后就把蛋放
        放進去，炒一下再放飯，最後   进去，炒一下再放饭，最后放
        放醬油jiàngyóu和鹽yán，再炒幾下   酱油和盐，再炒几下就好了。

就好了。

Li: 天啊！我回宿舍吃好了！   天啊！我回宿舍吃好了！

Li: Wang Hua, do you know how to make Mapo tofu? I love eating tofu!

Wang: Watch out, or I will teach you a lesson!

Li: I don't mean that.

Wang: What do you mean?

Li: I want to learn how to cook. It's so miserable having dorm food.

Wang: Well, then I will teach you how to make fried rice. It's delicious to eat and easy to make. First, you pour some oil in the wok. After the oil is hot, you put in the egg and stir it a little bit. Then you put in the rice. The last thing is to add soy sauce and salt. Stir everything a few times, and it's done.

Li: My God! I'll go back to my dorm to eat!

小故事 Stories

Read the following tale for your own enjoyment and for your understanding of the highlighted expression that is relevant to the theme of the chapter.

 囫圇吞棗 húlún tūn zǎo

❀ 他無論吃飯或讀書都是囫圇吞棗。

囫圇	húlún	whole, entire
吞	tūn	to swallow
棗兒	zǎor	date
年輕人	niánqīngrén	young man
梨	lí	pear
牙	yá	teeth
好處	hǎochu	benefit
胃	wèi	stomach
嚼	jiáo	to chew
肚子	dùzi	stomach

從前有個年輕人買了一些水果，有梨也有棗兒，坐在路邊大口大口地吃。有個老人看見了，就對他說：「梨不能多吃，雖然這東西對牙有好處，可是吃太多對胃不好。」

年輕人就問：「棗兒怎麼樣？」老人說：「棗兒對胃好，可是對牙不好，也不能多吃。」

這個年輕人聽了老人的話，就說：「那容易，我吃梨就只用牙嚼，不吞到肚子裏去；吃棗兒就不嚼，把它整個兒吞下去。」

✐ 囫圇吞棗的意思是＿＿＿＿＿＿＿＿＿＿＿＿＿＿＿＿＿＿

囫囵吞枣 húlún tūn zǎo

❀　他无论吃饭或读书都是囫囵吞枣。

从前有个年轻人买了一些水果，有梨也有枣儿，坐在路边大口大口地吃。有个老人看见了，就对他说："梨不能多吃，虽然这东西对牙有好处，可是吃太多对胃不好。"

年轻人就问："枣儿怎么样？"老人说："枣儿对胃好，可是对牙不好，也不能多吃。"

这个年轻人听了老人的话，就说："那容易，我吃梨就只用牙嚼，不吞到肚子里去；吃枣儿就不嚼，把它整个儿吞下去。"

囫囵	húlún	whole, entire
吞	tūn	to swallow
枣儿	zǎor	date
年轻人	niánqīngrén	young man
梨	lí	pear
牙	yá	teeth
好处	hǎochu	benefit
胃	wèi	stomach
嚼	jiáo	to chew
肚子	dùzi	stomach

漢字 Characters

Study the following selected characters for further enrichment of your writing and vocabulary.

酉 yǒu 'wine'
+ 夋 qún
phonetic

酸

酸辣	suānlà	hot and sour
酸辣湯	suānlàtāng	hot and sour soup
酸奶	suānnǎi*	yogurt

A: 你今天吃了什麼？

B: 早上喝酸奶，中午吃酸辣湯。

suān 14
sour

舌 shé 'tongue'
+ 甘 gān
'sweet'

甜

| 甜酸 | tiánsuān* | sweet and slightly sour |
| 甜食 | tiánshí* | sweetmeats, dessert |

A: 你吃甜食嗎？

B: 不吃，我怕胖。

tián 11
sweet, agreeable

艹 cǎo 'grass'
+ 古 gǔ
phonetic

苦

吃苦	chīkǔ	to bear hardship
辛苦	xīnkǔ*	hard, to work hard
痛苦	tòngkǔ*	pain, suffering

A: 你學中文吃了很多苦吧！

B: 辛苦是辛苦，可是很有意思。

Compare: 花 huā　故 gù

kǔ 9
bitter, hardship

辛 xīn 'bitter
suffering' + 束
shù 'bundle'

辣

辣椒	làjiāo*	hot pepper, chili
酸辣	suānlà	hot and sour
麻辣	málà*	with chili peppers, sesame oil and brown pepper

A: 你做飯的時候，放不放辣椒？

B: 放，我喜歡吃麻辣的東西。

là 14
peppery, hot, biting

亻 rén 'person'
+ 建 jiàn
'establish'

健

jiàn 10
healthy, strong, to
invigorate

健康	jiànkāng	health
健美操	jiànměicāo*	aerobics
健身	jiànshēn*	to keep fit
健身房	jiànshēnfáng	gymnasium

A: 你常去健身房健身嗎？
B: 不常去，只是在家做做健美操。

Compare: 建 jiàn

Originally 庚
gēng 'threshing
tool' + 米 mǐ
'rice'—to chaff

康

kāng 11
healthy, peaceful

| 康復 | kāngfù* | to restore to health, recovery (from illness) |

A: 他的病好了沒有？
B: 快康復了。

Picture of a
sturdy vessel
with feet and lid

食

shí 9
to eat, meal, edible

食物	shíwù	food
食堂	shítáng*	dining room, canteen
主食	zhǔshí*	staple/principal food

A: 你覺得中國的食物怎麼樣？
B: 很不錯，連學生食堂的飯都很好。

Compare: 飯 fàn 館 guǎn 飽 bǎo

牛 niú 'ox' +
勿 wù phonetic

物

wù 8
thing, matter, world

動物	dòngwù	animal
生物	shēngwù*	living thing
植物	zhíwù*	plant, flora
人物	rénwù*	character, personage

A: 月球上沒有生物嗎？
B: 動物我想沒有，植物可能有。

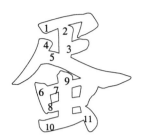

虫 chóng
'reptile' + 疋
shǔ phonetic

蛋糕	dàn'gāo	cake
蛋白	dànbái*	white of egg
雞蛋	jīdàn*	hen's egg
完蛋	wándàn*	to be finished/destroyed

蛋

A: 這種蛋糕怎麼做？一次用幾個雞蛋？

B: 用四個，而且只能用蛋白。

dàn 11
egg, egg-shaped

木 mù 'tree' +
攸 yōu
phonetic

薯條兒	shǔtiáor	french fries
字條	zìtiáo*	brief note
麵條	miàntiáo*	noodles
條件	tiáojiàn	condition, terms

条

A: 她的字條上說什麼？

B: 她叫我中午自己吃麵條。

tiáo 11
strip, item, short note

禾 hé 'grain' +
日 rì, which
was originally
甘 gān 'sweet'
—the sweet
scent of grain

香煙	xiāngyān*	cigarette, incense smoke
香水	xiāngshuǐ*	perfume, scent
吃香	chīxiāng*	popular, well-liked
口香糖	kǒuxiāngtáng	chewing gum

香

A: 她對香水、香煙都過敏guòmǐn。

B: 在她面前，你也不能吃口香糖。

xiāng 9
fragrant, perfume,
spice

食 shí 'food' +
包 bāo
phonetic

| 吃飽 | chībǎo* | to eat one's fill |
| 半飽 | bànbǎo* | half full |

饱

A: 你吃飽了嗎？

B: 不太飽，但是吃得半飽對身體好。

Compare: 包 bāo   抱 bào

bǎo 13
full, satiated

忄 xīn 'heart' +
圣 an obsolete
character used
as a phonetic

怪

怪不得	guàibude	no wonder
奇怪	qíguài	strange, odd, amazing
難怪	nánguài	no wonder
怪人	guàirén*	eccentric

A: 奇怪，怎麼都沒看到他？
B: 你沒來學校，怪不得不知道。他病了。

guài 8
strange, to blame, very

土 tǔ 'land' +
成 chéng
'become'
phonetic

城

中國城	Zhōngguóchéng	Chinatown
長城	Chángchéng*	Great Wall
城市	chéngshì	town, city

A: 美國哪幾個城市有中國城？
B: 大的城市裏都有。

Compare: 成 chéng

chéng 9
wall, city wall, city

氵 shuǐ 'water'
+ 齊 qí
phonetic—to
help someone
cross a river;
then, just to
help someone in
need

濟

済

| 經濟 | jīngjì | economy, economical |
| 經濟學 | jīngjìxué* | economics |

A: 你覺得明年的經濟會怎麼樣？
B: 我不搞經濟學，沒有什麼看法。

Compare: 齊 qí 擠 jǐ

jì 17
to cross (river), aid,
benefit

Character
analogous to 氏
shì 'clan,
family'

民

移民	yímín	immigrant, to emigrate
人民	rénmín	the people
公民	gōngmín*	citizen
民主	mínzhǔ	democracy
民歌	míngē	folk song

A: 他想移民到哪兒去？
B: 他說他要民主，想做美國公民。

mín 5
people, masses, civilian

不 bù 'no' +
口 kǒu 'mouth'

否

fǒu 7
no, to negate

否則	fǒuzé	otherwise
否定	fǒudìng*	to negate, deny
是否	shìfǒu*	whether or not

A: 明天我們要開會，你是否能來？

B: 除非我把這些事辦完，否則來不了。

Compare: 歪 wāi

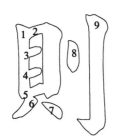

貝 bèi 'money'
+ 刂 dāo 'knife'
—to carve a
shell: pattern

則

zé 9
rule, in that case

| 原則 | yuánzé* | principle |
| 規則 | guīzé* | rule, regulation, regular |

A: 除非我寫完我的功課，否則我不出去。

B: 你這個人真有「原則」。

Compare: 廁 cè 測 cè

言 yán 'words'
+ 冓 gòu
phonetic

讲

jiǎng 17
to speak, to explain

講究	jiǎngjiu	to be particular about
講話	jiǎnghuà*	to speak, speech, talk
講師	jiǎngshī*	lecturer

A: 你喜歡那個講師嗎？

B: 不喜歡，我一聽他講話就想睡。

Compare: 說 shuō 話 huà 語 yǔ

舟 zhōu 'boat'
+ 殳 shū 'beat'
— to propel a
boat, distribute,
category

般

bān 10
sort, kind, way

| 一般 | yìbān | ordinary, common |
| 一般說來 | yìbān shuōlái* | generally speaking |

A: 一般的美國人喜歡吃中國飯嗎？

B: 一般說來，他們很喜歡。

Compare: 搬 bān 船 chuán

語法和用法 Grammar and Usage

Pay attention to the function of the structure and then study the example sentences.

1. Describing a general status through a range of alternatives

（要）不是…就是…	(yào)bushì…jiùshì…	If it isn't…then it's…or
（再）不然就…	(zài)bùrán jiù…	else it's…

一般所謂的中國飯也不地道，炒的菜**要不是**太生，**就是**太老，**再不然**就是太鹹。

1. 你最近怎麼樣？忙
不忙？

   你最近怎么样？忙
不忙？

   How are you doing
lately? Are you busy?

   忙死了，我不是學
習中文，就是做實
驗，再不然就是寫
報告。

   忙死了，我不是学
习中文，就是做实
验，再不然就是写
报告。

   I am terribly busy. If I
am not studying Chinese,
then I am doing an
experiment, or else I am
writing a paper.

2. 明天我來找你，行
嗎？

   明天我来找你，行
吗？

   Is it O.K. if I come to see
you tomorrow?

   行，我不是在辦公
室，就是在圖書
館，不然就在系上
的休息室。

   行，我不是在办公
室，就是在图书
馆，不然就在系上
的休息室。

   Yes. If I am not in my
office, then I am in the
library, or else I will be in
the department lounge.

3. 你喜歡那家餐廳的
菜嗎？

   你喜欢那家餐厅的
菜吗？

   Do you like that
restaurant's food?

   不喜歡，不是太
鹹，就是太甜，再
不然就是太油。

   不喜欢，不是太
咸，就是太甜，再
不然就是太油。

   No. Their food is too
salty, or too sweet, or else
too oily.

Note that if there are only two alternatives, one uses the structure 不是…就是. If
there are three options, one can use this pattern. Furthermore, the pattern is used to
express literal possibilities as in example 2, or as parallel examples to describe an
overall situation, as in examples 1 and 3.

2. Expressing an indispensable condition

除非condition, 否則 action	chúfēi…fǒuzé	Unless…, otherwise…
除非condition,（要）不然 action	chúfēi…(yào)bùrán	
action, 除非condition	…, chúfēi	S will (not) do sth. unless…

除非上中國城去，**否則**不管怎麼吃都吃不飽。

1.	我怎麼樣可以瘦一點兒？	我怎么样可以瘦一点儿？	How can I lose a little weight?
	除非你不吃蛋糕，否則瘦不了。	除非你不吃蛋糕，否則瘦不了。	You've got to give up eating cake; otherwise you can't lose weight.
2.	你能不能幫我的忙？	你能不能帮我的忙？	Can you help me?
	除非你請我吃飯，要不然我不能幫你的忙。	除非你请我吃饭，要不然我不能帮你的忙。	Unless you take me out for dinner, I can't help you.
3.	你教我下棋，好不好？	你教我下棋，好不好？	Can you teach me how to play chess?
	我不能教你下棋，除非我先把功課做完。	我不能教你下棋，除非我先把功课做完。	I can't teach you how to play chess unless I finish my homework first.

除非 often occurs in the first clause of a two-clause sentence that has 否則 or 要不然 in the second clause. In many cases, the second-clause 除非 indicates an afterthought.

3. Describing a quality by comparison

像…這樣/那樣Adj的N	xiàng…zhèyàng/nàyang…de	(Adj) somebody/
像…這麼/那麼Adj的N	xiàng…zhème/nàme…de…	something like this/that…

像我**這樣**不講究吃**的**人在這兒住半年都受不了，真不知道那些中國來的移民是怎麼過日子的？

1. 你為什麼不喜歡你　　你为什么不喜欢你　　Why don't you like your
   的同屋？　　　　　　的同屋？　　　　　　roommate?

   我受不了像他那麼　　我受不了象他那么　　I can't stand people as
   愛管閒事的人。　　　愛管闲事的人。　　　nosy as he is.

2. 你怎麼那麼喜歡那　　你怎么那么喜欢那　　Why do you like that
   個學生？　　　　　　个学生？　　　　　　student so much?

   像她那麼愛學習的　　象她那么爱学习的　　Nowadays you can't find
   人現在真不多了。　　人现在真不多了。　　many students as diligent
   　　　　　　　　　　　　　　　　　　　　as she is.

3. 像我這麼好的人，　　象我这么好的人，　　Where can you find a
   你到哪兒去找？　　　你到哪儿去找？　　　person as good as I am?

   你真是老王賣瓜，　　你真是老王卖瓜，　　You are really blowing
   自賣自誇Lǎo Wáng mài 自卖自夸。　　　your own horn (Lao
   guā, zì mài zì kuā。　　　　　　　　　　Wang, selling melons,
   　　　　　　　　　　　　　　　　　　　　praises his own goods).

In Chinese, the modifier precedes the modified. In this pattern, the relative clause modifying a noun can be very long. Typically, the subject (e.g., person, place) of the relative clause is identified after 像 and the adjective or verb phrase goes after 這樣/這麼 or 那樣/那麼.

4. Expressing a strong contradiction

S 不但沒/不…反而…　　búdànméi/bù…fǎn'ér…　　not only not…, on the contrary…

我在這兒雖然吃得少，**不但沒瘦，反而**越來越胖了。

1. 你今天考得怎麼　　你今天考得怎么　　How did you do on
   樣？　　　　　　　样？　　　　　　　today's test?

   我昨天花了很長時　　我昨天花了很长时　　Yesterday I spent a long
   間準備，可是不但　　间准备，可是不但　　time preparing. Even so, I
   沒考好，反而考得　　没考好，反而考得　　did poorly, worse than my
   比平常差。　　　　　比平常差。　　　　　usual performance.

2. 你羨慕她什麼？   你羡慕她什么？   Why do you envy her?

她吃那麼多東西，不但不胖，反而瘦得很。   她吃那么多东西，不但不胖，反而瘦得很。   She eats so much. Yet she does not gain weight; on the contrary, she is quite slim.

3. 你為什麼這麼生氣？   你为什么这么生气？   Why are you so angry?

我幫了他的忙，他不但沒謝我，反而說我多管閑事。   我帮了他的忙，他不但没谢我，反而说我多管闲事。   I helped him, but he didn't thank me. Instead, he said that I was too meddlesome.

反而, an adverb, indicates something contrary to one's expectation, assumption or common sense/logic. Don't confuse this pattern with 不但…而且 'not only...but also...'

5. Expressing obligation/necessity/inevitability with double negation

不得不V	bùdé bù…	cannot not V; can't help but; must
不能不V	bùnéng bù…	cannot not V; can't help but; must
不會不V	búhuìbù…	will certainly V

現在**不得不**學美國人，拼命減肥。

1. 你為什麼這麼用功？   你为什么这么用功？   Why do you study so hard?

我平常沒念書，下星期有大考，現在不得不拼命學習。   我平常没念书，下星期有大考，现在不得不拼命学习。   I usually don't study much, and there is an exam coming next week, so I must study really hard now.

2. 你不能少打幾通 tōng 電話嗎？   你不能少打几通电话吗？   Can't you make fewer phone calls?

不行，我不能不和我的朋友聊聊。   不行，我不能不和我的朋友聊聊。   No. I must chat with my friends.

3.	你不是都騎自行車來上課嗎？	你不是都骑自行车来上课吗？	You normally ride your bike to school, don't you?
	我的自行車壞了，我不得不坐公共汽車來上課。	我的自行车坏了，我不得不坐公共汽车来上课。	My bike is broken, so I have no choice but to take a bus to school.

The double negation can go with auxiliary verbs in Chinese and is more emphatic than 一定.

6. Expressing a rapid turn of events

S 才V₁(Time Span) (S)就V₂	…cái…jiù…	It's only…, S already…
S 剛V₁ (Time Span) (S)就V₂	…gāng…jiù…	

你看……**才**來兩個月，**就**把中國的「酸甜苦辣」全都嚐了。

1.	老師，這句話是什麼意思？	老师，这句话是什么意思？	Teacher, what does this sentence mean?
	才放了三個月的假，你就把中文全忘了！	才放了三个月的假，你就把中文全忘了！	You've only been on vacation for three months, and you have forgotten everything about Chinese.
2.	我想把經濟學的課退了。	我想把经济学的课退了。	I want to drop the economics course.
	你才上了一個星期的課，就想把它退了？	你才上了一个星期的课，就想把它退了？	You've only had it for one week, and you want to drop it?
3.	我想出去吃點兒東西。	我想出去吃点儿东西。	I want to go out and eat something.
	你怎麼才吃了午飯就餓了呢？	你怎么才吃了午饭就饿了呢？	You just had your lunch. How come you are already hungry again?
4.	她在這兒適應嗎？	她在这儿适应吗？	Is she used to it here?

退 tuì
retreat

她剛來一個星期就交了很多朋友了。	她刚来一个星期就交了很多朋友了。	After just one week, she has already made a lot of friends.

5. 你的中文真不錯，才學兩年就能看故事了。　　你的中文真不错，才学两年就能看故事了。　　Your Chinese is really good. You can read a story after studying for only two years.

哪裏、哪裏。	哪里、哪里。	It's nothing.

This pattern expresses that an action takes a shorter period of time than expected.

文化點滴 Culture Notes

1. **Varieties of food**: There are eight major kinds of dishes in China. They are:

Variety	Pinyin	Taste
山東菜 (魯菜)	Shāndōngcài (lǔcài)	fresh and delicate
四川菜 (川菜)	Sìchuāncài (chuāncài)	hot and spicy, strong-flavored
廣東菜 (粵菜)	Guǎngdōngcài (yuècài)	light-flavored and crispy
江蘇菜 (蘇菜)	Jiāngsūcài (sūcài)	light-flavored and scented
浙江菜 (浙菜)	Zhèjiāngcài (zhècài)	fresh, crispy, soft, and smooth, original taste
福建菜 (閩菜)	Fújiàncài (mǐncài)	sweet and sour, fresh and good-looking
湖南菜 (湘菜)	Húnáncài (xiāngcài)	heavily seasoned and delicately cooked
安徽菜 (徽菜)	Ānhuīcài (huīcài)	emphasizing oil, color, and time of cooking

2. **Names of dishes**: Although most Chinese dishes are quite delicious, it can be difficult to figure out what to order in a restaurant, even for native Chinese. This has to do with the creative and often extremely figurative names the dishes have. Thus, it is good to learn what one can usually expect in the name of a dish. In general, names of dishes have four characters, but sometimes three or five characters. The name usually indicates the ingredients 原料 yuánliào, the method of preparation 作法 zuòfǎ, taste 味道 wèidào, and forms 形狀 xíngzhuàng. Typical ingredients include chicken 雞 jī, fish 魚 yú, pork 豬 zhū, mutton 羊 yáng, tomato 蕃茄 fānqié, etc. The various methods of preparation, taste, and forms are listed in the charts below. After looking at those charts, can you picture the following dishes: 咖哩雞塊 jiālǐ jīkuài, 油烹大蝦 yóu pēng dàxiā, 蔥燒海參 cōng shāo hǎishēn, 清蒸桂魚 qīngzhēn guìyú, 魚香肉絲 yúxiāng ròusī, 蔥爆羊肉 cōng bào yángròu, 糖醋鯉魚 tángcù lǐyú, 番茄肉片 fānqié ròupiàn?

Method of Preparation		Pinyin	English
炒	炒	chǎo	to stir-fry, to fry, to sauté
爆	爆	bào	to quick-fry, to quick-boil
熘	熘	liū	to quick-fry (with thick gravy)
烹	烹	pēng	to boil, to fry quickly in hot oil and stir in sauce
清蒸	清蒸	qīngzhēng	to steam in clear soup (usually without soy sauce)
紅燒	红烧	hóngshāo	to braise in soy sauce
煎	煎	jiān	to fry in shallow oil
炸	炸	zhá	to fry in deep fat or oil, deep-fry
烤	烤	kǎo	to roast, to toast, to bake
燜	焖	mèn	to boil in a covered pot over a slow fire, to braise
炖	炖	dùn	to stew
熬	熬	áo	to boil, to stew

Taste		Pinyin	English	Taste		Pinyin	English
酸	酸	suān	sour	麻	麻	má	numbingly hot
辣	辣	là	spicy	甜	甜	tián	sweet
鹹	咸	xián	sauty	穌	酥	sū	short, shortbread
香	香	xiāng	fragrant	滑	滑	huá	smooth
鮮	鲜	xiān	fresh (often of seafood)	苦	苦	kǔ	bitter
澀	涩	sè	astringent	脆	脆	cuì	crisp
焦	焦	jiāo	burnt, charred	軟	软	ruǎn	soft
硬	硬	yìng	hard	淡	淡	dàn	plain
濃	浓	nóng	thick				

Form		Pinyin	English	Form		Pinyin	English
片	片	piàn	slice	段	段	duàn	part
絲	丝	sī	shredded meat	丸子	丸子	wánzi	a round mass of food
丁	丁	dīng	cubes	塊	块	kuài	chunk
條	条	tiáo	strips	卷	卷	juǎn	roll

Seasoning		Pinyin	English	Seasoning		Pinyin	English
油	油	yóu	oil	糖	糖	táng	sugar
醬油	酱油	jiàngyóu	soy sauce	鹽	盐	yán	salt
麻油	麻油	máyóu	sesame oil	醋	醋	cù	vinegar
蔥	葱	cōng	onion	咖哩	咖哩	kāli	curry
薑	姜	jiāng	ginger	太白粉	太白粉	tàibáifěn	corn starch
蒜	蒜	suàn	garlic				

3. **Expressions related to eating**:   Since cooking and food are so important in Chinese culture, the verb "to eat," as "to do or to make" in English, is very common.   Listed below are some interesting terms associated with 吃 "to eat."

Terms with "to eat"		Pinyin	English
吃苦	吃苦	chīkǔ	to bear hardship
吃香	吃香	chīxiāng	to be very popular, to be well-liked
吃醋	吃醋	chīcù	to be jealous (usually of a rival in love)
吃力	吃力	chīlì	to be a strain
吃水	吃水	chīshuǐ	to absorb water
吃虧	吃亏	chīkuī	to suffer losses, to come to grief
吃驚	吃惊	chījīng	to be startled, to be shocked, to be taken aback
吃緊	吃紧	chījǐn	to be critical, to be hard pressed
吃素	吃素	chīsù	to be a vegetarian
吃葷	吃荤	chīhūn	to eat meat
吃官司	吃官司	chī guānsī	to be sued
吃耳光	吃耳光	chī ěrguāng	to take a blow
吃館子	吃馆子	chī guǎnzi	to go to a restaurant
吃大鍋飯	吃大锅饭	chī dàguōfàn	to eat food prepared in a large cauldron (the same as everyone else)
吃不開	吃不开	chībukāi	to be unpopular, not to be much sought after
吃不上	吃不上	chībushàng	not to be in time for a meal, not able to get a meal
吃不起	吃不起	chībuqǐ	can afford to eat

歌兒 Songs

國外的食物
Food Abroad

Allegretto

詞、曲：李毓真

一 個 人 在 國 外，　吃 不 到 媽媽 燒 的 菜，不 但 沒 變瘦 反而 變胖
Yí　ge rén zài guówài　　chībudào māma shāo de cài,　búdàn méi biàn shòu fǎn'ér biàn pàng
Being abroad by myself, I can't eat the dishes Mother cooks.　It's so strange that rather than

真 奇 怪。　本 來 我 對 我 的 體 重 一 直 是 無 所 謂　　但 現
zhēn　qíguài.　　Běnlái　wǒ duì wǒde tǐzhòng yìzhí　shì wúsuǒwèi,　　dàn xiàn
getting thinner, I'm getting fat. Before, I never cared about my weight.　　But now,

在 我 胖 得 不 得 不 減 肥。　　有 人 說 是 因 為
zài wǒ pàng de　bùdebù　jiǎnféi.　　Yǒurén shuō shì　yīnwèi
I'm so fat that I must lose weight.　　People say that this is because

吃 的 食 物 太 有 營 養，怪 不 得 天 天 沒 吃 飽 也 發 胖 其
chīde　shíwù　tài yǒu yíngyǎng, guàibudé　tiāntiān　méi chī bǎo　yě　fāpàng.　Qí
the food I eat is too nutritious.　　No wonder that even though I don't eat much each day, I'm still

實 我 對 吃 的 東 西 並 不 是 很 挑 剔　　只 要 食 物 健 康 價 錢 又 經
shí wǒ duì chīde dōngxi bìng bú shì hěn tiāotì,　zhǐyào shíwù　jiànkāng jiàqián yòu jīng
getting fatter. Actually, I'm not very picky about the food I eat　as long as the price is

濟
jì.
economical.

<table>
<tr><td>第六課</td><td>

Theme Fashion and Leisure

Communicative Objectives
- Talking about hobbies
- Commenting on songs and pop stars
- Discussing movies
- Asking for and giving advice

</td><td>

Grammar Focus
- 千萬別／要／得V
- S本來／原來…現在／後來
- 一來…二來…（三來）
- 多（麼）Adj啊
- 向來…；從來不；從來沒…過
- …就好了／就行了／就可以了

</td></tr>
</table>

Focus on Characters
- 世紀偉愛、導演拍片、清楚精彩、失望認靠、象足土目

現在流行什麼？

生詞 Vocabulary

Study the following words for their pronunciation and meaning. When an area is shaded, guess at the meaning of the word based on its constituent characters and then fill in the blank. Read the usage of words and related terms (antonyms, synonyms, compounds sharing the constituent characters, etc.) and try to answer the sample questions in Chinese. Note that proper nouns or incidental terms are not numbered.

◎ By Order of Appearance

1.	秘密	mìmì	N/	secret, confidential	[secret-close]
			Adj	你會跟誰說你的秘密？	
				你会跟谁说你的秘密？	
2.	千萬 千万	qiānwàn	Adv	by all means, absolutely	[thousand-ten million]
				去中國千萬得帶什麼？	
				去中国千万得带什么？	
3.	網 网	wǎng	N	net	
				→網上 'online'、上網 'to log on'	
				你喜歡在網上做什麼？	
				你喜欢在网上做什么？	
4.	網友 网友	wǎngyǒu	N	▨▨▨▨▨▨▨▨▨▨	[net-friend]
				你跟你的網友常常談什麼？	
				你跟你的网友常常谈什么？	
5.	之間 之间	zhī jiān	Suf	between, among	[of-between]
				同學之間應該怎麼樣？	
				同学之间应该怎么样？	
6.	完全	wánquán	Adv	completely, absolutely	[finish-whole]
				我完全不知道他最近在搞什麼，你知道他的事嗎？	
				我完全不知道他最近在搞什么，你知道他的事吗？	
7.	距離 距离	jùlí	N/V	distance, to be away from	[away from-apart from]
				你跟你的父母之間有很大的距離嗎？	
				你跟你的父母之间有很大的距离吗？	
8.	年紀 年纪	niánjì	N	age	[year-age]
				你父親多大年紀了？	

你父亲多大年纪了？

| 9. | 共同 | gòngtóng | Adj | common, joint | [share-same] |

你們倆有沒有共同的興趣？

你们俩有没有共同的兴趣？

| 10. | 愛好
爱好 | àihào | N/V | hobby, interest, to be keen on | [love-like] |

你有什麼愛好？

你有什么爱好？

| 11. | 迷 | mí | V/N/
Adj | to be enchanted with, fan,
enchanted | |

為什麼美國人那麼迷「星際大戰」xīngjì dàzhàn 'Star Wars'？

为什么美国人那么迷"星际大战"？

| 12. | 足球 | zúqiú | N | | [foot-ball] |

你喜歡看美式足球還是英式足球？為什麼？

你喜欢看美式足球还是英式足球？为什么？

| | 張藝謀
张艺谋 | Zhāng
Yìmóu | N | name of a director | |

| 13. | 拍 | pāi | V | to shoot film, to take a
picture | |

你喜歡看誰拍的片子？

你喜欢看谁拍的片子？

| 14. | 片子 | piānzi | N | film, movie | [slice-suffix] |

你喜歡看誰演的片子？

你喜欢看谁演的片子？

| | 鞏俐
巩俐 | Gǒng Lì | N | name of an actress | |

| 15. | 演戲
演戏 | yǎnxì | VO | to act in a play | [perform-play] |

你覺得誰很會演戲？

你觉得谁很会演戏？

Characters with Many Strokes

秘　密　萬　網　距　離　愛　演　戲

16.	精彩	jīngcǎi	Adj	brilliant, splendid	[skilled-colorful]

你覺得誰演的戲很精彩？

你觉得谁演的戏很精彩？

17.	明星	míngxīng	N	(movie, etc.) star	[bright-star]

→歌星、影星、球星

你最喜歡哪個男明星？哪個女明星？

你最喜欢哪个男明星？哪个女明星？

18.	導演 导演	dǎoyǎn	N		[guide-performance]

你覺得哪一個美國導演最行？

你觉得哪一个美国导演最行？

19.	討厭 讨厌	tǎoyàn	V/ Adj	to be disgusted with, disgusting, nasty	[denounce-detest]

你討厭做什麼事？討厭什麼樣的人？

你讨厌做什么事？讨厌什么样的人？

20.	節目 节目	jiémù	N	program, item (on program)	[part-section]

你喜歡看哪一台 tái 'station' 的節目？

你喜欢看哪一台的节目？

21.	好感	hǎogǎn	N		[good-feeling]

你對誰有好感？

你对谁有好感？

22.	本來 本来	běnlái	Adv/ Adj	originally, at first, original	[root-come]

你的專業是什麼？本來就對那個專業有興趣嗎？

你的专业是什么？本来就对那个专业有兴趣吗？

23.	約會 约会	yuēhuì	VO/ N	to date, engagement	[invite-meet]

你怎麼跟一個女孩子約會？

你怎么跟一个女孩子约会？

24.	多(麼) 多(么)	duō(me)	Adv	how, what	[many-suffix]

這個地方多麼美啊！

这个地方多么美啊！

25.	認為 认为	rènwéi	V	to think/believe that	[consider-by]

你認為二十世紀最偉大的發明是什麼？

你认为二十世纪最伟大的发明是什么？

26.	土包子	tǔbāozi	N	rube, hick	[earth-bundle]

你覺得誰是個土包子？

你觉得谁是个土包子？

27.	向來 向来	xiànglái	Adv	always, all along	[always-come]

她向來就不喜歡運動，你不知道嗎？

她向来就不喜欢运动，你不知道吗？

28.	打扮	dǎbàn	V	to dress/make up	[get-dress up as]

你覺得哪個明星最會打扮？

你觉得哪个明星最会打扮？

29.	衣服	yīfu	N	clothes, clothing	[clothing-dress]

你喜歡穿什麼顏色 yánsè 'color' 的衣服？

你喜欢穿什么颜色的衣服？

30.	鞋子	xiézi	N	shoes	[shoe-suffix]

你的鞋子都在哪兒買的？

你的鞋子都在哪儿买的？

31.	清楚	qīngchu	Adj/ V	clear, distinct, to understand clearly	[clear-clear]

你對他的事情清楚嗎？

你对他的事情清楚吗？

32.	說不定 说不定	shuōbudìng	Adv	perhaps, maybe	[say-not-decide]

說不定她不來了，別等了！

说不定她不来了，别等了！

33.	失望	shīwàng	V		[lose-hope]

你來了這兒以後，對什麼很失望？

你来了这儿以后，对什么很失望？

34.	心事	xīnshì	N		[mind-thing]

她最近有什麼心事？

她最近有什么心事？

心里的心事
something on your mind that bother you

35.	談戀愛 谈恋爱	tán liàn'ài	VO	to court, to woo	[talk-love]

在那個電影裏，誰跟誰談戀愛？

在那个电影里，谁跟谁谈恋爱？

Characters with Many Strokes

精　彩　導　厭　感　鞋　楚　望　戀

| 36. | 世紀
世纪 | shìjì | N | century | [generation-century] |

你覺得二十世紀最偉大的人是誰？為什麼？

你觉得二十世纪最伟大的人是谁？为什么？

| 37. | 偉大
伟大 | wěidà | Adj | great, mighty | [great-big] |

誰是上個世紀最偉大的發明家？

谁是上个世纪最伟大的发明家？

| 38. | 發明
发明 | fāmíng | N/V | invention, to invent | [develop-brightness] |

電燈 diàndēng 'electric light' 是誰發明的？

电灯是谁发明的？

| 39. | 靠 | kào | V | to rely on, to lean on | |

你是靠什麼找到這個工作的？

你是靠什么找到这个工作的？

| 40. | 對象
对象 | duìxiàng | N | boy/girlfriend, target | [right-image] |

你現在有對象了嗎？你想什麼時候開始找對象？

你现在有对象了吗？你想什么时候开始找对象？

| 41. | 時髦
时髦 | shímáo | Adj | fashionable | [time-stylish] |

誰總是穿得很時髦？

谁总是穿得很时髦？

| 42. | 大方 | dàfāng | Adj | elegant and composed, generous | [big-upright] |

你覺得這件衣服大方嗎？

你觉得这件衣服大方吗？

Characters with Many Strokes

偉　發　對　象　髦

靠山吃山，靠海吃海

◎ By Grammatical Categories

Nouns/Pronouns/Measure Words

網	wǎng	net
網友	wǎngyǒu	net pal
對象	duìxiàng	boy/girlfriend, target
明星	míngxīng	(movie, etc.) star
導演	dǎoyǎn	director
片子	piānzi	film, movie
節目	jiémù	program, item (on program)
足球	zúqiú	soccer
衣服	yīfu	clothes, clothing
鞋子	xiézi	shoes

年紀	niánjì	age
愛好	àihào	hobby, interest, to be keen on
好感	hǎogǎn	favorable impression
心事	xīnshì	weight on one's mind, worry
秘密	mìmì	secret, confidential
世紀	shìjì	century
發明	fāmíng	invention, to invent
距離	jùlí	distance, to be away from
土包子	tǔbāozi	rube, hick, outsider

Verbs/Stative Verbs/Adjectives

拍	pāi	to shoot film, to take a picture
靠	kào	to rely on, to lean on
迷	mí	to be enchanted with, fan, enchanted
認為	rènwéi	to think/believe that
失望	shīwàng	to become disappointed
討厭	tǎoyàn	to be disgusted with, disgusting, nasty
演戲	yǎnxì	to act in a play
打扮	dǎbàn	to dress/make up

約會	yuēhuì	to date, engagement
談戀愛	tán liàn'ài	to court, to woo
共同	gòngtóng	common, joint
偉大	wěidà	great, mighty
清楚	qīngchu	clear, distinct, to understand clearly
精彩	jīngcǎi	brilliant, splendid
時髦	shímáo	fashionable
大方	dàfāng	elegant and composed, generous

Adverbs and Others

千萬	qiānwàn	by all means, absolutely
完全	wánquán	completely, absolutely
多(麼)	duō(me)	how, what
本來	běnlái	originally, at first, original

向來	xiànglái	always, all along
說不定	shuōbudìng	perhaps, maybe
之間	zhī jiān	between, among

◎ By Pinyin

Entries with * indicate lexical items used in Mini-Dialogues and of possible interest for supplemental study.

àihào	爱好	hobby, interest	qiānwàn	千万	by all means
běnlái	本来	originally	qīngchu	清楚	clear, distinct
dǎbàn	打扮	to dress/make up	rènwéi	认为	to think that
dàfāng	大方	elegant and composed	shìjì	世纪	century
dǎoyǎn	导演	director	shímáo	时髦	fashionable
diàoyú*	钓鱼	to fish	shīwàng	失望	to become disappointed
duìxiàng	对象	boy/girlfriend, target	shuōbudìng	说不定	perhaps
duō(me)	多（么）	how, what	tán liàn'ài	谈恋爱	to court, to woo
fāmíng	发明	invention	tǎoyàn	讨厌	to be disgusted with
gòngtóng	共同	common	tī*	踢	to kick
hǎogǎn	好感	favorable impression	tǔbāozi	土包子	rube, hick
huáchuán*	划船	to row a boat	wǎng	网	net
huàzhuāng*	化妆	to apply makeup	wǎngyǒu	网友	net pal
jiémù	节目	program	wánquán	完全	completely
jīngcǎi	精彩	brilliant	wěidà	伟大	great, mighty
jùlí	距离	distance	xiànglái	向来	always, all along
kào	靠	to rely on, to lean on	xiézi	鞋子	shoes
mí	迷	to be enchanted with, fan, enchanted	xīnshì	心事	weight on one's mind, worry
mìmì	秘密	secret	yǎnxì	演戏	to act in a play
míngxīng	明星	star	yīfu	衣服	clothing
niánjì	年纪	age	yuēhuì	约会	to date
pāi	拍	to shoot film, to take a picture	zhī jiān	之间	between
piānzi	片子	film	zúqiú	足球	soccer
pīngpāngqiú*	乒乓球	ping-pong			

課文 Text

Use the following questions to guide your reading of the text.

1. 王華的秘密是什麼？

2. 王華為什麼現在不想和她的網友約會？

3. 美英對王華的約會有什麼看法？

美英：

跟你說一個秘密，你[1]**千萬別**告訴別人。我最近在網上交了一個朋友。知道嗎？就是所謂的「網友」。我們認識才兩個多月，就像老朋友一樣什麼都談，我跟他之間好像完全沒有距離。我們年紀差不多，而且有很多共同的愛好：我迷籃球、他迷足球；我覺得張藝謀拍的片子很好、他覺得鞏俐演的

戲精彩；我喜歡的明星、導演他都喜歡，我討厭的電視節目他也討厭。老實說，我對他真有好感。我們[2]**本來**約了下星期見個面，**現在**我卻不想去了。[3]**一來**我怕跟人約會，[4]**多**不好意思**啊**！**二來**我怕他會認為我是個土包子。你知道我[5]**向來**不愛打扮，今年流行什麼樣的衣服、鞋子，我也不清楚。說不定見面以後，他會很失望。你說我該怎麼辦呢？

王華

王華:

　　怪不得你最近總是有心事的樣子，原來是在談戀愛！電腦真是二十世紀最偉大的發明，連你這麼內向的人都靠它找到了對象。我看，你還是去見見他。穿得時髦不時髦沒有什麼關係，自然、大方[6]就好了，可能他也是個土包子呢！

　　　　　　　　　　　　　　　　　　　　　　　　　　美英

课文 Text

Use the following questions to guide your reading of the text.

1. 王华的秘密是什么？

2. 王华为什么现在不想和她的网友约会？

3. 美英对王华的约会有什么看法？

 美英：

跟你说一个秘密，你[1]**千万别**告诉别人。我最近在网上交了一个朋友。知道吗？就是所谓的"网友"。我们认识才两个多月，就象老朋友一样什么都谈，我跟他之间好象完全没有距离。我们年纪差不多，而且有很多共同的爱好：我迷篮球、他迷足球；我觉得张艺谋拍的片子很好、他觉得巩俐演的戏精彩；我喜欢的明星、导演他都喜欢，我讨厌的电视节目他也讨厌。老实说，我对他真有好感。我们[2]**本来**约了下星期见个面，**现在我却不想去了。**[3]**一来**我怕跟人约会，[4]**多**不好意思**啊**！二来我怕他会认为我是个土包子。你知道我[5]**向来**不爱打扮，今年流行什么样的衣服、鞋子，我也不清楚。说不定见面以后，他会很失望。你说我该怎么办呢？

王华

王华：

怪不得你最近总是有心事的样子，原来是在谈恋爱！电脑真是二十世纪最伟大的发明，连你这么内向的人都靠它找到了对象。我看，你还是去见见他。穿得时髦不时髦没有什么关系，自然、大方⁶就好了，可能他也是个土包子呢！

美英

小對話 Mini-Dialogues

Read the supplementary dialogues for a better understanding of the text. See if you can memorize one and perform it in class.

(1) Talking about hobbies

A:　沒事的時候，你喜歡做什麼？

Wang:　我喜歡看籃球賽——雖然我自己不會打籃球。

A:　我也喜歡看球賽，我喜歡看足球賽。我會踢tī足球，但是沒時間玩，不過看人踢球也是一種享受！

Wang:　就是。除了足球，你還喜歡什麼？

A:　我喜歡下棋，有時候打打乒乓球pīngpāngqiú、釣釣魚diàoyú，或划划船huáchuán也不錯。

A:　没事的时候，你喜欢做什么？

我喜欢看篮球赛——虽然我自己不会打篮球。

我也喜欢看球赛，我喜欢看足球赛。我会踢足球，但是没时间玩，不过看人踢球也是一种享受！

就是。除了足球，你还喜欢什么？

我喜欢下棋，有时候打打乒乓球、钓钓鱼，或划划船也不错。

A:　What do you like to do when you are free?

Wang: I like to watch a basketball game, though I myself cannot play basketball.

A:　I like to watch ball games, too. I like football. I can play football, but have no time to do so. Yet watching other people play is also a great enjoyment.

Wang: That's right. In addition to football, what else do you like?

A:　I like to play chess. Sometimes it is also fun to play ping-pong, go fishing or row a boat.

(2) Commenting on songs and pop stars

A:　你聽過「吻別」Wěnbié嗎？張學

你听过"吻别"吗？张学友的歌

友的歌真不錯。

Gao: 他是誰？

A: 你連他都不知道，他是香港的「歌神」！

Gao: 我只知道美國有個「貓王」。難道「歌神」唱得比「貓王」好？

A: 這就難說了，根本沒辦法比較嘛！

真不错。

他是谁？

你连他都不知道，他是香港的"歌神"！

我只知道美国有个"猫王"。难道"歌神"唱得比"猫王"好？

这就难说了，根本没办法比较嘛！

A: Have you ever heard the song "Kiss Good-bye"? Zhang Xueyou's songs are really good.

Gao: Who is he?

A: You don't even know who he is. He is the "God of Songs" from Hong Kong.

Gao: I've only heard about the "King of Cats" (Elvis Presley) in the U.S. Are you telling me that this "God" sings better than "the King"?

A: That is hard to say. There is no way to compare them.

(3) Discussing movies

Wang: 你喜歡看電影嗎？

A: 當然喜歡。鞏俐的電影我全看過。

Wang: 你這麼迷她？她演戲演得不太自然，是張藝謀拍得好。

A: 是嗎？我覺得她演得很好，人又長得漂亮。

Wang: 我想你是在看人，不是在看戲！

你喜欢看电影吗？

当然喜欢。巩俐的电影我全看过。

你这么迷她？她演戏演得不太自然，是张艺谋拍得好。

是吗？我觉得她演得很好，人又长得漂亮。

我想你是在看人，不是在看戏！

Wang: Do you like movies?

A: Of course I do. I have seen all the
        movies in which Gong Li had a role.

Wang: Are you such a fan of hers? Her acting is
        not very natural. It is Zhang Yimou who
        has done a great job.

A: Is that right? I think her acting is great, and
        she is beautiful.

Wang: I think you are just enjoying the look of the actress, and not the whole production.

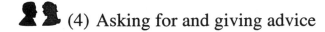 (4) Asking for and giving advice

Wang: 明天我有個約會，應該怎麼打扮   明天我有个约会，应该怎么打扮
        呢？   呢？

Lin: 你千萬別穿你的運動鞋，像土包   你千万别穿你的运动鞋，象土包
        子一樣。   子一样。

Wang: 可是穿得太時髦，我又不舒服。   可是穿得太时髦，我又不舒服。
        我要不要化妝huàzhuāng？   我要不要化妆？

Lin: 化一點妝，看起來自然、大方就   化一点妆，看起来自然、大方就
        好了。   好了。

Wang: I have a date tomorrow. How should I dress?

Lin: By all means, don't wear your tennis shoes.
        You'll look like a hick.

Wang: But if what I wear is too fashionable, I don't feel
        comfortable. Do I need to put on makeup?

Lin: Apply just a little makeup. As long as you look
        natural and elegant, it will be all right.

小故事 Stories

Read the following tale for your own enjoyment and for your understanding of the highlighted expression that is relevant to the theme of the chapter.

 東施效顰 Dōngshī xiào pín

✿ 她對自己了解不夠，卻學著別人的樣子打扮，所以總是東施效顰。

古時候有一個姑娘，長得很漂亮。她家住在一條河的西岸，所以人們叫她西施。河的東岸也有一個姑娘，長得很難看，大家都叫她東施。

東施看見西施長得漂亮，很想跟她學。西施怎麼打扮，她就怎麼打扮；西施怎麼走路，她就怎麼走路。

東施	Dōngshī	name of a girl
效	xiào	to follow the example of
顰	pín	to knit one's brows
古時候	gǔshíhou	ancient times
姑娘	gūniang	girl
河	hé	river
岸	àn	bank (of a river)
皺	zhòu	to frown
眉頭	méitou	brows
按住	ànzhù	to press
胸口	xiōngkǒu	pit of one's stomach

西施的身體不太好，一不舒服，就皺起眉頭，按住胸口。大家看到她這個樣子，覺得她比平常更漂亮了。

東施也希望別人說她好看，就學西施皺起眉頭，按住胸口，以為自己這樣就和西施一樣漂亮了。可是沒有人說她好看，反而說她越學越難看。

✑ 東施效顰的意思是_____

东施效颦 Dōngshī xiào pín

❀ 她对自己了解不够，却爱学着别人的样子打扮，所以总是东施效颦。

古时候有一个姑娘，长得很漂亮。她家住在一条河的西岸，所以人们叫她西施。河的东岸也有一个姑娘，长得很难看，大家都叫她东施。

东施	Dōngshī	name of a girl
效	xiào	to follow the example of
颦	pín	to knit one's brows
古时候	gǔshíhou	ancient times
姑娘	gūniang	girl
河	hé	river
岸	àn	bank (of a river)
皱	zhòu	to frown
眉头	méitou	brows
按住	ànzhù	to press
胸口	xiōngkǒu	pit of one's stomach

东施看见西施长得漂亮，很想跟她学。西施怎么打扮，她就怎麼打扮；西施怎么走路，她就怎么走路。西施的身体不太好，一不舒服，就皱起眉头，按住胸口。大家看到她这个样子，觉得她比平常更漂亮了。

东施也希望别人说她好看，就学西施皱起眉头，按住胸口，以为自己这样就和西施一样漂亮了。可是没有人说她好看，反而说她越学越难看。

漢字 Characters

Study the following selected characters for further enrichment of your writing and vocabulary.

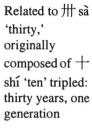

Related to 卅 sà 'thirty,' originally composed of 十 shí 'ten' tripled: thirty years, one generation

世紀	shìjì	century
世界	shìjiè	world
世上	shìshàng*	in the world, on earth
去世	qùshì*	to die, to pass away

A: 你想這個世紀會變得怎麼樣？
B: 世界上的事很難說。

Compare: 也 yě

世

shì 5
generation, life, age

糸 sī 'silk thread' + 己 jǐ—to unravel threads, to arrange, to regulate, law, to record, year

年紀	niánjì	age
經紀	jīngjì*	to manage (business)
經紀人	jīngjìrén*	manager, broker

A: 他看起來太年輕，怕經驗不夠。
B: 好的經紀人年紀不一定大。

Compare: 記 jì　計 jì

紀

jì 9
century, to record

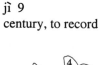

亻 rén 'person' + 韋 wěi phonetic

| 偉大 | wěidà | great, mighty |
| 偉人 | wěirén* | great man |

A: 你覺得美國歷史上最偉大的人是誰？
B: 林肯 Lín Kěn，他真是一個偉人。

偉

wěi 11
great, mighty

爫 zhǎo 'hand' + 冖 mì 'cover' + 心 xīn 'heart' + 夂 zhǐ 'walk slowly' —once meant 'to walk on tiptoe' or 'gracious gait'

愛好	àihào	hobby, interest
愛人	àirén	husband, wife, lover
愛情	àiqíng	romantic love
熱愛	rè'ài*	to love ardently

A: 她的愛人有什麼愛好？
B: 他熱愛籃球，每一場比賽都看。

愛

ài 13
love, to like, to cherish

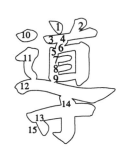

道 dào 'path' +
寸 cùn 'hand'

导

dǎo 15
to guide, to lead, to
instruct

導演	dǎoyǎn	director
導遊	dǎoyóu	tourist guide
報導	bàodǎo*	to report

A: 你看了今天的新聞報導沒有？
B: 看了，有個法國大導演去世了。

氵 shuǐ 'water'
+ 寅 yín
phonetic —
originally a
river getting
wider and
extending
towards the sea

演

yǎn 14
to evolve, to perform

演戲	yǎnxì	to act in a play
演員	yǎnyuán	performer
表演	biǎoyǎn*	to perform, to act

A: 你為什麼不喜歡那個演員演的戲？
B: 他的表演實在不好。

扌 shǒu 'hand'
+ 白 bái
phonetic

拍

pāi 8
to clap, to shoot film,
to bat

| 拍手 | pāishǒu* | to applaud |
| 球拍 | qiúpāi | racket |

A: 去年吳宇森John Woo拍了什麼片子？
B: 他拍了一部功夫片。

Compare: 拉 lā 打 dǎ

The right side
of a 木 mù tree
sliced in half

片

piàn 4
slice, part, partial

片子	piànzi	film, movie
片面	piànmiàn*	one-sided
影片	yǐngpiàn*	film, movie
照片	zhàopiàn	photograph, picture

A: 我覺得這種片子都不好。
B: 你的看法太片面。

氵 shuǐ 'water' + 青 qīng phonetic

清楚	qīngchu	to understand clearly
清早	qīngzǎo*	early morning
弄清	nòngqīng*	to make clear, to clarify

A: 你怎麼一大清早就起來？

B: 我得把這個問題搞清楚。

Compare: 情 qíng　晴 qíng

qīng　11
to clear up, pure, fresh

林 lín 'forest' + 疋 shū 'picture of a foot' phonetic — dense bushes, rich, detailed, distinct

| 一清二楚 | yìqīng-èrchǔ* | to be very clear about sth. |

A: 你怎麼對那個演員的生活一清二楚？

B: 我最近才迷上他的。

Compare: 是 shì　定 dìng　走 zǒu

chǔ　13
clear, suffering

米 mǐ 'rice' + 青 qīng phonetic—rice is perfect every time, the essence of Chinese food

精彩	jīngcǎi	brilliant, splendid
精神	jīngshen	animated
精力	jīnglì*	energy, vigor

A: 你覺得哪個節目最精彩？

B: 「六十分鐘」。

jīng　14
refined, essence, very

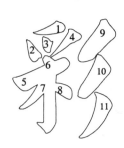

采 cǎi 'pick' and 彡 shān 'feathers'

彩色	cǎisè*	color
彩電	cǎidiàn*	color TV
水彩	shuǐcǎi*	watercolor

A: 他很奇怪，特別愛看黑白片。

B: 彩色的不一定拍得比黑白的好啊！

Compare: 形 xíng　影 yǐng

cǎi　11
color, colorful

手 shǒu 'hand'
+ 丶
'something
falling from it'

失

shī 5
to lose, to miss, to let
slip, mishap

失望　　　shīwàng　　　to become disappointed
失業　　　shīyè*　　　　to be out of work
消失　　　xiāoshī*　　　to disappear, to vanish

A: 他消失了嗎？怎麼最近都沒看到他？
B: 聽說他失業了，不想和朋友見面。

Compare: 矢 shǐ　跌 dié　光 guāng　先 xiān

月 yuè 'moon'
+ 王 tǐng + 亡
wáng phonetic
—a person
standing on the
土 tǔ, a vantage
point for moon-
gazing

望

wàng 11
look, full moon, hope

希望　　　xīwàng　　　to hope, to wish

A: 你對那個球隊失望了嗎？
B: 不，我覺得他們還是有希望贏的。

言 yán 'words'
+ 忍 rěn
phonetic

认

rèn 14
to recognize, to know,
to admit

認為　　　rènwéi　　　to think/believe that
認識　　　rènshi　　　to know, to recognize
認真　　　rènzhēn　　　to take seriously, earnest

A: 你認為小高這個人怎麼樣？
B: 我不認識他，聽說他做事很認真。

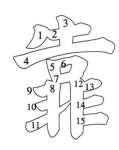

非 fēi 'wrong'
+ 告 gào
phonetic

靠

kào 15
to lean on, to get near,
to rely on

可靠　　　kěkào*　　　reliable, trustworthy
靠近　　　kàojìn*　　　to be nearby, to be close to
靠不住　　kàobuzhù*　　unreliable

A: 你看他這個人可靠嗎？
B: 我看靠不住。

Picture of an elephant—figure cut in ivory, figure, image, form, similar, symbol

對象	duìxiàng	target, boy/girlfriend to
好像/象	hǎoxiàng	to seem, to be like
想像/象	xiǎngxiàng	to imagine, to fancy
大象	dàxiàng*	elephant

象

A: 你好像對她很有意思的樣子？
B: 人家已經有對象了。

Compare: 像 xiàng

xiàng 12
elephant, image, to be like

Picture of a 止 zhǐ 'foot'—It's not clear what the 口 over the toes is for.

足球	zúqiú	soccer
滿足	mǎnzú*	to be satisfied, to satify

足

A: 我看他真個足球迷。
B: 對，他無論看多少場比賽都不滿足。

Compare: 路 lù 跟 gēn 跑 pǎo 跳 tiào

zú 7
foot, base, sufficient, fully

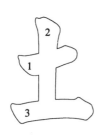

Picture of a clod of dirt, or a plant growing up out of the ground

土包子	tǔbāozi	rube, hick
土氣	tǔqì*	rustic, uncouth
土豆片兒	tǔdòupiànr*	potato chips

土

A: 他居然沒吃過土豆片兒！
B: 所以我說他是個土包子。

Compare: 在 zài 地 dì 時 shí 去 qù

tǔ 3
earth, land, local, uncouth

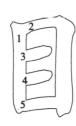

Picture of an eye, turned sideways

節目	jiémù	program, item
目的	mùdì	purpose, aim, goal

目

A: 你為什麼整天看這些中文節目？
B: 我的目的是想多練習聽中文。

Compare: 自 zì 看 kàn 相 xiāng 想 xiǎng

mù 5
eye, item, list

語法和用法 Grammar and Usage

Pay attention to the function of the structure and then study the example sentences.

1. Making an exhortation

S千萬別/要/得V	…qiānwàn bié/yào/děi…	by all means…; must (not) V

跟你說一個秘密，你可**千萬別**告訴別人。

1.	你去了中國以後，千萬得給我寫信。	你去了中国以后，千万得给我写信。	After you go to China, by all means write to me.
	沒問題，我會給你發電子郵件。	没问题，我会给你发电子邮件。	No problem; I will send you an e-mail.
2.	你千萬不要在路上買東西吃。	你千万不要在路上买东西吃。	By no means should you buy food from the street.
	吃了就會拉肚子嗎？	吃了就会拉肚子吗？	Will I have diarrhea if I do so?
3.	你千萬別告訴她我喜歡她。	你千万别告诉她我喜欢她。	Please don't ever tell her I like her.
	你什麼時候才要告訴她呢？	你什么时候才要告诉她呢？	When are you going to tell her?

千萬, literally 'a thousand and ten thousand,' is an adverb used to warn or urge people to do or not to do something. Therefore, the subject is often the second person pronoun 你, seldom the first person pronoun 我.

2. Expressing changed circumstances

S本來/原來…,現在/後來	…běnlái/yuánlái…,	Formerly/originally…
本來/原來S…,現在/後來	xiànzài/hòulái…	now/later on

我們**本來**約了下星期見個面，**現在**我卻不想去了。

1.	你的專業是什麼？	你的专业是什么？	What is your major?
	我本來學的是歷史，現在學的是文學。	我本来学的是历史，现在学的是文学。	Originally, I majored in history; now I major in literature.
2.	你有什麼心事？	你有什么心事？	What's on your mind?
	本來我不太喜歡她，後來卻發現她這個人挺可愛的。	本来我不太喜欢她，后来却发现她这个人挺可爱的。	I never used to like her very much, but later I found her to be very charming.
3.	那個明星本來演得不怎麼樣，後來卻越演越好。	那个明星本来演得不怎么样，后来却越演越好。	That star's performance was so-so in the beginning, but his acting is getting better with experience.
	你怎麼對他演的戲那麼清楚？	你怎么对他演的戏那么清楚？	Why do you know the films in which he played so well?

本來/原來/現在/後來 are movable adverbs comparable to time expressions such as 今天/明天. Their position can occur before or after the subject.

3. Enumerating reasons

一來…二來…（三來…）	yīlái…èrlái…(sānlái…)	First..., second..., third...

一來我怕跟人約會，多不好意思啊！**二來**我怕他認為我是個土包子。

1.	你為什麼不想去中國？	你为什么不想去中国？	Why don't you want to go to China?
	一來我沒有錢，二來我馬上要畢業了，沒有時間。	一来我没有钱，二来我马上要毕业了，没有时间。	On the one hand, I don't have the money; on the other, I am going to graduate soon and have no time.

2. | 你為什麼還不「上網」？ | 你为什么还不"上网"？ | Why don't you "log on"? |
| 一來我不會中文打字，二來我沒有電腦。 | 一来我不会中文打字，二来我没有电脑。 | For one thing, I don't know how to type in Chinese; for another, I don't have a computer. |

3. | 你為什麼不告訴父母，你去打工？ | 你为什么不告诉父母，你去打工？ | Why don't you tell your parents that you have a part-time job? |
| 我一來怕他們擔心，二來怕他們不讓我工作。 | 我一来怕他们担心，二来怕他们不让我工作。 | On the one hand, I am afraid that they will worry; on the other hand, I fear that they won't let me work. |

This pattern is used to enumerate one's reasons or arguments. 一來 and 二來 can go before the subject, as in examples 1 and 2, or after the subject, as in example 3. Sometimes, 來 in 一來 and 二來 can even be omitted.

4. Expressing a special quality in an exclamation

| 多（麼）Adj 啊 | duō (me) …a | How…! So…! |

一來我怕跟人約會，**多**不好意思**啊**！

1. | 那個孩子多可愛啊！ | 那个孩子多可爱啊！ | That kid is so cute! |
| 可不是嗎？她有張圓圓的臉 liǎn 和一雙大大的眼睛。 | 可不是吗？她有张圆圆的脸和一双大大的眼睛。 | How could she not be? She has a round face and big eyes. |

2. | 這個校園多美啊！ | 这个校园多美啊！ | How beautiful this campus is! |
| 秋天 qiūtiān 葉子 yèzi 紅的時候就更漂亮了。 | 秋天叶子红的时候就更漂亮了。 | It will be even more beautiful when the leaves turn red in the fall. |

3. 多不好意思啊！請   多不好意思啊！请   How embarrassing! We
    你幫忙，你還帶東   你帮忙，你还带东   ask for your help, and you
    西來。   西来。   even bring us something.

    這是應該的。   这是应该的。   This is what I should do.

This pattern is used to express emotions, e.g., when one sighs with sympathy or
exclaims with admiration. 麼 is often omitted in colloquial speech. The final sentence
particle 啊 may change depending on the ending of the preceding syllable. It is 哇 wa
after u or ao, 呀 ya after a, e, i, o, ü, 哪 na after n, or ng.

5. Expressing habitual action or untried experience

S 向來(不)V	…xiànglái (bù)…	S always V/never V
S 從來不V	…cónglái bù…	S never V
S 從來沒V過(O)	…cónglái méi…guò…	S has never V-ed

你知道我**向來**不愛打扮⋯⋯

1. 她剛買了幾件衣   她刚买了几件衣   She just bought some
    服，現在又出去逛   服，现在又出去逛   clothes, and yet she went
    街了。   街了。   out shopping again.

    你知道她向來愛趕   你知道她向来爱赶   You know that she always
    gǎn時髦。   时髦。   tries to keep up with
                                          fashion.

2. 現在大家喜歡看什   现在大家喜欢看什   What program does
    麼節目？   么节目？   everyone like to watch
                                          nowadays?

    你知道我向來/從來   你知道我向来/从来   You know that I never
    不看電視，對電視   不看电视，对电   watch TV, and I have no
    節目一點兒興趣也   视节目一点儿兴趣也   interest in TV programs
    沒有。   没有。   at all.

3. 你吃過北京烤鴨   你吃过北京烤鸭   Have you ever had
    嗎？   吗？   Peking duck?

從來沒吃過，可能我今天應該試試看。	从来没吃过，可能我今天应该试试看。	I have never had it. Perhaps I should try it today.

The adverb 向來 can have either positive or negative construction after it. But 從來 is often used with a negative 不 or 沒. 從來不 indicates that one has not done something in the past and would not do so in the present or future. 從來沒 always has an experiential marker 過 and implies only that one has not done something in the past; there is no implication about the present or future.

6. Expressing a minimal requirement

（只要）…就好了／就行了／就可以了	（zhǐyào）....jiù hǎole/ jiù xíngle/jiù kěyǐle	…then it will be all right …then it should be fine

穿得時髦不時髦沒有什麼關係，自然、大方**就好了**……

1.	我今天應該做哪些事情？	我今天应该做哪些事情？	What should I do today?
	你把功課做完就好了。	你把功课做完就好了。	If you can just finish your homework, it will be fine.
2.	你什麼時候能跟我出去玩？	你什么时候能跟我出去玩？	When can you and I go out and have some fun?
	我把課文看完就可以了。	我把课文看完就可以了。	After I finish reading the text, it will be all right.
3.	明天我有個約會，真不知道該穿哪一件衣服好！	明天我有个约会，真不知道该穿哪一件衣服好！	I have a date tomorrow, but really I don't know what clothes to wear.
	你別穿那件迷你裙就行了。	你别穿那件迷你裙就行了。	Whatever you do, don't wear that mini-skirt.

Note that 就好了／就行了／就可以了 always comes at the end of a sentence. It's a short form for 只要...就 (L4, G5). This pattern is often used when offering a suggestion or solution.

文化點滴 Culture Notes

1. **Color:** As in many other cultures, Chinese people are taken with colors. Some colors are considered "appropriate" and others "deviant," based on the predilections of different dynasties. Red has been the orthodox representation of good fortune, yet there are derogatory terms associated with red also. It is interesting to note that Chinese see brown sugar as "red sugar," 紅糖 hóngtáng, and whole-wheat bread as "black bread," 黑麵包 hēimiànbāo.

Color	Complimentary Terms	Derogatory Terms
Red	symbolizes happiness, luck, popularity 紅包 hóngbāo 'red envelope' 紅運 hóngyùn 'good luck' 紅利 hónglì 'bonus' 走紅 zǒuhóng 'to be popular'	symbolizes envy, jealousy 眼紅 yǎnhóng 'to be jealous' 紅眼病 hóngyǎnbìng 'to be jealous'
Yellow	symbolizes holiness 黃袍 huángpáo 'Imperial (Yellow) robe' 黃金 huángjīn 'gold'	symbolizes decadence, obscenity 黃色小說 huángsè xiǎoshuō 'pornographic novel' 黃色電影 huángsè diànyǐng 'pornographic movie'
Green	symbolizes spring, peace, hope 綠色工程 'foresting project' 綠色食品 'organic food'	symbolizes lowliness and degradation 帶綠帽子 dài lǜmàozi 'cuckold'
Black	symbolizes dignity, fairness, mystery In operas, judges wear black facial makeup.	symbolizes ingloriousness, illegality 抹黑 mǒhēi 'to smear' 黑社會 hēishèhuì 'underground society'
White	symbolizes purity, brightness	symbolizes low status, ominousness, decline, failure 白眼 báiyǎn 'look... with disdain' 白痴 báichī 'idiot' 豎白旗 shùbáiqí 'to surrender'

2. **Fashion:** With the impact of mass media and globalization today, one can expect to see Chinese youth, particularly in Taiwan, dressed like those in Tokyo, New York, or Paris. Young people are especially keen on keeping abreast of trends, and imitating idols. If you see a Chinese woman with blond or even green hair, don't be surprised. Traditional clothes such as *qipao* 旗袍, a close-fitting dress with high neck and slit skirt, and

zhongshanzhuang 中山裝, a military uniform-like dress with closed collar, have become outmoded, and mostly worn only on special occasions.

3. **Leisure**: Chinese people, as those in other countries, enjoy going to movies, watching sports, and hanging out with their friends while window-shopping or having tea in a teahouse. Among these leisure activities, surfing the internet is the latest fad. With this phenomenon, many new terms have been created.

Chinese Terms		*Pinyin*	*English*
網址	网址	URL	wǎngzhǐ
網頁	网页	web page	wǎngyè
網站	网站	web site	wǎngzhàn
網吧	网吧 <PRC>	internet café	wǎngbā
網咖	网咖 <TW>	internet café	wǎngkā
網友	网友	net pal	wǎngyǒu
上傳	上传	to upload	shàngchuán
下載	下载	to download	xiàzài
上網	上网	to log on	shàngwǎng
下網	下网	to log off	xiàwǎng

歌兒 Songs

我的秘密
My Secret

Moderato

詞、曲：李毓真

我 有 一 個 秘 密，　　不 敢 告 訴 你。　　我 怕 讓 你　知 道 了 以 後
Wǒ yǒu yí ge mì　mì,　　bù gǎn gàosù nǐ.　　Wǒ pà ràng nǐ　zhīdào le yǐ hòu,
I have a secret that I dare not tell you.　　I'm afraid that if you knew,

你 會 和 我 有 距 離。　　可 能 我 該 大 方 一 點　　你 喜 歡 也 說 不
Nǐ huì hé wǒ yǒu jùlí.　　Kěnéng wǒ gāi dàfāng yì diǎn.　　Nǐ xǐhuān yě shuōbú
there would be distance between us.　Perhaps I should be more open-minded, and you would like me.

定。　　如 果 不 說 會 多 麼 痛 苦，　　就 把 事 情 說 清　　楚
dìng.　　Rúguǒ bù shuō huì duóme tòngkǔ,　　jiù bǎ shìqíng shuō qīngchǔ.
　　　　How I will suffer if I don't tell you!　　So, let me make things clear.

我 知 道　　我 的 打 扮 有 點 土，　　可 是 我　　　　肯
Wǒ zhī dào　　wǒde dǎbàn yǒudiǎn tǔ,　　kě shì wǒ　　　kěn
I know that my attire looks a bit gauche.　　However, I'm willing to

為 你 吃 苦。　　雖 然 有　　很 多 人 追 求 時 髦
wèi nǐ chī kǔ.　　Suī rán yǒu　　hěnduō rén zhuī qiú shí máo,
suffer for you.　　Though many people go for fashion,

但 我 想　　那 一 點 兒 都 不　　好。　　在 開 放
dàn wǒ xiǎng　　nà yì diǎnr dōu bù　　hǎo.　　Zài kāi fàng
I don't think　　it's good at all.　　In this open

✎ **Effective learning strategies:**

第七課

Theme Dating and Making Friends

Communicative Objectives
- Asking someone out
- Meeting an old friend
- Talking about appearance & personality
- Talking about a date

Focus on Characters
- 竟遇姑娘、互罵呆聰、惜戴鏡架、印滿咖啡、猜伙排班

Grammar Focus
- 到底…(呢)
- A對B的印象…
- 竟然…
- V出(O)來
- …，要不然/要不/不然S也/就
- 難怪/怪不得…

他到底長什麼樣子？

生詞 Vocabulary

Study the following words for their pronunciation and meaning. When an area is shaded, guess at the meaning of the word based on its constituent characters and then fill in the blank. Read the usage of words and related terms (antonyms, synonyms, compounds sharing the constituent characters, etc.) and try to answer the sample questions in Chinese. Note that proper nouns or incidental terms are not numbered.

◎By Order of Appearance

1. 到底　　　dàodǐ　　　Adv　　after all, to the end　　[reach-bottom]

   你到底在想什么?
   what on earth are you thinking?

   明天你到底來不來我家玩？
   明天你到底来不来我家玩？

2. 見到　　　jiàndào　　RV　　to see, to meet　　[see-completion of action]

   见到　*can see from far away*

   你昨天見到了誰？
   你昨天见到了谁？

3. 帥　　　　shuài　　　Adj　　handsome

   帅

   你覺得哪個男演員最帥？
   你觉得哪个男演员最帅？

4. 印象　　　yìnxiàng　　N　　impression　　[print-appearance]

   complete　*empty*
   满 ≠ 空

   你對誰的印象很好？為什麼？
   你对谁的印象很好？为什么？

5. 滿意　　　mǎnyì　　　Adj　　satisfied, pleased　*w/ service/attention*　　[complete-desire]
   滿意　*full feeling*

   满足
   content, internal feeling physical

   你對你住的地方滿意嗎？
   你对你住的地方满意吗？

6. 說來話長　shuōlái huà　IE　[say-come-word-long]
   说来话长　cháng

   說來話長，這件事不說也好。
   说来话长，这件事不说也好。

7. 咖啡館　　kāfēiguǎn　N　　café　　[coffee-building]
   咖啡馆

   你喜歡去星巴xīngbā咖啡館喝咖啡嗎？
   你喜欢去星巴咖啡馆喝咖啡吗？

8. 緊張　　　jǐnzhāng　　Adj　　nervous, tense　　[tight-stretch]
   紧张

   什麼情況下你會很緊張？
   什么情况下你会很紧张？

9. 竟然　　　jìngrán　　　Adv　　unexpectedly, to one's surprise　　[actually-so]

今天有聽寫，你竟然没準備？

今天有听写，你竟然没准備？

| 10. | 遇到 | yùdào | RV | to run into, to meet | [encounter-completion of action] |

你在哪兒遇到她的？

你在哪儿遇到她的？

正好遇到下雨

| 11. | 對面 | duìmiàn | N/ | opposite, right in front | [right-face] |
| | 对面 | | Adj | | |

你家對面住什麼人？

你家对面住什么人？

面对面讲比邮件清楚

| 12. | 外號 | wàihào | N | | [other-name] |
| | 外号 | | | | |

你有没有外號？你的外號是什麼？

你有没有外号？你的外号是什么？

| 13. | 牛 | niú | N | ox | |

→牛肉、牛奶、牛排、牛仔褲

你喜歡吃牛排嗎？

你喜欢吃牛排吗？

| 14. | 男孩兒 | nánháir | N | boy | [male-child] |
| | 男孩儿 | | | | |

你家有幾個男孩兒、幾個女孩兒？

你家有几个男孩儿、几个女孩儿？

| 15. | 吵架 | chǎojià | VO | to quarrel | [make noise-withstand] |

你常和誰吵架？你們為什麼吵架？

你常和谁吵架？你们为什么吵架？

| 16. | 老 | lǎo | Adv | always | |

誰老笑你？

谁老笑你？

colloq.
老是 ~ 总是

| 17. | 排骨 | páigǔ | N | spareribs | [row-bone] |

你喜歡吃糖醋 cù 'vinegar, sour' 排骨嗎？

你喜欢吃糖醋排骨吗？

三 pái

| 18. | 罵 | mà | V | to call names, to scold | |
| | 骂 | | | | |

小孩兒常喜歡罵人什麼？

小孩儿常喜欢骂人什么？

挨骂
āi mà?
to get a scolding

骂人
to call sb.
names

Characters with Many Strokes

帥　滿　館　緊　竟　遇　號　架　骨　罵

骂小孩
to be strict w/ kids

	四眼田雞 四眼田鸡	sìyǎn tiánjī	IE	four-eyes, one who wears glasses	[four-eye-frog]
19.	戴	dài	V	to put on, to wear (glasses, watch, etc.)	

手表 (handwritten)

你戴的眼鏡是在哪兒買的？

你戴的眼镜是在哪儿买的？

厚厚的 ≠ 薄 báo (handwritten)

| 20. | 厚 | hòu | Adj | thick |

那兒冷不冷？要不要帶一件厚的大衣去？

那儿冷不冷？要不要带一件厚的大衣去？

鏡子 mirror (handwritten)

| 21. | 眼鏡
眼镜 | yǎnjìng | N | glasses (M: 副 fù) | [eye-lens] |

你什麼時候開始戴眼鏡的？

你什么时候开始戴眼镜的？

| 22. | 一下子 | yíxiàzi | N | at once, in one fell swoop | [one-down-suffix] |

一次性 one sitting
yí cì xìng (handwritten)

今天的功課不多，我一下子就做完了。

今天的功课不多，我一下子就做完了。

| 23. | 認
认 | rèn | V | to recognize |

三個月沒見，你還認得我嗎？

三个月没见，你还认得我吗？

| 24. | 毛病 | máobing | N | shortcoming, fault, illness | [small-disease] |

你的車毛病多不多？

你的车毛病多不多？

| 25. | 改 | gǎi | V | to change |

你能不能把你這毛病改一改？

你能不能把你这毛病改一改？

| 26. | 互相 | hùxiāng | Adv | mutually, each other | [each other-each other] |

你跟誰常常互相幫忙？

你跟谁常常互相帮忙？

| 27. | 研究生 | yánjiūshēng | N | graduate student | [grind-investigate-student] |

你是研究生還是本科生 běnkēshēng？

你是研究生还是本科生？

| 28. | 書呆子
书呆子 | shūdāizi | N | *nerd* | [book-idiot] |

書呆子常常喜歡做什麼？

书呆子常常喜欢做什么？

29.	吹牛	chuīniú	VO	to brag, to boast	[blow-cow]

誰愛吹牛？他/她愛吹什麼？

谁爱吹牛？他/她爱吹什么？

30.	溫柔	wēnróu	Adj	gentle and soft *sweet*	[mild-soft]

emptytalk
空話

這個女孩兒溫柔嗎？

这个女孩儿温柔吗？

31.	可愛 可爱	kě'ài	Adj	lovely, likeable	[able-love]

你覺得誰特別可愛？

你觉得谁特别可爱？

32.	姑娘	gūniang	N	girl, daughter	[father's sister-young woman]

你喜歡什麼樣的姑娘？

你喜欢什么样的姑娘？

33.	聰明 聪明	cōngming	Adj	intelligent	[clever-bright]

聰明的學生都做什麼？

聪明的学生都做什么？

34.	幽默	yōumò	Adj/ N	humorous, humor	[secluded-silent]

你覺得我們班誰最幽默？

你觉得我们班谁最幽默？

35.	年輕 年轻	niánqīng	Adj	young	[year-light]

你希望你的對象比你年輕嗎？年輕幾歲？

你希望你的对象比你年轻吗？年轻几岁？

36.	小伙子	xiǎohuǒzi	N	young fellow, lad	[small-fellow-suffix]

你喜歡的小伙子應該長什麼樣子？

你喜欢的小伙子应该长什么样子？

37.	可惜	kěxī	IE/ Adj	It's a pity! unfortunately	[able-feel sorry for]

worth sighing for

你覺得沒做過什麼、沒吃過什麼很可惜？

你觉得没做过什么、没吃过什么很可惜？

38.	猜到	cāidào	RV	to figure out, to guess right	[guess-hit target]

猜到了那個問題能得幾分？

猜到了那个问题能得几分？

Characters with Many Strokes

戴　厚　鏡　究　溫　柔　娘　聰　默　猜

| 39. | 難怪 | nánguài | Adv | no wonder | [hard-strange] |
| | 难怪 | | | | |

他昨天沒來上課，難怪不懂。

他昨天没来上课，难怪不懂。

| 40. | 唉 | ài | Inter | Oh! | |

唉，我又沒考好。

唉，我又没考好。

| 41. | 感情 | gǎnqíng | N | feeling, emotion | [sense-feeling] |

你跟誰的感情最好？為什麼？

你跟谁的感情最好？为什么？

Characters with Many Strokes

難 唉 感 情

◎ By Grammatical Categories

Nouns/Pronouns/Measure Words

牛	niú	ox	姑娘	gūniang	girl, daughter
印象	yìnxiàng	impression	小伙子	xiǎohuǒzi	young fellow, lad
感情	gǎnqíng	feeling, emotion	研究生	yánjiūshēng	graduate student
外號	wàihào	nickname	書呆子	shūdāizi	bookworm
排骨	páigǔ	spareribs	咖啡館	kāfēiguǎn	café
眼鏡	yǎnjìng	glasses	對面	duìmiàn	opposite, right in front
毛病	máobing	shortcoming, fault, illness	一下子	yíxiàzi	at once, in one fell swoop
男孩兒	nánháir	boy			

Verbs/Stative Verbs/Adjectives

戴	dài	to put on, to wear (glasses, watch, etc.)	厚	hòu	thick
認	rèn	to recognize	帥	shuài	handsome
改	gǎi	to change	溫柔	wēnróu	gentle and soft
罵	mà	to call names, to scold	可愛	kě'ài	lovely, likable
吵架	chǎojià	to quarrel	聰明	cōngming	intelligent
吹牛	chuīniú	to brag, to boast	幽默	yōumò	humorous, humor
見到	jiàndào	to see, to meet	年輕	niánqīng	young
遇到	yùdào	to run into, to meet	滿意	mǎnyì	satisfied, pleased
猜到	cāidào	to figure out, to guess right	緊張	jǐnzhāng	nervous, tense

Adverbs and Others

老	lǎo	always	難怪	nánguài	no wonder
到底	dàodǐ	after all, to the end	可惜	kěxī	It's a pity! unfortunately
竟然	jìngrán	unexpectedly, to one's surprise	說來話長	shuōlái huà cháng	it's a long story
互相	hùxiāng	mutually, each other	唉	ài	Oh!

◎ By Pinyin

Entries with * indicate lexical items used in Mini-Dialogues and of possible interest for supplemental study.

ài	唉	Oh!	máobing	毛病	shortcoming
bú jiàn bú sàn*	不见不散	won't leave without seeing each other	mà	骂	to call names
			nánguài	难怪	no wonder
cāidào	猜到	to figure out	nánháir	男孩儿	boy
chǎojià	吵架	to quarrel	niánqīng	年轻	young
chuīniú	吹牛	to brag	niú	牛	ox
cōngming	聪明	intelligent	páigǔ	排骨	spareribs
dài	戴	to wear (glasses)	rèn	认	to recognize
dàodǐ	到底	after all	shūdāizi	书呆子	bookworm
duìmiàn	对面	opposite	shuài	帅	handsome
gǎi	改	to change	shuōlái huà cháng	说来话长	it's a long story
gǎnqíng	感情	feeling	wàihào	外号	nickname
gūniang	姑娘	girl	wēnróu	温柔	gentle and soft
hòu	厚	thick	xiǎohuǒzi	小伙子	young fellow
hùxiāng	互相	mutually	yǎnjìng	眼镜	glasses
jiàndào	见到	to see	yánjiūshēng	研究生	graduate student
jìngrán	竟然	unexpectedly	yìnxiàng	印象	impression
jǐnzhāng	紧张	nervous, tense	yīnyuèhuì*	音乐会	concert
kāfēiguǎn	咖啡馆	café	yíxiàzi	一下子	at once
kě'ài	可爱	lovely	yōumò	幽默	humorous
kěxī	可惜	It's a pity!	yùdào	遇到	to run into
lǎo	老	always			
mǎnyì	满意	satisfied			

課文 Text

Use the following questions to guide your reading of the text.

1. 美英想知道關於王華的什麼事情？

2. 王華的約會順利嗎？她遇到了誰？

3. 王華的網友到底是個什麼樣的人？他長什麼樣子？

王華：

　　你見到「他」了嗎？他[1]**到底**長什麼樣子？帥不帥？你[2]**對**他**的印象**怎麼樣？他對你滿意嗎？你們是在哪兒見面的？快告訴我吧！

美英

美英：

　　說來話長，那天我們約好了五點在校門口那家咖啡館見面，我因為緊張，就決定早半個小時去。誰知道[3]**竟然**遇到我的小學同學，就是從前住在我們家對

面，外號小牛的那個男孩兒。我們小時候整天吵架：因為我很瘦，他老叫我「排骨」；我呢？就罵他是「四眼田雞」！到現在他還戴著很厚的眼鏡，所以我一下子就[4]**認出**他**來**了。這麼多年沒見，我們還是像從前一樣，老毛病不改，一直互相開玩笑。他現在是研究生了，我笑他是個「書呆子」，笑他愛吹牛，因為他說他認識了一個溫柔、可愛的姑娘。我告訴他：「我也認識了一個聰明、幽默的年輕小伙子。我正在等他呢！可惜人還沒來，[5]**要不你也**可以見見我的對象。」猜到了吧！原來我的「網友」就是這個「大牛」，[6]**難怪**我總覺得我們像老朋友一樣。唉！說說你和小高吧！你們倆的感情怎麼樣了？

王華

课文 Text

Use the following questions to guide your reading of the text.

1. 美英想知道关于王华的什么事情？

2. 王华的约会顺利吗？她遇到了谁？

3. 王华的网友到底是个什么样的人？他长什么样子？

王华：

你见到"他"了吗？他¹**到底**长什么样子？帅不帅？你²**对**他**的印象**怎么样？他对你满意吗？你们是在哪儿见面的？快告诉我吧！

美英

美英：

说来话长，那天我们约好了五点在校门口那家咖啡馆见面，我因为紧张，就决定早半个小时去。谁知道³**竟然**遇到我的小学同学，就是从前住在我们家对面，外号小牛的那个男孩儿。我们小时候整天吵架：因为我很瘦，他老叫我"排骨"；我呢？就骂他是"四眼田鸡"！到现在他还戴着很厚的眼镜，所以我一下子就⁴**认出**他**来**。这么多年没见，我们还是象从前一样，老毛病不改，一直互相开玩笑。他现在是研究生了，我笑他是个"书呆子"，笑他爱吹牛，因为他说他认识了一个温柔、可爱的姑娘。我告诉他："我也认识了一个聪明、幽默的年轻小伙子。我正在等他呢！可惜人还没来，⁵**要不**你**也**可以见见我的对象。"猜到了吧！原来我的"网友"就是这个"大牛"，⁶**难怪**我总觉得我们象老朋友一样。唉！说说你和小高吧！你们俩的感情怎么样了？

王华

小對話 Mini-Dialogues

Read the supplementary dialogues for a better understanding of the text. See if you can memorize one and perform it in class.

(1) Asking someone out

A:	你這個星期五有沒有空？	你这个星期五有没有空？
Wang:	什麼事？	什么事？
A:	這兩個月來我們在網上聊得很開心，出來見個面怎麼樣？	这两个月来我们在网上聊得很开心，出来见个面怎么样？
Wang:	可以啊！	可以啊！
A:	我們可以先喝喝咖啡，再去看個電影或聽個音樂會yīnyuèhuì。	我们可以先喝喝咖啡，再去看个电影或听个音乐会。
Wang:	不是去看鞏俐的電影吧？	不是去看巩俐的电影吧？
A:	不是，去看你喜歡的老片子。	不是，去看你喜欢的老片子。
Wang:	咱們在哪兒見？	咱们在哪儿见？
A:	在學校門口的那家咖啡館，怎麼樣？	在学校门口的那家咖啡馆，怎么样？
Wang:	好，不見不散bú jiàn bú sàn。	好，不见不散。

A: Are you free this Friday?

Wang: What's up?

A: We have had a great time chatting on the net for the past two months. How about seeing each other?

Wang: O.K.

A: We can have coffee first and then go see a movie or go to a concert.

Wang: We are going to see a Gong Li movie, aren't we?

A: No. We will watch the old films that you like.

Wang: Where shall we meet?

A: How about the café at the entrance of the university?

Wang: All right. We won't leave without seeing each other.

(2) Meeting an old friend

Wang: 你不是那個、那個「小牛」嗎？ | 你不是那个、那个"小牛"吗？

A: 是，現在是「大牛」了。 | 是，现在是"大牛"了。

Wang: 我們有多少年沒見了？ | 我们有多少年没见了？

A: 十多年了吧！ | 十多年了吧！

Wang: 時間過得真快。你也來這兒念書嗎？怎麼我在校園裏從來沒見過你？ | 时间过得真快。你也来这儿念书吗？怎么我在校园里从来没见过你？

A: 我是上個學期來的。平時忙著做研究，很少參加中國同學會的活動。 | 我是上个学期来的。平时忙着做研究，很少参加中国同学会的活动。

Wang: 你還是老樣子啊，整天就知道看書，「四眼田雞」！ | 你还是老样子啊，整天就知道看书，"四眼田鸡"！

A: 你也沒長肉，還是個「排骨」！ | 你也没长肉，还是个"排骨"！

Wang: Aren't you that, that "Little Ox"?

A: Yes. Now I am "Big Ox."

Wang: How many years has it been since we last saw each other?

A: More than ten years.

Wang: Time really flies. Have you also come here to study? How come I have never seen you on campus?

A: I came here last semester. I am busy doing research and rarely participate in the activities organized by the Chinese Student Association.

Wang: You haven't changed a bit. You have your mind on books all the time, "Four-eyed Frog"!

A: You haven't gained any weight, either. You are still "spareribs."

(3) Talking about appearance and personality

Lin: 他到底長什麼樣子？高嗎？

Wang: 高高瘦瘦的，也很精神。

Lin: 多大年紀了？

Wang: 看上去二十七、八歲的樣子，是個研究生。

Lin: 他不會是個書呆子吧？

Wang: 就是，他還戴了很厚的眼鏡！

Lin: 那不是跟你一樣可愛嗎？

他到底长什么样子？高吗？

高高瘦瘦的，也很精神。

多大年纪了？

看上去二十七、八岁的样子，是个研究生。

他不会是个书呆子吧？

就是，他还戴了很厚的眼镜！

那不是跟你一样可爱吗？

Lin: What does he look like? Is he tall?

Wang: Yes, he is tall and slim, and also very energetic.

Lin: How old is he?

Wang: He looks about 27 or 28 years old. He is a graduate student.

Lin: He wouldn't happen to be a bookworm, would he?

Wang: Yes, indeed. Also, he wears a pair of very thick glasses.

Lin: Isn't he just as cute as you?

(4) Talking about a date

Lin: 你聽說了嗎？王華上個週末跟她的網友約會了。

A: 聽說她以前對他很有好感，現在怎麼樣？

Lin: 現在很難說了。

你听说了吗？王华上个周末跟她的网友约会了。

听说她以前对他很有好感，现在怎么样？

现在很难说了。

A: 怎麼了？

怎么了？

Lin: 原來那個人竟然是她的小學同學，從前整天在一起。

原来那个人竟然是她的小学同学，从前整天在一起。

A: 那不是更好嗎？

那不是更好吗？

Lin: 可是聽說那個人很內向，王華要找一個外向一點兒的人。

可是听说那个人很内向，王华要找一个外向一点儿的人。

Lin: Have you heard? Wang Hua went out for a date with her net pal last weekend.

A: I heard that previously she liked him a lot. How is it now?

Lin: It's hard to say now.

A: What happened?

Lin: The guy turned out to be her elementary school classmate. They were together all the time.

A: Isn't that even better?

Lin: But I heard that guy is very introverted. Wang Hua wants to find someone a bit more outgoing.

小故事 Stories

Read the following tale for your own enjoyment and for your understanding of the highlighted expression that is relevant to the theme of the chapter.

 其貌不揚 qí mào bù yáng

❀ 他長得其貌不揚，真讓我失望！

從前鄭國有個很有學問的人叫然明，他長得很不好看。有一次，一個學者叫叔向來到鄭國，然明跟著很多人去看他。

那時叔向正在喝酒，聽到人群中有人說話，就想：「是誰說話這麼有學問、有教養？」一定是然明了。他立刻走到人群中，一問，果然是然明。他就對然明說：「你看起來一點兒也不出眾，如果你不開口，我根本不知道你來了。」以後他們兩個人變成了非常好的朋友。

其	qí	his
貌	mào	appearance
揚	yáng	to raise
鄭國	Zhèng guó	name of a state
學問	xuéwèn	knowledge
然明	Ránmíng	name of a person
學者	xuézhě	scholar
叔向	Shúxiàng	name of a person
人群	rénqún	crowd
教養	jiàoyàng	upbringing, culture
果然	guǒrán	as expected
出眾	chūzhòng	outstanding
開口	kāikǒu	to open one's mouth
變成	biànchéng	to become

✎ 其貌不揚的意思是_____

其貌不扬 qí mào bù yáng

❀　他长得其貌不扬，真让我失望！

　　从前郑国有个很有学问的人叫然明，他长得很不好看。有一次，一个学者叫叔向来到郑国，然明跟着很多人去看他。

　　那时叔向正在喝酒，听到人群中有人说话，就想："是谁说话这么有学问、有教养？"一定是然明了。他立刻走到人群中，一问，果然是然明。他就对然明说："你看起来一点儿也不出众，如果你不开口，我根本不知道你来了。"以后他们两个人变成了非常好的朋友。

其	qí	his
貌	mào	appearance
扬	yáng	to raise
郑国	Zhèng guó	name of a state
学问	xuéwèn	knowledge
然明	Ránmíng	name of a person
学者	xuézhě	scholar
叔向	Shúxiàng	name of a person
人群	rénqún	crowd
教养	jiàoyǎng	upbringing, culture
果然	guǒrán	as expected
出众	chūzhòng	outstanding
开口	kāikǒu	to open one's mouth
变成	biànchéng	to become

漢字 Characters

Study the following selected characters for further enrichment of your writing and vocabulary.

音 xīn 'sound'
+ 儿 rén 'person'—the song is over?

竟然　　　　jìngrán　　　　unexpectedly
究竟　　　　jiūjìng　　　　after all, in the end

A: 你竟然不認識那個小伙子？
B: 他究竟是誰？

Compare: 鏡 jìng

jìng 11
to finish, actually

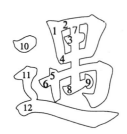

辶 chuò 'go' +
禺 yú phonetic

遇到　　　　yùdào　　　　to run into, to encounter
遇見　　　　yùjiàn*　　　　to meet, to come across

A: 你是在哪兒遇到那個書呆子的？
B: 當然是圖書館了。

Compare: 寓 yù

yù 12
to meet, to treat

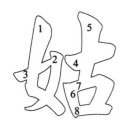

女 nǚ 'woman'
+ 古 gǔ phonetic

小姑　　　　xiǎogū*　　　　husband's younger sister
姑姑　　　　gūgu*　　　　father's sister

A: 你認得那個姑娘嗎？
B: 怎麼不認得？她是我的小姑。

Compare: 故 gù

gū 8
father's/husband's sister

女 nǚ 'woman'
+ 良 liáng phonetic

姑娘　　　　gūniang　　　　girl, daughter
新娘　　　　xīnniáng*　　　　bride

A: 那個新娘真漂亮！
B: 快去找一個跟她一樣的姑娘吧！

Compare: 很 hěn　恨 hèn

niáng 10
mother, aunt

Symbol of two hooks gripping each other

| 互相 | hùxiāng | each other |
| 互愛 | hù'ài* | to love each other |

A: 你們總是互相開玩笑嗎？

B: 對，我們是老朋友了。

hù 4
mutual, each other

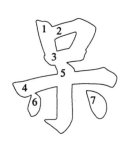

口 口 kǒu 'mouth' doubled + 馬 mǎ phonetic— to reprimand sb. caught for some offense

| 罵人 | màrén* | to curse (at people) |
| 被罵 | bèi mà* | to get a scolding |

A: 他為什麼這麼不高興？

B: 沒做功課，剛才被父母罵了一頓。

mà 16
to curse, to call names, to scold

A conventional abbreviation for 獃

書呆子	shūdāizi	pedant, bookworm
呆子	dāizi*	idiot, simpleton
發呆	fādāi*	to stare blankly, to be in a daze

A: 你在發什麼呆啊？

B: 我在想那個書呆子，他呆是呆，可是很可愛。

dāi 7
silly, foolish

Compare: 保 bǎo

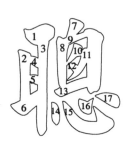

耳 ěr 'ear' + 恩 cōng phonetic

| 聰明 | cōngming | intelligent, bright |
| 小聰明 | xiǎocōngming* | cleverness in trivial matters |

A: 你覺得他聰明嗎？

B: 有一點兒小聰明，可是不夠努力。

Compare: 總 zǒng

cōng 17
clever, intelligent, bright

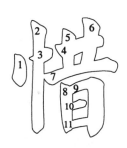

忄 xīn 'heart'
+ 昔 xī
phonetic

惜

| 可惜 | kěxī | It's a pity! |
| 愛惜 | àixī* | to cherish, to treasure |

A: 你應該好好愛惜東西。

B: 這種東西有什麼好可惜的？

Compare: 錯 cuò

xī 11
to cherish, to feel sorry
for sb.

異 yì
'different' +
戈 zái phonetic
—You become
different when
you put on a hat
or glasses.

戴

| 戴眼鏡 | dài yǎnjìng | to put on glasses |
| 戴高帽子 | dài gāomàozi* | to wear a tall hat, to flatter |

A: 你戴了這副眼鏡特別好看。

B: 別給我戴高帽子了。

dài 17
to wear, to put on
(accessories)

金 jīn 'metal'
+ 竟 jìng
phonetic

镜

眼鏡	yǎnjìng	glasses, spectacles
鏡子	jìngzi*	mirror
鏡片	jìngpiàn*	lens
放大鏡	fàngdàjìng*	magnifying glass

A: 你戴了眼鏡還看不見，要不要放大鏡？

B: 不用，是我的鏡片不乾淨。

jìng 19
mirror, lens, glass

木 mù 'wood'
+ 加 jiā
phonetic

架

吵架	chǎojià	to quarrel
打架	dǎjià*	to fight, to scuffle
書架	shūjià	bookshelf, bookcase
衣架	yījià*	coat hanger, clothes rack

A: 那個孩子常常跟人打架嗎？

B: 還好，他不打架，只跟人吵架。

jià 9
to put up, to fight, frame,
shelf

爪 zhǎo 'a hand, turned sideways' + 卩 jié 'a person kneeling'—the hand is pushing the person down: to press down

印

yìn 5
seal, stamp, to print

印象	yìnxiàng	impression
複印	fùyìn*	to duplicate
打印機	dǎyìnjī*	printer

A: 你對那個年輕人的印象怎麼樣？
B: 我忙著複印，沒時間跟他多談。

Compare: 節 jié

氵 shuǐ 'water' + 㒼 mán phonetic

滿

mǎn 14
full, satisfied, entirely, to fill

滿意	mǎnyì	satisfied, pleased
不滿	bùmǎn	dissatisfied, resentful
滿分	mǎnfēn*	perfect scores

A: 這次考試他滿分，一定很滿意吧。
B: 他還有很多不滿呢。

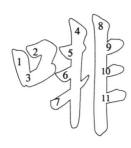

口 kǒu 'mouth' + 加 jiā phonetic

咖

kā 8

咖啡館	kāfēiguǎn	café
咖啡	kāfēi	coffee
咖啡因	kāfēiyīn*	caffeine

A: 你要不要跟我去那家咖啡館？
B: 不行，喝太多咖啡我睡不著覺。

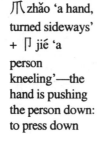

口 kǒu 'mouth' + 非 fēi phonetic

啡

fēi 11

| 咖啡色 | kāfēisè* | coffee color |

A: 你喜歡那件咖啡色的毛衣嗎？
B: 不喜歡，樣子太老。

犭 quǎn 'dog' +
青 qīng 'green'—a curiously colored dog?

猜想	cāixiǎng*	to suppose, to suspect
猜謎	cāimí*	to guess riddle
猜中	cāizhòng*	to guess right

A: 你猜他有多大年紀？

B: 別猜謎了，猜中了也沒用，他已經有對象了。

Compare: 清 qīng　晴 qíng　情 qíng

猜
cāi 11
to guess, to suspect

亻 rén 'person' + 火 huǒ 'fire'

| 小伙子 | xiǎohuǒzi | (coll.) lad, young fellow |
| 大伙兒 | dàhuǒr* | us, we all, everyone |

A: 你要和那些小伙子一起做生意嗎？

B: 對，大伙兒一塊搞，人多好辦事。

伙
huǒ 6
partner, group, to join

扌 shǒu 'hand' + 非 fēi phonetic

排骨	páigǔ	spareribs
牛排	niúpái*	beefsteak
排球	páiqiú*	volleyball
排隊	páiduì*	to stand in line

A: 你喜歡吃牛排嗎？咱們去那兒吃吧！

B: 別去了，那兒已經排了很長的隊。

排
pái 11
to arrange, row, line

玉 yù 'jade' + 刂 dāo 'knife'—to cut up pieces of jade and bestow them upon feudal lords

同班	tóngbān	classmate
上班	shàngbān*	to go to work
加班	jiābān*	to work overtime

A: 你們是同班同學嗎？

B: 不，我們是上班的時候認識的。

班
bān 10
class, team, duty

to leave smth

語法和用法 Grammar and Usage

Pay attention to the function of the structure and then study the example sentences.

1. Asking for definitive information

S到底QW(呢)	…dàodǐ…(ne)	actually…?

你見到「他」了嗎？他**到底**長什麼樣子？

1.	你們的約會到底有 沒有結果？	你们的约会到底有 没有结果？	What in the world happened on your date?
	我想沒有，我覺得 他一點兒幽默感也 沒有。	我想没有，我觉得 他一点儿幽默感也 没有。	Nothing. I think that he has no sense of humor at all.
2.	昨天的比賽到底哪 一隊贏了？	昨天的比赛到底哪 一队赢了？	Which team actually won the game yesterday?
	兩隊打成平手。	两队打成平手。	There was a tie.
3.	明天我請客，你到 底來不來？	明天我请客，你到 底来不来？	I am going to give a party tomorrow; are you coming or not?
	要是飯好吃，我就 一定來。	要是饭好吃，我就 一定来。	If you've got good food, I will certainly come.

到底, literally 'reach bottom,' is an adverb meaning "after all," or "after all is said and done." It's often used to ask for clarification on some matter or decision, and thus typically occurs in interrogative sentences. When replying to a question with 到底, remember not to repeat 到底 in the answer. For example, the answer to the question "你到底來不來？" shouldn't be 我到底不來. It's a synonym of 究竟 (L15, G6).

2. Expressing one's impression

A對B的印象Adj	…duì… de yìnxiàng…	A's impression of B is…
A對B有Adj的印象	…duì …yǒu…de yìnxiàng	A has a…impression of B
B給A留下了Adj的印象	…gěi …liúxiàle…de yìnxiàng	B leaves A with a… impression

你**對**他**的印象**怎麼樣？

1. 你對那個小伙子的
   印象怎麼樣？

   你对那个小伙子的
   印象怎么样？

   What is your impression
   of that young man?

   我對他的印象很不
   錯，他很幽默。

   我对他的印象很不
   错，他很幽默。

   I have a good impression
   of him. He is very
   humorous.

2. 你對那個學校有什
   麼印象？

   你对那个学校有什
   么印象？

   What impression do you
   have of that school?

   我對那個學校沒有
   什麼特別的印象。

   我对那个学校没有
   什么特别的印象。

   I don't have any particular
   impression of that school.

3. 誰給你留下了很深
   的印象？

   谁给你留下了很深
   的印象？

   Who has left you with a
   deep impression?

   你的女朋友，她很
   可愛。

   你的女朋友，她很
   可爱。

   Your girlfriend. She is
   very cute.

Note the various ways one can use 印象. Remember this pattern is used to indicate
one's impression of some place, or someone after initial acquaintance. Thus it
shouldn't be someone with whom one is very familiar. So, a sentence like 我對爸爸/
我男朋友的印象很好 is odd. Don't confuse 印象 with 影響 yǐngxiǎng 'influence.'

3. Indicating something contrary to expectation or common sense

S竟然(不/沒)V	…jìngrán (bù/méi)…	unexpectedly; surprisingly

誰知道**竟然**遇到我的小學同學……

1. 他就是我的中學同
   學。

   他就是我的中学同
   学。

   He was my middle school
   classmate.

   沒想到過了八年
   了，你竟然還認得
   rènde 他。

   没想到过了八年
   了，你竟然还认得
   他。

   To my surprise, you still
   recognized him after
   eight years.

2. 今天不是你的生日
   嗎？

   今天不是你的生日
   吗？

   Today is your birthday,
   isn't it?

我竟然把自己的生日給忘了。	我竟然把自己的生日给忘了。	Surprisingly, I forgot my own birthday.

3. 你竟然不認識這個明星？ / 你竟然不认识这个明星？ — It's surprising that you don't recognize this star.

我從來不看電影、電視。 / 我从来不看电影、电视。 — I never watch films or TV.

竟然, just like 居然 (L2, G5), is used to indicate surprise.

4. Expressing a change of state

S V(不)出(O)來	…(bù) chū…lái	S (cannot) V out (O)
S （沒）V 出(O)來	(méi)…chū…lái	S (didn't) V out (O)

到現在他還戴著很厚的眼鏡，所以我一下子就認**出**他**來**了。

1. 我不相信你有對象了。 / 我不相信你有对象了。 — I don't believe that you have a girlfriend.

我現在就拿出照片來給你看看。 / 我现在就拿出照片来给你看看。 — I will take out her picture and show it to you.

2. 你為什麼不說話呢？ / 你为什么不说话呢？ — Why don't you say something?

我太緊張了，一下子說不出話來。 / 我太紧张了，一下子说不出话来。 — I am too nervous to say anything at this moment.

3. 看到沒有？從屋子裏走出兩個人來了。 / 看到没有？从屋子里走出两个人来了。 — Do you see that? There are two people coming out of that house.

你喝醉了嗎？那兒只有一個人。 / 你喝醉了吗？那儿只有一个人。 — Are you drunk? There is only one person.

出來, literally 'come out,' is used to indicate the change of a state from hidden to obvious. This can be applied to the concrete physical movement (see examples 1 and

3) or abstract ideas, e.g., 想出答案來了 "to figure out an answer." Note that if there is an object, it should be placed between 出 and 來.

5. Expressing a regrettable condition

…要不然S也/就…	…yàobùrán…yě/jiù…	If it were not for a regrettable condition, one would otherwise do something else.
…要不S也/就…	…yàobù…yě/jiù…	
…不然S也/就…	…bùrán…yě/jiù…	

可惜人還沒來，**要不**你**也**可以見見我的對象。

1. 我剛到這個地方，你對這兒熟悉嗎？

我刚到这个地方，你对这儿熟悉吗？

I am new here. Are you familiar with this place?

很熟悉。我今天沒空，要不然我也可以帶你出去走走。

很熟悉。我今天没空，要不然我也可以带你出去走走。

Ycs, but I am busy today. Otherwise I would take you out and show you around.

2. 今天怎麼沒看到小李的對象？

今天怎么没看到小李的对象？

Why didn't I see Xiao Li's girlfriend today?

她生病了，要不你就能見到她。

她生病了，要不你就能见到她。

She is sick, otherwise you would have been able to meet her.

3. 我後天要坐飛機回家。

我后天要坐飞机回家。

I am flying home the day after tomorrow.

我的車子有毛病，不然我就送你到機場去。

我的车子有毛病，不然我就送你到机场去。

My car has some problems. Otherwise I would take you to the airport.

The clause preceding 要不然/不然/要不 often indicates the reason/cause for the regret. The clause following 要不然/不然/要不 states what one would like to do otherwise. Don't confuse this pattern with 要不是…就… (L1, G2).

6. Expressing a sudden realization

| 難怪/怪不得 S… | nánguài/guàibude… | No wonder… |

難怪我總覺得我們像老朋友一樣。

1.	他不吃青菜，也不吃水果。	他不吃青菜，也不吃水果。	He eats neither vegetables nor fruit.
	他吃東西那麼挑剔，難怪身體不好。	他吃东西那么挑剔，难怪身体不好。	He is so picky about food; no wonder he is not very healthy.
2.	我申請到一個獎學金，可以去中國留學。	我申请到一个奖学金，可以去中国留学。	I have applied for and received a scholarship which will allow me to study in China.
	怪不得你那麼開心。	怪不得你那么开心。	No wonder you are so happy.
3.	他兩年沒回家了。	他两年没回家了。	He hasn't been home for two years.
	怪不得他那麼想家。	怪不得他那么想家。	No wonder he is so homesick.

文化點滴 Culture Notes

1. **Dating**: Although arranged marriage is not as common as it was in the past, matchmakers 紅娘 hóngniáng or 媒人 méirén are still in need for those who don't seem to be able to find their dream lovers. It is worth noting that Chinese students, before getting into college, are not encouraged to have boyfriends or girlfriends, as it is believed that this has an adverse effect on students' performance in school. Despite this, students still find ways to express their affections.

2. **Beauty**: It has been said that "beauty is in the eye of beholder" 情人眼裏出西施 qíngrén yǎnlǐ chū xīshī. When it comes to models and stars as the measure of "beauty," one has to admit that what is considered "beautiful" in modern Chinese society is similar to that in the West. However, ideals of beauty have changed over time. In the Tang dynasty, full-figured women were considered beautiful. In the Song dynasty, a beautiful woman had to

be skinny. In general, those with black silky hair and fair skin are considered "beautiful." Thus, it is common to see women holding onto their parasols, whenever they go outside.

3. **Emotions**: In general, Chinese people have less conspicuous body language. They usually do not shrug their shoulders to express disbelief or stare into people's eyes to check their sincerity. What is normal and natural to Chinese might be considered "low-key" in Western society. The tendency to use understatement can also make Westerners feel frustrated and puzzled. When Chinese teachers say "not bad 不錯," it actually means "good." Following are a few more terms expressing emotions in Chinese.

Chinese Terms		*Pinyin*	*English*
高興	高兴	gāoxìng	happy
開心	开心	kāixīn	happy
興奮	兴奋	xīngfèn	excited
難過	难过	nánguò	sad
傷心	伤心	shāngxīn	aggrieved, brokenhearted
灰心	灰心	huīxīn	discouraged, disheartened
沮喪	沮丧	jǔsàng	frustrated
生氣	生气	shēngqì	mad, angry
憤怒	愤怒	fènnù	furious

4. **Names**: In addition to the last name 姓 xìng and first name 名 míng, traditional Chinese also have 字 zì, a name taken at the age of twenty (for boys) or fifteen (for girls) to complement their first names, or 號 hào, studio names used by scholars, poets, calligraphers, painters, etc. Nowadays 字 and 號 have become obsolete, but children still have "childhood names," 小名 xiǎomíng or 乳名 rǔmíng, or tend to give each other "nicknames," 外號 wàihào or 綽號 chuòhào. A few common nicknames are listed below.

Chinese Terms		*Pinyin*	*English*
四眼田雞	四眼田鸡	sìyǎn tiánjī	four-eyes
排骨	排骨	páigǔ	spareribs
夫子	夫子	fūzǐ	pedant
小嘴	小嘴	xiǎozuǐ	small mouth
小胖	小胖	xiǎopàng	chubby
小白菜	小白菜	xiǎobáicài	little cabbage (referring to young and pretty girls)
大頭	大头	dàtóu	big head

歌兒 Songs

戀愛故事
Love Story

Andante

詞：劉雅詩　　曲：馬定一

1. 聽　說　你　遇　見　他，　　　幽　默　年　輕　的　　小　伙　子。
   Tīng shuō nǐ　yù　jiàn　tā,　　　yōu mò nián qīng de　xiǎo huǒ zi.
   I heard that you ran into him,　　that humorous young lad.

2. 聽　說　你　遇　見　她，　　　聰　明　溫　柔　的　　美　姑　娘。
   Tīng shuō nǐ　yù　jiàn　tā,　　　cōngmíng wēnróu de　měi gū niang.
   I heard that you ran into her,　　that smart, gentle, pretty girl.

1. 兩人老是互相 笑罵，你遇見他，幽默年輕小　伙　子。　　你　笑　他
   Liǎng rén lǎo shì hùxiāng xiào mà, nǐ yùjiàn tā, yōumò niánqīng xiǎohuǒzi.　　Nǐ　xiào tā
   You two always tease and laugh at each other. You ran into him, that humorous young lad. You joke

2. 雖然你們常常 吵架，你遇見她，聰明 溫柔美　姑　娘。　　你　怪　她
   Suīrán nǐmen chángcháng chǎojià, nǐ yùjiàn tā, cōngmíng wēnróu měi gūniang.　　Nǐ　guài tā
   Although you always fight, you ran into her, that smart, gentle, pretty girl.　　You complain

1. 戴著眼鏡像青蛙，　他　笑　你　臉兒長長像匹馬。其　實　你　心　　裏
   dàizhe yǎnjìng xiàng qīngwā, tā xiào nǐ　liǎnr chángcháng xiàng pī mǎ. Qíshí nǐ　xīn　lǐ
   that he wears glasses like a frog. He jokes that your long face is like a horse's.　Actually you are

2. 念 東念西像老媽，　她　怪　你　管 這管那像老 爸。其　實　你　早　已
   niàn dōng niàn xī xiàng lǎomā, tā guài nǐ　guǎn zhè guǎn nà xiàng lǎobà. Qí shí nǐ　zǎo　yǐ
   that her nagging about this and that is like your mom's. She complains that you bother her about
   this and that like her dad.　Actually you have already

1. 十　分　滿　意　他，　難　怪　看　見　他　只　會　笑　哈　哈。
   shí fēn mǎn yì　tā,　nán　guài　kàn jiàn tā　zhǐ　huì xiào hā hā.
   pretty happy in your heart. No wonder you always laugh when you see him.

2. 深　深　愛　上　她，　怪　不　得　一　心　想　娶　她　回　　家。
   shēnshēn àishàng tā,　guài　bu　dé　yì　xīn xiǎng qǔ tā huí　jiā.
   fallen deeply in love with her. No wonder you want to marry her with all your heart.

第八課

Theme Love and Marriage

Communicative Objectives
- Expressing surprise
- Showing disapproval
- Relating an event
- Sharing a concern

Focus on Characters
- 洋化背景、幸福保守、將白勸醒、歧觀偏嫌、克困代件

Grammar Focus
- 能少…就少；能 V…就 V
- 非…不可
- …再說…
- A 嫌 B…
- A 為 B Adj/VO
- A 受到 B 的歧視/影響/歡迎

你說你愛上了誰？

生詞 Vocabulary

Study the following words for their pronunciation and meaning. When an area is shaded, guess at the meaning of the word based on its constituent characters and then fill in the blank. Read the usage of words and related terms (antonyms, synonyms, compounds sharing the constituent characters, etc.) and try to answer the sample questions in Chinese. Note that proper nouns or incidental terms are not numbered.

◎ By Order of Appearance

1. 愛上　　　àishang　　RV　　　　　　　　　　　　　　[love-up]
   愛上

   在那個節目裏，現在是誰愛上了誰？

   在那个节目里，现在是谁爱上了谁？

2. 白人　　　báirén　　N　　Caucasian　　　　　[white-people]

   現在在美國，白人和黑人之間還有很多問題嗎？

   现在在美国，白人和黑人之间还有很多问题吗？

3. 文學　　　wénxué　　N　　literature　　　[literary-study]
   文学

   你對文學感興趣嗎？喜歡誰的小說？

   你对文学感兴趣吗？喜欢谁的小说？

4. 長大　　　zhǎngdà　　RV　　to grow up, to mature　　[grow-big]
   长大

   小時候你希望長大以後做什麼？

   小时候你希望长大以后做什么？

5. 平時　　　píngshí　　Adv　　in ordinary times　　[ordinary-time]
   平时

   你平時幾點起床？幾點睡覺？

   你平时几点起床？几点睡觉？

6. 句　　　jù　　N/M　　sentence, measure word for poems/songs

   你少說兩句，你們就不會吵架了。

   你少说两句，你们就不会吵架了。

7. 非…不可　　fēi…bùkě　　IE　　must　　　[not…not-approve]

   明天有考試，現在我非複習不可了。

   明天有考试，现在我非复习不可了。

8. 提醒　　　tíxǐng　　V　　to remind, to alert to　　[mention-wake up]

   老師常提醒你們什麼？

   老师常提醒你们什么？

9. 洋人   yángrén   N   [foreign-person]

他雖然是個洋人，可是已經完全中國化
了。

他虽然是个洋人，可是已经完全中国化
了。

10. 一起   yìqǐ   Adv   together, in the same place   [one-start]

=一塊兒

你常常和誰一起念書？

你常常和谁一起念书？

11. 歧視   qíshì   N/V   discrimination, to treat with [divergent-look]
    歧视   bias

什麼人在社會上常受到歧視？

什么人在社会上常受到歧视？

12. 影響   yǐngxiǎng   N/V   influence, to influence   [shadow-sound]
    影响

A對B有影響；B受到A的影響

誰對你有很大的影響？

谁对你有很大的影响？

13. 文化   wénhuà   N   culture, education (PRC)   [writing-culture]

你覺得中國文化裏，最有趣的是什麼？

你觉得中国文化里，最有趣的是什么？

14. 背景   bèijǐng   N   background   [back-view]

那個人的家庭背景怎麼樣？

那个人的家庭背景怎么样？

15. 將來   jiānglái   N/   future, in the future   [shall-come]
    将来   Adv   你將來想在哪兒生活？為什麼？

你将来想在哪儿生活？为什么？

16. 離婚   líhūn   N/   [separate-marriage]
    离婚   VO   →結婚、再婚

現在離婚的人越來越多還是越來越少？

现在离婚的人越来越多还是越来越少？

Characters with Many Strokes

愛　醒　歧　視　影　響　景　將　離　婚

| 17. | 再說
再说 | zàishuō | IE | besides, furthermore | [again-say] |

你們的文化背景完全不同；再說，你的
年紀也太小，怎麼可以和他一起生活？
你们的文化背景完全不同；再说，你的
年纪也太小，怎么可以和他一起生活？

| 18. | 嫁 | jià | V | (of a woman) to marry |

↔娶 qǔ '(of a man) to marry'
你想嫁給什麼樣的人？
你想嫁给什么样的人？

| 19. | 愛情
爱情 | àiqíng | N | romantic love | [love-feeling] |

你覺得男女之間只有愛情沒有友情 'friendship'
嗎？
你觉得男女之间只有爱情没有友情吗？

| 20. | 勸
劝 | quàn | V | to advise, to urge |

你父母常勸你做什麼？
你父母常劝你做什么？

| 21. | 醫
医 | yī | N | medical science |

→文、法 fǎ, 理 lǐ, 工 gōng, 農 nóng, 商 shāng
你想學醫還是學工？
你想学医还是学工？

| 22. | 華裔
华裔 | Huáyì | N | ethnic Chinese of other
nationalities | [Chinese-descendents] |

→日裔、美裔、法裔、德裔
美國的華裔常常會遇到什麼問題？
美国的华裔常常会遇到什么问题？

| 23. | 嫌 | xián | V | to dislike the fact that |

你為什麼不跟他交朋友？你嫌他什麼？
你为什么不跟他交朋友？你嫌他什么？

AA BB

| 24. | 囉嗦
罗嗦 | luōsuo | Adj | longwinded, wordy |

你覺得誰很囉唆？
你觉得谁很罗唆？

| 25. | 分手 | fēnshǒu | VO | | [part-hand] |

你為什麼和他/她分手？
你为什么和他/她分手？

| 26. | 觀念
观念 | guānniàn | N | concept, sense, idea | [view-thought] |

你的父母有「重男輕女」zhòng nán qīng nǔ 'value boys over girls' 的觀念嗎？

你的父母有"重男轻女"的观念吗？

| 27. | 保守 | bǎoshǒu | Adj | conservative | [protect-guard] |

你的父母保守嗎？他們不讓你做什麼？

你的父母保守吗？他们不让你做什么？

| 28. | 代溝
代沟 | dàigōu | N | generation gap | [generation-ditch] |

你和父母之間有很大的代溝嗎？

你和父母之间有很大的代沟吗？

| 29. | 接受 | jiēshòu | V | to accept | [receive-accept] |

你能不能接受你父母對交朋友的看法？

你能不能接受你父母对交朋友的看法？

| 30. | 偏見
偏见 | piānjiàn | N | bias, prejudice | [slanting-view] |

你覺得別人對你有偏見嗎？為什麼？

你觉得别人对你有偏见吗？为什么？

| 31. | 受到 | shòudào | V | to receive | [receive-completion of action] |

A受到B的影響/歧視/歡迎

你受到了誰很大的影響？

你受到了谁很大的影响？

| 32. | 算 | suàn | V | to consider, to regard as | |

你覺得自己算不算個保守的人？

你觉得自己算不算个保守的人？

| 33. | 反對
反对 | fǎnduì | V | to oppose | [turn over-opposite] |

你的父母反對你做什麼？為什麼反對？

你的父母反对你做什么？为什么反对？

| 34. | 原因 | yuányīn | N | reason, cause | [origin-cause] |

你討厭他的原因是什麼？

你讨厌他的原因是什么？

Characters with Many Strokes

嫁 勸 醫 裔 嫌 囉 唆 觀 溝 算

| 35. | 收入 | shōurù | N | income | [collect-enter] |

做什麼樣的工作收入比較高？

做什么样的工作收入比较高？

| 36. | 看法 | kànfǎ | N | view | [see-way] |

你對移民問題有什麼看法？

你对移民问题有什么看法？

| 37. | 同意 | tóngyì | V | | [same-idea] |

你同意我的看法嗎？

你同意我的看法吗？

| 38. | 講
讲 | jiǎng | V | to speak, to stress | |

美國人講獨立 dúlì 'independent' 中國人呢？

美国人讲独立，中国人呢？

| 39. | 條件
条件 | tiáojiàn | N | condition, term, requirement | [item-item] |

你找對象有些什麼條件？

你找对象有些什么条件？

| 40. | 幸福 | xìngfú | N/
Adj | happiness, happy | [luck-blessing] |

你覺得幸福的生活應該是怎麼樣的？

你觉得幸福的生活应该是怎么样的？

| 41. | 相愛
相爱 | xiāng'ài | V | to love each other | [mutually-love] |

你覺得兩個人相愛一定要結婚嗎？

你觉得两个人相爱一定要结婚吗？

| 42. | 克服 | kèfú | V | to surmount, to put up with (hardship, etc.) | [overcome-submit] |

想學中文的人要克服什麼困難？

想学中文的人要克服什么困难？

| 43. | 困難
困难 | kùnnán | N/
Adj | difficulty | [tired-difficult] |

你學中文的時候，遇到了什麼困難？

你学中文的时候，遇到了什么困难？

| 44. | 敬上 | jìngshàng | IE | respectfully submitted | [respect-submit] |

Characters with Many Strokes

講　條　幸　福　難　敬

◎ By Grammatical Categories

Nouns/Pronouns/Measure Words

醫	yī	medical science
白人	báirén	Caucasian
洋人	yángrén	foreigner
華裔	Huáyì	ethnic Chinese of other nationalities
文化	wénhuà	culture, education (PRC)
文學	wénxué	literature
背景	bèijǐng	background
條件	tiáojiàn	condition, term, requirement
收入	shōurù	income
將來	jiānglái	future, in the future
愛情	àiqíng	romantic love

幸福	xìngfú	happiness, happy
離婚	líhūn	divorce
困難	kùnnán	difficulty
觀念	guānniàn	concept, sense, idea
看法	kànfǎ	way of looking at sth., view
偏見	piānjiàn	bias, prejudice
歧視	qíshì	discrimination, to treat with bias
影響	yǐngxiǎng	influence, to influence
原因	yuányīn	reason, cause
代溝	dàigōu	generation gap
句	jù	sentence, measure word for poems/songs

Verbs/Stative Verbs/Adjectives

嫁	jià	(of a woman) to marry
勸	quàn	to advise, to urge
嫌	xián	to dislike the fact that
講	jiǎng	to speak, to stress
算	suàn	to consider, to regard as
接受	jiēshòu	to accept
受到	shòudào	to receive
提醒	tíxǐng	to remind, to alert to
同意	tóngyì	to agree

反對	fǎnduì	to oppose
相愛	xiāng'ài	to love each other
愛上	àishang	to fall in love with
長大	zhǎngdà	to grow up, to mature
分手	fēnshǒu	to break up
克服	kèfú	to surmount, to put up with (hardship, etc.)
囉嗦	luōsuo	longwinded, wordy
保守	bǎoshǒu	conservative

Adverbs and Others

平時	píngshí	in ordinary times
一起	yìqǐ	together, in the same place
再說	zàishuō	besides, furthermore

非…不可	fēi…bùkě	must
敬上	jìngshàng	respectfully submitted

◎By Pinyin

Entries with * indicate lexical items used in Mini-Dialogues and of possible interest for supplemental study.

àiqíng	爱情	romantic love	luōsuo	罗嗦	wordy
àishang	爱上	to fall in love with	piānjiàn	偏见	bias
báirén	白人	Caucasian	píngshí	平时	in ordinary times
bǎoshǒu	保守	conservative	qíshì	歧视	discrimination
bèijǐng	背景	background	quàn	劝	to advise
bìngrén*	病人	patient	shòudào	受到	to receive
chángtú*	长途	long distance	shōurù	收入	income
dàigōu	代沟	generation gap	suàn	算	to regard as
fǎnduì	反对	to oppose	tiáojiàn	条件	condition
fēi...bùkě	非…不可	must	tíxǐng	提醒	to remind
fēnshǒu	分手	to break up	tóngyì	同意	to agree
guānniàn	观念	concept	wénhuà	文化	culture
Huáyì	华裔	ethnic Chinese of other nationalities	wénxué	文学	literature
jiānglái	将来	future	xián	嫌	to dislike the fact that
jiǎng	讲	to stress	xiāng'ài	相爱	to love each other
jià	嫁	(of a woman) to marry	xìngfú	幸福	happiness
jiēshòu	接受	to accept	yángrén	洋人	foreigner
jìngshàng	敬上	respectfully submitted	yī	医	medical science
jù	句	sentence	yǐngxiǎng	影响	influence, to influence
kànfǎ	看法	view	yìqǐ	一起	together, in the same place
kèfú	克服	to surmount	yuányīn	原因	reason
kùnnán	困难	difficulty	zàishuō	再说	besides
líhūn	离婚	divorce	zhǎngdà	长大	to grow up

課文 Text

Use the following questions to guide your reading of the text.

1. 美英的媽媽想不想讓她和高德中在一起？為什麼？

2. 美英覺得自己和高德中有沒有距離？為什麼？

3. 美英對愛情有什麼看法？

美英：

　　昨天在電話裏你說你愛上了誰？那個叫什麼高德中的男孩。他是個美國白人吧？聽你說他現在人在中國，學的是比較文學。孩子，媽知道你已經長大了，所以我平時[1]能少說兩句，就少說兩句。可是現在我[2]非提醒你不可——千萬別跟洋人在一起。不是我對那個高德中有什麼特別的歧視，而是洋人跟我們在文化背景和生活習慣上的距離太大，將來你們可能會離婚的。[3]再說，他是個學文的，嫁給他，一定會吃苦。愛情雖好，可是麵包更重要啊！我勸你好好想一想，還是讓我給你介紹一個念醫的華裔吧！不要[4]嫌媽囉嗦，早點兒跟小高分手吧！

翻譯
fān yì
to translate

　　　　　　　　　　　　　　　　　　　　媽媽

媽：

　　沒想到您的觀念這麼保守，我們之間的代溝居然這麼大。我不明白您為什麼不能接受「美國人」，為什麼對他們有偏見？您知道嗎？我也是個美國人啊！從前您和爸總是說中國移民在美國生活不容易，常[5]受到歧視，現在是誰歧視誰呢？而且到底什麼人才算「中國人」呢？小高對中國文化很感興趣，又能說地道的中文，他可能比很多中國人還中國呢！您反對我們在一起的另外一個原因，是怕他將來沒有好的收入。這種看法，我更不同意。我覺得愛情是不應該講條件的。麵包雖然重要，沒有愛情兩個人又怎麼可能幸福呢？我相信只要我們相愛，就沒有克服不了的困難。別[6]為我擔心了，媽。

女兒
美英敬上

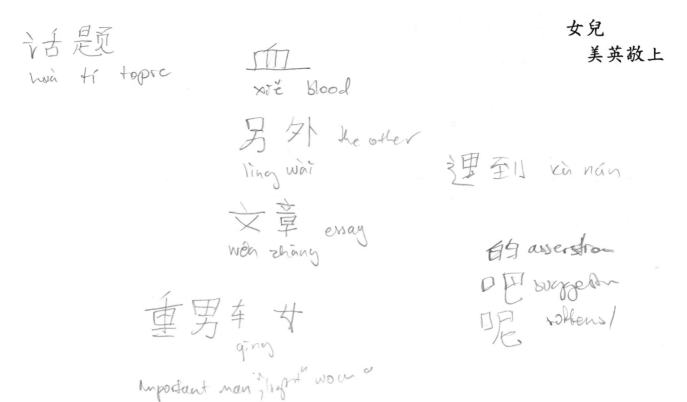

课文 Text

Use the following questions to guide your reading of the text.

1. 美英的妈妈想不想让她和高德中在一起？为什么？

2. 美英觉得自己和高德中有没有距离？为什么？

3. 美英对爱情有什么看法？

 美英：

　　昨天在电话里你说你爱上了谁？那个叫什么高德中的男孩。他是个美国白人吧？听你说他现在人在中国，学的是比较文学。孩子，妈知道你已经长大了，所以我平时[1]**能**少说两句，**就**少说两句。可是现在我[2]**非**提醒你**不可**——千万别跟洋人在一起。不是我对那个高德中有什么特别的歧视，而是洋人跟我们在文化背景和生活习惯上的距离太大，将来你们可能会离婚的。[3]**再说**，他是个学文的，嫁给他，一定会吃苦。爱情虽好，可是面包更重要啊！我劝你好好想一想，还是让我给你介绍一个念医的华裔吧！不要[4]**嫌**妈罗嗦，早点儿跟小高分手吧！

妈妈

妈：

　　没想到您的观念这么保守，我们之间的代沟居然这么大。我不明白您为什么不能接受"美国人"，为什么对他们有偏见？您知道吗？我也是个美国人啊！从前您和爸总是说中国移民在美国生活不容易，常[5]**受到**歧视，现在是谁歧视谁呢？而且到底什么人才算"中国人"呢？小高对中国文化很感兴趣，又能说地道的中文，他可能比很多中国人还中国呢！您反对我们在一起的另外一个原因，是怕他将来没有好的收入。这种看法，我更不同意。我觉得爱情是不应该讲条件的。面包虽然重要，没有爱情两个人又怎么可能幸福呢？我相信只要我们相爱，就没有克服不了的困难。别[6]**为**我担心了，妈。

女儿

美英敬上

小對話 Mini-Dialogues

Read the supplementary dialogues for a better understanding of the text. See if you can memorize one and perform it in class.

(1) Expressing surprise

Lin:	喂，是媽嗎？我是美英啊！	喂，是妈吗？我是美英啊！
Mom:	美英啊！怎麼好久沒打電話回家了？	美英啊！怎么好久没打电话回家了？
Lin:	我這幾個星期功課多得要命，忙不過來嘛！	我这几个星期功课多得要命，忙不过来嘛！
Mom:	那你今天打電話有什麼事嗎？是不是錢花完了？	那你今天打电话有什么事吗？是不是钱花完了？
Lin:	不是，我有一件重要的事要告訴您和爸。	不是，我有一件重要的事要告诉您和爸。
Mom:	什麼事快說啊！長途chángtú電話很貴的。	什么事快说啊！长途电话很贵的。
Lin:	我愛上了一個人。	我爱上了一个人。
Mom:	什麼？	什么？
Lin:	一個白人。他是我去年認識的，念比較文學。今年他去了中國，我才發現我很想他。我想我愛上他了。	一个白人。他是我去年认识的，念比较文学。今年他去了中国，我才发现我很想他。我想我爱上他了。

Lin: Hello, Mom? This is Meiying.

Mom: Meiying, why haven't you called home for such a long time?

Lin: I have had a lot of homework for the last few weeks, and I am almost falling behind.

Mom: Then why are you calling today? Is there something going on? Are you out of money?

Lin: No. I have something important to tell you and Dad.

Mom: What's going on? Tell me. A long-distance phone call is quite expensive.

Lin: I have fallen in love.

Mom: What?

Lin: He is a white man. I got to know him last year. He studies Comparative Literature. I didn't realize that I would miss him so much till he went to China this year. I think I am in love with him.

(2) Showing disapproval

Mom:	今天美英來電話了。
Dad:	她現在怎麼樣了？感恩節的時候回來過節嗎？
Mom:	她說她愛上了一個小伙子。
Dad:	女兒大了總是留不住的。
Mom:	他不是個中國人！而且他是念文的。
Dad:	那怎麼行呢？一定不能讓他們在一起，快給美英介紹別的對象吧！
Mom:	說得容易，你應該知道你女兒的脾氣。

今天美英来电话了。

她现在怎么样了？感恩节的时候回来过节吗？

她说她爱上了一个小伙子。

女儿大了总是留不住的。

他不是个中国人！而且他是念文的。

那怎么行呢？一定不能让他们在一起，快给美英介绍别的对象吧！

说得容易，你应该知道你女儿的脾气。

Mom: Meiying phoned home today.

Dad: How is she doing? Is she coming back for Thanksgiving?

Mom: She said that she fell in love with a guy.

Dad: Our daughter is going to leave the nest someday.

挺 的
tǐng...

Mom: But he is not a Chinese! Besides, he is a literature major.

Dad:　That won't work. We certainly can't let them be together. Let's quickly find someone else for Meiying.

俩 liǎ

Mom: That's easy to say. But you should know your daughter's temperament.

sā
我们仨
three ppl

(3) Relating an event

Wang:　小李，美英愛上了一個男的，你
　　　　知道嗎？

小李，美英爱上了一个男的，你
知道吗？

Li:　　這有什麼奇怪的？

这有什么奇怪的？

Wang:　這個男的你也很熟悉，現在人在
　　　　中國。

这个男的你也很熟悉，现在人在
中国。

Li:　　不會是小高吧！

不会是小高吧！

Wang:　正是小高！他們倆現在感情很不
　　　　錯。

正是小高！他们俩现在感情很不
错。

Li:　　好極了！他們倆挺合適的。

好极了！他们俩挺合适的。

Wang:　可是美英的父母反對。一是因為
　　　　小高是個白人；二是因為他的專
　　　　業不對。

可是美英的父母反对。一是因为
小高是个白人；二是因为他的专
业不对。

Wang:　Xiao Li, Meiying has taken a shine to a man. Have you heard?

Li:　　What's so strange about that?

Wang:　You know this man very well, too.
　　　　He is now in China.

Li:　　Are you talking about Xiao Gao?

Wang:　That's right. Their relationship is pretty good right now.

Li:　　That's terrific! They are a good match.

Wang:　But Meiying's parents do not approve. First, Xiao Gao is a white man; second, his major is not "right."

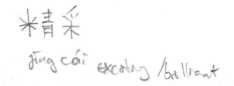

※精采
jīng cǎi exciting /brilliant

Handwritten annotations at top:
看什么书！ridiculous to do
what's the point of reading
why bother?

哭有什么用
what's the use of crying

学数书有什么用?

(4) Sharing a concern

Lin:	德中，我把我們的事告訴我爸媽了。	德中，我把我们的事告诉我爸妈了。
Gao:	好啊！應該早一點讓父母知道。	好啊！应该早一点让父母知道。
Lin:	可是他們反對我跟你在一起，嫌你不是個中國人。	可是他们反对我跟你在一起，嫌你不是个中国人。
Gao:	可是我會說中文，我也了解中國文化。	可是我会说中文，我也了解中国文化。
Lin:	那有什麼用，他們嫌你不是學醫的。	那有什么用，他们嫌你不是学医的。
Gao:	學醫有什麼好？我爸爸就是個醫生，每天看到的都是難過的病人 bìngrén。	学医有什么好？我爸爸就是个医生，每天看到的都是难过的病人。
Lin:	他們不這麼想啊！他們覺得醫生的收入高。	他们不这么想啊！他们觉得医生的收入高。
Gao:	收入高，可是兩個人不相愛也不會幸福。	收入高，可是两个人不相爱也不会幸福。

Lin: Dezhong, I have told my parents about you.

Gao: Good! We should not keep this from our parents any longer.

Lin: But they don't want me to be with you, because you are not a Chinese.

Gao: But I can speak Chinese and I also understand Chinese culture.

Lin: That won't help. They also dislike that fact that you are not a medical school student.

Gao: What's so great about studying medicine? My father is a doctor, and all he sees every day are sad patients.

Lin: They don't see it that way. They think a doctor's salary is high.

Gao: Even if one's salary is high, if two people don't love each other, they can't be happy together.

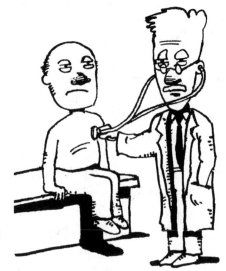

小故事 Stories

Read the following tale for your own enjoyment and for your understanding of the highlighted expression that is relevant to the theme of the chapter.

 月下老人 yuèxià lǎorén

✿　誰是你們倆的月下老人啊？

唐朝的時候，有一個人叫韋固，有一次他到宋城去旅行，看到一個老人在月光下翻一本書。他問這個老人：「您在看什麼書？」老人說：「這是天下男女婚姻的記錄。」

韋固又問：「那你袋子裏的紅線是做什麼用的？」老人說：「我用那些線，把將來會結婚的男女繫在一起。無論他們之間的距離有多遠，只要繫上了，就一定會成為夫妻。」老人指著一個老婆婆抱著的孩子說：「那就是你的妻子。」

韋固不希望自己和沒有錢的人家有關係，就派人去殺那個女孩。結果沒有成功，只傷了她的額頭。十四年以後，他和一個有錢的女子結婚了，發現她頭上有一個疤。原來她就是自己從前派人殺傷的女孩。

唐朝	Tángcháo	Tang dynasty
韋固	Wěigù	a person's name
宋城	Sòngchéng	Song city
月光	yuèguāng	moonlight
翻	fān	to flip
天下	tiānxià	world
記錄	jìlù	record
袋子	dàizi	bag
紅線	hóngxiàn	red string
繫	xì	to tie
成為	chéngwéi	to become
夫妻	fūqī	couple
指	zhǐ	to point at
老婆婆	lǎopópo	old woman
抱	bào	to hold
妻子	qīzi	wife
派	pài	to send
殺	shā	to kill
成功	chénggōng	successful
傷	shāng	to injure
額頭	étóu	forehead
女子	nǚzǐ	woman
疤	bā	scar

✎月下老人的意思是

月下老人 yuèxià lǎorén

❀ 谁是你们俩的月下老人啊？

唐朝的时候，有一个人叫韦固，有一次他到宋城去旅行，看到一个老人在月光下翻一本书。他问这个老人："您在看什么书？"老人说："这是天下男女婚姻的记录。"

韦固又问："那你袋子里的红线是做什么用的？"老人说："我用那些线，把将来会结婚的男女系在一起。无论他们之间的距离有多远，只要系上了，就一定会成为夫妻。"老人指着一个老婆婆抱着的孩子说："那就是你的妻子。"

韦固不希望自己和没有钱的人家有关系，就派人去杀那个女孩。结果没有成功，只伤了她的额头。十四年以后，他和一个有钱的女子结婚了，发现她头上有一个疤。原来她就是自己从前派人杀伤的女孩。

唐朝	Tángcháo	Tang dynasty
韦固	Wěigù	a person's name
宋城	Sòngchéng	Song city
月光	yuèguāng	moonlight
翻	fān	to flip
天下	tiānxià	world
记录	jìlù	record
袋子	dàizi	bag
红线	hóngxiàn	red string
系	xì	to tie
成为	chéngwéi	to become
夫妻	fūqī	couple
指	zhǐ	to point at
老婆婆	lǎopópo	old woman
抱	bào	to hold
妻子	qīzi	wife
派	pài	to send
杀	shā	to kill
成功	chénggōng	successful
伤	shāng	to injure
额头	étóu	forehead
女子	nǚzǐ	woman
疤	bā	scar

漢字 Characters

Study the following selected characters for further enrichment of your writing and vocabulary.

氵 shuǐ 'water'
+ 羊 yang
phonetic

洋

洋人	yángrén	foreigner
洋房	yángfáng*	Western-style building
洋化	yánghuà*	to westernize

A: 她跟洋人交往，所以很洋化了。
B: 你的觀念太保守了。

yáng 9
ocean, vast, foreign

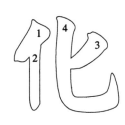

The picture of a person 亻 and a person upside down—who flips and changes

化

文化	wénhuà	culture, civilization
變化	biànhuà	to change, change
化學	huàxué*	chemistry

A: 他對中國文化有研究嗎？
B: 有，他特別感興趣的是語言的變化。

Compare: 花huā 靴xuē

huà 4
to change, to melt

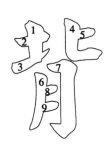

北 běi 'north (the back side)'
+ 月 ròu 'flesh'

背

背景	bèijǐng	background, backdrop
背後	bèihòu*	behind, in the rear
背心	bèixīn*	vest
背書	bèishū*	to recite a lesson from memory

A: 站在她背後、穿背心的那個人是誰？
B: 是個只會背書的呆子。

bèi, bēi 9
back, to shoulder

日 rì 'sun' +
京 jīng
phonetic

景

風景	fēngjǐng*	scenery, landscape
景氣	jǐngqì*	prosperity, boom
不景氣	bùjǐngqì*	in recession/depression

A: 你看今年的經濟怎麼樣？
B: 不太好，可能會不景氣。

Compare: 影yǐng

jǐng 12
view, scene, great

Uncertain
explanation

幸

幸福	xìngfú	happiness, happy
幸好	xìnghǎo*	fortunately
不幸	búxìng*	unfortunately, misfortune

A: 你現在生活很幸福吧？

B: 幸好沒跟那個書呆子結婚。

Compare: 報 bào　辛 xīn

xìng　8
luck, good fortune

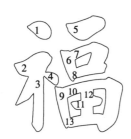

衤 shì 'spirit' +
畐 fú phonetic

福

福氣	fúqì*	happy lot, good fortune
發福	fāfú*	to put on weight
口福	kǒufú	gourmet's luck

A: 你真有福氣，她很會做飯。

B: 口福是有的，可是我也發福了。

fú　13
blessing, happiness

亻 rén 'person' +
呆 originally 子
zǐ 'child'; two
strokes 八 were
added to the
sides,
representing
swaddling
clothes

保

| 保守 | bǎoshǒu | conservative |
| 保持 | bǎochí | to keep, to maintain |

A: 你為什麼不喜歡他？

B: 他太保守了。

Compare: 堡 bǎo

bǎo　9
to protect, to keep, to
guarantee

宀 mián 'roof' +
寸 cùn 'hand'—
someone on hand
to guard the
house

守

| 守時 | shǒushí* | to show up on time |
| 守法 | shǒufǎ* | to abide by the law |

A: 他跟人約會從來不守時。

B: 有時候還不守法呢！

shǒu　6
to guard, to observe

寸 cùn 'to offer
月 meat' + 爿
qiáng phonetic

將

jiāng 11
shall, to take, just

| 將來 | jiānglái | future, in the future |
| 將要 | jiāngyào* | going to, will, shall |

A: 你對自己的將來有什麼打算？
B: 沒什麼打算，先畢業了再說。

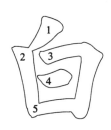

日 rì sun with a
point at the top
→sun pointing
upwards, rising

白

bái 5
white, clear, in vain

白人	báirén	Caucasian
白天	báitiān	daytime, day
白色	báisè*	white (color)
明白	míngbái	to understand, to know

A: 我不明白你為什麼要嫁給那個白人？
B: 他愛我，我也愛他啊。

Compare: 百 bǎi 怕 pà 的 de 原 yuán

力 lì 'strength'
+ 雚 guàn
phonetic

劝

quàn 19
to exhort, to urge, to
advise

| 勸告 | quàngào* | to advise, to exhort |

A: 你去看病，醫生給你什麼勸告？
B: 他勸我不要再吸煙。

Compare: 觀 guān 歡 huān

酉 yǒu 'wine' +
星 xīng
phonetic

醒

xǐng 16
to sober up, to wake up

提醒	tíxǐng	to remind, to warn
叫醒	jiàoxǐng*	to wake up, to awaken
睡醒	shuìxǐng*	to wake up

A: 你睡醒了，就把我叫醒，好嗎？
B: 你自己沒有鬧鐘嗎？

止 zhǐ 'stop' +
支 zhī phonetic

歧視　　qíshì　　　　to treat with bias,
　　　　　　　　　　　　discrimination

A: 你為什麼歧視他？

B: 我對他一點兒歧視也沒有。

qí 8
fork, branch, divergent

見 jiàn 'see' +
雚 guan
phonetic

觀念　　guānniàn　　concept
觀點　　guāndiǎn*　　point of view

A: 你父母的觀念很保守嗎？

B: 對，他們不太能了解我的觀點。

Compare: 歡 huān

guan 25
to observe, view,
concept

亻 rén 'person'
+ 扁 biǎn
phonetic

偏見　　piānjiàn　　prejudice, bias
偏偏　　piānpiān　　just, but, only
偏食　　piānshí*　　to be particular about food

A: 不是我對你有偏見，你經驗不夠。

B: 你有偏見，卻偏偏說我不行。

Compare: 遍 biàn

piān 11
slanting, partial,
stubbornly

女 nǚ 'woman'
+ 兼 jiān
phonetic

嫌麻煩　xián máfan*　not to want to take the trouble

A: 你為什麼不在家自己做飯吃？

B: 我嫌做飯太麻煩。

xián 13
to dislike, to mind,
suspicion

kè 7
can, to restrain, to overcome

Used to look like 皮 pí 'skin' minus 又, resembled 革 gé 'leather, an animal being flayed'—to overcome an animal

克

克服   kèfú   to surmount
巧克力   qiǎokèlì   chocolate

A: 你怎麼克服困難，讓他聽你的？
B: 我送了他一盒巧克力。

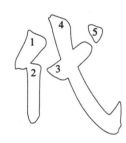

kùn 7
to surround, hard-pressed

木 mù 'tree' + 囗 wéi 'surround'—a tree railed in

困

困難   kùnnán   difficulty

A: 你覺得學中文困難嗎？
B: 說不太難，寫很難。

Compare: 因 yīn

dài 5
to take the place of, period

亻 rén 'person' + 弋 yì phonetic

代

代溝   dàigōu   generation gap
現代   xiàndài*   modern times, modern
時代   shídài*   times, age, era

A: 你和你的父母有代溝嗎？
B: 沒有，他們的想法很現代。

Compare: 袋 dài

jiàn 6
measure word for items, document

亻 rén 'person' + 牛 niú 'ox'

件

條件   tiáojiàn   condition, term
郵件   yóujiàn   postal items, post
信件   xìnjiàn*   letter, mail
軟件   ruǎnjiàn*   software

A: 你一天收到多少電子郵件？
B: 五十封吧！

語法和用法 Grammar and Usage

Pay attention to the function of the structure and then study the example sentences.

1. Expressing the capacity to act

能少…，就少	néng shǎo…, jiù shǎo…	if one can avoid…then don't…
能不…，就不	néng bù…, jiù bù…	
能V…，就V	néng…, jiù…	if one can possibly V…then V

所以我平時能少說兩句，就少說兩句。

1.	他現在忙得要命！	他现在忙得要命！	He is terribly busy now!
	所以我能不找他，就不找他。	所以我能不找他，就不找他。	So if I can avoid bugging him, I won't.
2.	原來她現在在拼命減肥。	原来她现在在拼命减肥。	It turns out that she is working hard to stay on a diet.
	所以你能少買蛋糕，就少買蛋糕。	所以你能少买蛋糕，就少买蛋糕。	So if you can buy fewer cakes, buy fewer cakes.
3.	我的錢快用完了。	我的钱快用完了。	I am running out of money.
	所以我勸你，能不出去吃飯，就不出去吃飯。	所以我劝你，能不出去吃饭，就不出去吃饭。	So here is my advice: if you can, avoid dining out.

In this pattern 能…就… means '(if)... can, then....' "If" is implied in the first clause and the verbs in the two clauses are often the same. The omission of the conditional conjunction in Chinese is quite common. While this pattern is often used to give advice (see examples 2 and 3), it can be used to realize many other language functions, for example, in offering encouragement (e.g., 能做就做) or a promise (e.g., 能幫就幫).

2. Expressing necessity or obligation with double negation

S非(要/得)VO不可	…fēi (yào/děi)…bùkě	S absolutely must VO

可是現在我非提醒你不可——千萬別跟洋人在一起。

1. 他講究吃嗎？　　　　他讲究吃吗？　　　　Is he particular about food?

　　很講究，他每天非　　很讲究，他每天非　　Yes, he has to go to that
　　去那個飯館不可。　　去那个饭馆不可。　　restaurant every day.

2. 你要不要跟我去看　　你要不要跟我去看　　Do you want to go to the
　　電影？　　　　　　电影？　　　　　　movie with me?

　　我現在非學習不　　我现在非学习不　　I absolutely have to study
　　可，要不然我就完　　可，要不然我就完　　now; otherwise I will be
　　了。　　　　　　了。　　　　　　finished.

eg. 我完蛋了
I'm afraid egg ypner

3. 你為什麼非要和　　你为什么非要和　　Why do you have to be
　　他在一起不可呢？　　他在一起不可呢？　　with him?

　　因為我愛他。　　　因为我爱他。　　Because I love him.

非…不可, literally '(if) not..., then it is not permissible,' is a pattern using double-negation to indicate a very strong statement or resolution. 非 and 不可 enclose a phrase stating that something must be done.

3. Introducing an additional reason

reason 1, (2, 3,...),再說 another reason	…zàishuō…	moreover; furthermore

將來你們一定會離婚的。**再說**，他是個學文的，嫁給他，一定會吃苦……

1. 你為什麼不找她談　　你为什么不找她谈　　Why don't you talk to her
　　談這件事？　　　　谈这件事？　　　　about this matter?

　　她很囉唆，再說，　　她很罗唆，再说，　　She is wordy. Besides,
　　她對我有偏見。我　　她对我有偏见。我　　she is biased against me.
　　不想找她談。　　　不想找她谈。　　I don't want to seek her
　　　　　　　　　　　　　　　　out and talk with her.

2. 你為什麼要學中文　　你为什么要学中文　　Why do you study
　　呢？　　　　　　呢？　　　　　　Chinese?

_接受 你的_
挑 战 challenge
/war/
tǎo zhàn

因為我對中國文化一直很感興趣，再說，我的專業是歷史，中國的歷史很長、可以好好地研究。

因为我对中国文化一直很感兴趣，再说，我的专业是历史，中国的历史很长、可以好好地研究。

Because I have always been interested in Chinese culture. Besides, my major is history. China has a very long history which awaits further research.

3. 你為什麼不喜歡他？

你为什么不喜欢他？

Why don't you like him?

因為我們沒有共同的興趣，再說，他也不是我喜歡的那種男孩。

因为我们没有共同的兴趣，再说，他也不是我喜欢的那种男孩。

Because we don't have anything in common. Besides, he is not the type of man that I like.

再說, a phrase used to introduce further reason/argument, supports the speaker's view and can make one's speech sound cohesive. In this context, it works like 而且.

4. Expressing the reason one dislikes something

A 嫌 B sth. negative	...xián...	A dislikes/minds/complains of B...

不要**嫌**媽囉嗦……

1. 你為什麼不去那兒吃飯？

你为什么不去那儿吃饭？

Why don't you go there to eat?

我嫌那兒的飯太貴。

我嫌那儿的饭太贵。

I think the food there is too expensive.

2. 那個學校的學費 xuéfèi 太貴、宿舍太小、停車 tíngchē 的地方也太少。

那个学校的学费太贵、宿舍太小、停车的地方也太少。

The tuition of that school is too high, and their dorms are too small. Also, there are very few places for parking.

你不要嫌這個不好、嫌那個不好，

你不要嫌这个不好、嫌那个不好，

Don't complain that this or that isn't right. You are lucky to have been

有學校要你就不錯了。	有学校要你就不错了。	accepted by a school at all.

3.

你不要嫌我難看，你也看看你自己的樣子吧！	你不要嫌我难看，你也看看你自己的样子吧！	Don't say that I am not good-looking. Take a look at yourself, too.
你說什麼！	你说什么！	What did you just say?

Though 嫌 is not a sentence pattern per se, its usage can be tricky. Make sure that the **reason** for one's dislike of something, someone, or some place is stated. Never just say 我嫌他.

5. Expressing the impact of something

A受到(B的)歧視	…shòudào (…de) qíshì	A is discriminated against by B
A受到(B的)影響	…shòudào (…de) yǐngxiǎng	A is influenced by B
A受到(B的)歡迎	…shòudào (…de) huānyíng	A is welcomed by B

從前您和爸總是說中國移民在美國生活不容易，常**受到**歧視……

1.

為什麼從前的人如果生活不幸福也不離婚？	为什么从前的人如果生活不幸福也不离婚？	Why didn't people in the past get divorced when they were not happy together?
因為離過婚的人常常受到別人的歧視。	因为离过婚的人常常受到别人的歧视。	Because those who were divorced were discriminated against by other people.

2.

為什麼現在的孩子問題這麼多？	为什么现在的孩子问题这么多？	Why do children today have so many problems?
因為他們看太多電視，受到很多不好的影響。	因为他们看太多电视，受到很多不好的影响。	Because they watch too much TV and are exposed to bad influences.

3.

什麼樣的老師容易受到學生的歡迎？	什么样的老师容易受到学生的欢迎？	What kind of teacher is popular among students?

不給學生太多功課的老師。	不给学生太多功课的老师。	Those who don't give their students a lot of homework.

受到, a verb literally meaning 'be given,' takes limited abstract objects (e.g., 歧視、影響、歡迎、批評、表揚、教育) to make common verb phrases. If B is the general public or can be easily inferred from the context, it is often omitted. Don't confuse 受到 shòudàowith 收到 shōudào 'to receive,' which takes concrete objects.

6. Expressing an action or feeling for another's sake

A 為 B Adj/VO	…wèi…	A Adj/VO for the sake of B

只要我們相愛，就沒有克服不了的困難。別**為**我擔心了，媽。

1.	不知道他們在學校吃得好不好？穿得夠不夠？	不知道他们在学校吃得好不好？穿得够不够？	I don't know if they eat well and dress warmly at school.
	孩子已經長大了，你不要再為他們擔心了。	孩子已经长大了，你不要再为他们担心了。	Our children have grown up. Don't keep worrying about them.
2.	聽說你們分手了？	听说你们分手了？	I heard that you two had broken up.
	你不必為我們難過，我們還是朋友。	你不必为我们难过，我们还是朋友。	You don't need to feel sorry for us. We are still friends.
3.	我贏了這場比賽，你怎麼反而哭kū了呢？	我赢了这场比赛，你怎么反而哭了呢？	I won this game. Why on earth are you crying?
	我是為你高興啊！	我是为你高兴啊！	I am so happy for you.

夠 gòu

In this pattern 為 is a co-verb meaning "to V for the sake of." B can be a noun, a pronoun (see examples 1, 2, 3), or a verb functioning as a noun. It has the same meaning as 為了 (see L10, G6), but 為了is a conjunction which indicates the purpose for a situation stated in the main clause of a sentence.

文化點滴 Culture Notes

1. **Marriage**: Chinese parents today assert less control over their children's marriages than in the past, when marriages were sometimes decided even before the children were born 指腹為婚 zhǐ fù wéi hūn. Nonetheless, parents still prefer to have their children marry someone of a similar social background, as noted in the idiom 門當戶對 méndāng hùduì 'equal gates and windows facing.' Contrary to the American custom, it is the groom's, 新郎 xīnláng, family instead of the bride's, 新娘 xīnniáng, which usually has to pay the expenses involved in the wedding ceremony.

2. **Interracial marriage**: Because of the frequent contact between Chinese and Westerners, interracial marriage has become more and more common nowadays. In fact, marriage between different ethnic groups was also prevalent in traditional Chinese society, although it was used mostly as a political attempt by the Han imperial family to cement relations with rulers of other nationalities in the border areas 和親 héqīn. The most famous example of a Han daughter marrying a foreign noble is the marriage of Wang Zhaojun 王昭君 to the Xiongnu 匈奴 chief, Chanyu 單于.

3. **Stereotypes**: Although often a hindrance to our understanding of people and reality, stereotypes, 刻板印象 kèbǎn yìnxiàng or 成見 chéngjiàn, are prevalent in Chinese society, as they are in any other. Many Chinese think that Westerners are less serious about relationships and that their marraiges do not last long. Some Chinese also have the impression that Westerns tend to squander their resources and don't know how to save money.

歌兒 Songs

幸福
Happiness

Adagio

詞：劉力嘉　曲：馬定一

1. 你 要 嫁 他 太 可 惜， 你 不 明 白 幸 福 的
　 Nǐ yào jià tā tài kě xí, nǐ bù míng bái xìng fú de
　 It's a shame you want to marry him.　　You simply don't know

2. 您 的 提 醒 我 同 意， 可 是 愛 情 很 難
　 Nín de tí xǐng wǒ tóng yì, kěshì ài qíng hěn nán
　 I agree with your advice.　　Yet, it's not

1. 意 義。 我 勸 你 千 萬 別 跟 他 在 一 起，
　 yì yì. Wǒ quàn nǐ qiānwàn bié gēn tā zài yì qǐ,
　 the meaning of happiness. I urge you by all means not to be with him.

2. 講 道 理。 再 說 我 倆 相 愛 觀 念 沒 距
　 jiǎng dào lǐ. Zàishuō wǒ liǎng xiāng ài guān niàn méi jù
　 to reason with love. Besides we two care for each other and think alike.

1. —— 收 入 條 件 不 好， 不 可 以。 別 嫌 我 囉唆
　 shōurù tiáo jiàn bù hǎo bù kě yǐ. Bié xián wǒ luōsuo,
　 It's not all right if salary and conditions are poor.　　Don't say that I'm longwinded

2. 離。 將 來 一 切 全 靠 自 己 努 力。 別 為 我 擔 心
　 lí. Jiānglái yí qiè quán kào zì jǐ nǔ lì. Bié wèi wǒ dānxīn,
　 Our future all depends on our own efforts.　　Don't worry about me

1. 別 生 氣， 背 景 不 同 將 來 生 活 不 容 易。
　 bié shēng qì, Bèi jǐng bù tóng jiāng lái shēnghuó bù róng yì.
　 and don't be mad. It won't be easy to live with different backgrounds in the future.

2. 別 著 急， 克 服 了 困 難 幸 福 就 在 手 裏。
　 bié zhāo jí, kè fú le kùn nán, xìng fú jiù zài shǒu lǐ.
　 and don't be anxious. I'll have happiness after overcoming difficulties.

第九課

Theme Family and Gender Roles

Communicative Objectives
- Indicating wishes
- Making concessions
- Asking for and responding to help
- Summarizing opinions

Grammar Focus
- （當）…的時候；（每）當…的時候
- …總之…
- 任何O(S)都V
- （等）V₁（了）（以後）再V₂
- 好（不）容易才V
- 為了A，B；B是為了A

Focus on Characters
- 任何夫婦、母顧庭務、職業由運、主幹爭願、需須燒之

誰不想要一個太太呢？

生詞 Vocabulary

Study the following words for their pronunciation and meaning. When an area is shaded, guess at the meaning of the word based on its constituent characters and then fill in the blank. Read the usage of words and related terms (antonyms, synonyms, compounds sharing the constituent characters, etc.) and try to answer the sample questions in Chinese. Note that proper nouns or incidental terms are not numbered.

◎By Order of Appearance

1.	太太	tàitai	N	wife, Mrs., madame	[great-great]

你有太太的話，希望她出去工作嗎？
你有太太的话，希望她出去工作吗？

2.	愛人 / 爱人	àiren	N	*(shaded)*	[love-person]

他的愛人叫什麼名字？
他的爱人叫什么名字？

píng
abstract
必需 (品)
concrete (necessities)

3.	必須 / 必须	bìxū	Aux	must, have to	[certainly-must]

學中文的學生必須常常做什麼？
学中文的学生必须常常做什么？

4.	能幹 / 能干	nénggàn	Adj	able, competent	[can-work]

你覺得誰很能幹？為什麼？
你觉得谁很能干？为什么？

5.	聽話 / 听话	tīnghuà	Adj/ VO	*(shaded)*	[listen-word]

你平常比較聽誰的話？
你平常比较听谁的话？

6.	家務 / 家务	jiāwù	N	household duties	[house-task]

=家事
你常幫你父母做什麼家務？
你常帮你父母做什么家务？

7.	工作	gōngzuò	N/V	job, to work	[work-do]

你希望自己找到什麼樣的工作？
你希望自己找到什么样的工作？

8.	整理	zhěnglǐ	V	to put in order, to arrange	[arrange-tidy up]

整理屋子/房間/東西/書
你什麼時候會整理你的房間？

成功
成熟

jià zhí guān
价值观
values

性格
性恪

你什么时候会整理你的房间？

9. 帶
    带   dài   V   to look after, to raise, to bring

你喜歡帶孩子嗎？你帶過誰的孩子？

你喜欢带孩子吗？你带过谁的孩子？

10. 燒
    烧   shāo   V   to cook, to roast, to burn

你會燒飯嗎？你燒的飯怎麼樣？

你会烧饭吗？你烧的饭怎么样？

(handwritten: 煮 zhǔ, 炸 chá fry, 炒 chǎo, 蒸 zhēng steam)

11. 需要   xūyào   V/N   to need, to want, to require   [need-want]

什麼時候你需要別人的幫助？

什么时候你需要别人的帮助？

12. 鼓勵
    鼓励   gǔlì   N/V   encouragement, to encourage   [inspire-encourage]

誰常常鼓勵你？她/他怎麼鼓勵你？

谁常常鼓励你？她/他怎么鼓励你？

13. 考慮
    考虑   kǎolǜ   V   to consider, to think over   [inspect-worry]

做什麼事情需要好好地考慮？

做什么事情需要好好地考虑？

14. 自由   zìyóu   N/   freedom, free   [self-let (sb. do sth.)]
                               Adj   在什麼地方你會覺得不太自由？

在什么地方你会觉得不太自由？

15. 總之
    总之   zǒngzhī   Conj   in a word, in short   [sum up-that]

總之，我不太喜歡他，不想和他交朋友。

总之，我不太喜欢他，不想和他交朋友。

16. 厲害
    厉害   lìhai   Adj   sharp, tough, ~~terrible~~ *(handwritten: impressive, awe)*   [harsh-harm]

你覺得哪個球員最厲害？為什麼？

你觉得哪个球员最厉害？为什么？

17. 任何   rènhé   Adj   any, whatever   [no matter-what]

我任何時候都可以來找你嗎？

我任何时候都可以来找你吗？

Characters with Many Strokes

須　幹　務　整　燒　鼓　勵　慮　總　厲

| 18. | 商量 | shāngliang | V | to consult, to talk over | [discuss-measure] |

你有問題的時候，會跟誰商量？

你有问题的时候，会跟谁商量？

| 19. | 女孩兒
女孩儿 | nǚháir | N | girl | [female-child] |

你喜歡男孩兒還是女孩兒？為什麼？

你喜欢男孩儿还是女孩儿？为什么？

| 20. | 争(着) *the*
争 (论)(炒) | zhēng | V | to fight for, to contend | |

孩子都喜歡爭著做什麼？

孩子都喜欢争着做什么？

| 21. | 看不起 | kànbuqǐ | RV | look down on | [look-not-up] |

你看不起什麼樣的人？

你看不起什么样的人？

| 22. | 小氣
小气 | xiǎoqi | Adj | stingy, mean | [small-attitude] |

↔大方

小氣的人常常不願意做什麼？

小气的人常常不愿意做什么？

| 23. | 男子漢
男子汉 | nánzǐhàn | N | a real man (in the he-mannish sense) | |

你覺得什麼樣的男人算是「男子漢」？

你觉得什么样的男人算是"男子汉"？

| 24. | 洗碗 | xǐwǎn | VO | | [wash-bowl] |

在你們家誰洗碗？

在你们家谁洗碗？

| 25. | 運氣
运气 | yùnqi | N | fortune, luck | [carry-air] |

你覺得自己運氣好嗎？為什麼？

你觉得自己运气好吗？为什么？

| 26. | 同時
同时 | tóngshí | Adv/
N | (at) the same time, meanwhile | [same-time] |

你除了學中文以外，同時還學什麼？

你除了学中文以外，同时还学什么？

| 27. | 份(兒)
份(儿) | fènr | M | measure word for copies, newspapers, jobs, etc. | |

你現在打工嗎？打幾份工？

你现在打工吗？打几份工？

28.	放棄 放弃	fàngqì	V	to give up	[release-discard]

你願意放棄自己的工作，跟著丈夫走嗎？

你愿意放弃自己的工作，跟着丈夫走吗？

29.	好容易	hǎoróngyì	Adv	with great difficulty, to have a hard time (doing sth.)	[good-hold-easy]

你好容易才把什麼事情做完？

你好容易才把什么事情做完？

30.	照顧 照顾	zhàogù	V	to look after, to care for	[take care of-attend to]

你不在的時候，誰照顧你的狗？

你不在的时候，谁照顾你的狗？

31.	職業 职业	zhíyè	N	occupation, profession	[post-job]

你希望自己將來的職業是什麼？

你希望自己将来的职业是什么？

32.	女性	nǚxìng	N	woman	[female-sex]

你覺得現代女性比傳統的女性幸福嗎？

你觉得现代女性比传统的女性幸福吗？

33.	家庭	jiātíng	N	family, household	

你覺得一個家庭中，最重要的是什麼？

你觉得一个家庭中，最重要的是什么？

34.	主婦 主妇	zhǔfù	N		[manage-woman]

你希望你的太太做個家庭主婦嗎？

你希望你的太太做个家庭主妇吗？

35.	成就	chéngjiù	N	achievement, success	[accomplish-undertake]

你認為什麼算是一種「成就」？

你认为什么算是一种"成就"？

36.	母親 母亲	mǔqin	N	mother	[mother-kin]

你父親、母親是做什麼工作的？

你父亲、母亲是做什么工作的？

Characters with Many Strokes

漢　碗　運　棄　顧　職　業　庭　婦

37.	妻子	qīzi	N	wife	[wife-suffix]

你希望做個什麼樣的妻子？

你希望做个什么样的妻子？

38.	願意 愿意	yuànyi	V	to be willing, to wish, to want	[wish-desire]

你願意待在家裏做家務嗎？

你愿意待在家里做家务吗？

39.	為了 为了	wèile	Prep	for, in order to, for the sake of	[for-particle]

你來這兒學習是為了什麼？

你来这儿学习是为了什么？

40.	事業 事业	shìyè	N	career, undertaking	[thing-profession]

你覺得家庭重要還是事業重要？

你觉得家庭重要还是事业重要？

41.	煮	zhǔ	V	to cook, to boil	

你媽媽常煮什麼菜給你吃？

你妈妈常煮什么菜给你吃？

42.	夫	fū	N	=丈夫husband, man	

她是怎麼認識她丈zhàngfu夫的？

她是怎么认识她丈夫的？

43.	平等	píngděng	Adj/ N	equal, equality	[level-grade]

你覺得現在男女平等了嗎？

你觉得现在男女平等了吗？

Characters with Many Strokes

妻　願　意　事　業　煮　等

◎ By Grammatical Categories

Nouns/Pronouns/Measure Words

夫	fū	husband, man
愛人	àiren	(PRC) spouse
太太	tàitai	wife, Mrs., madame
妻子	qīzi	wife
女孩兒	nǚháir	girl
女性	nǚxìng	woman
主婦	zhǔfù	housewife
母親	mǔqin	mother
男子漢	nánzǐhàn	a real man (in the he-mannish sense)
家庭	jiātíng	family, household

家務	jiāwù	household duties
工作	gōngzuò	job, to work
職業	zhíyè	occupation, profession
事業	shìyè	career, undertaking
成就	chéngjiù	achievement, success
運氣	yùnqi	fortune, luck
自由	zìyóu	freedom, free
鼓勵	gǔlì	encouragement, to encourage
份(兒)	fèn(r)	measure word for copies, newspapers, jobs, etc.

Verbs/Stative Verbs/Adjectives

帶	dài	to look after, to raise, to bring
燒	shāo	to cook, to roast, to burn
煮	zhǔ	to cook, to boil
爭	zhēng	to fight for, to contend
洗碗	xǐwǎn	to do dishes
整理	zhěnglǐ	to put in order, to arrange
照顧	zhàogù	to look after, to care for
考慮	kǎolǜ	to consider, to think over
商量	shāngliang	to consult, to talk over
放棄	fàngqì	to give up

願意	yuànyi	to be willing, to wish, to want
需要	xūyào	to need, to want, to require
必須	bìxū	must, have to
能	nénggàn	able, competent
屬害	lìhai	sharp, tough, terrible
聽話	tīnghuà	obedient
小氣	xiǎoqi	stingy, mean
平等	píngděng	equal, equality
任何	rènhé	any, whatever
看不起	kànbuqǐ	to scorn

Adverbs and Others

同時	tóngshí	(at) the same time, meanwhile
總之	zǒngzhī	in a word, in short
為了	wèile	for, in order to, for the sake of

好容易	hǎoróngyì	with great difficulty, to have a hard time (doing sth.)

◎ By Pinyin

Entries with * indicate lexical items used in Mini-Dialogues and of possible interest for supplemental study.

àiren	爱人	spouse	píngděng	平等	equal
bǎomǔ*	保姆	housekeeper, nanny	qīzi	妻子	wife
bìxū	必须	must	rènhé	任何	any
chéngjiù	成就	achievement	shāngliang	商量	to consult
cí*	辞	to quit (a job)	shāo	烧	to cook
dài	带	to look after	shìyè	事业	career
dàolǐ*	道理	reason, sense	tàitai	太太	wife, Mrs.
fàngqì	放弃	to give up	tīnghuà	听话	obedient
fèn(r)	份(儿)	measure word for jobs	tóngshí	同时	(at) the same time
fū	夫	husband	tuō'érsuǒ*	托儿所	child-care center
gōngzuò	工作	job, to work	wèile	为了	for
gǔlì	鼓励	encouragement	xiàbān*	下班	to get off work
hǎoróngyì	好容易	with great difficulty, to have a hard time (doing sth.)	xiǎoqi	小气	stingy
			xǐwǎn	洗碗	to do dishes
jiātíng	家庭	family	xūyào	需要	need
jiāwù	家务	household duties	yuànyi	愿意	to be willing
jièkǒu*	借口	excuse	yùnqi	运气	fortune, luck
kànbuqǐ	看不起	to scorn	zhàogù	照顾	to look after
kǎolǜ	考虑	to consider, to think over	zhēng	争	to fight for
			zhěnglǐ	整理	to put in order
lìhai	厉害	sharp	zhíyè	职业	occupation
mǔqin	母亲	mother	zhǔ	煮	to cook
nánzǐhàn	男子汉	a real man	zhǔfù	主妇	housewife
nénggàn	能干	competent	zìyóu	自由	freedom, free
nǚháir	女孩儿	girl	zǒngzhī	总之	in a word
nǚxìng	女性	woman			

課文 Text

Use the following questions to guide your reading of the text.

1. 小李想要找什麼樣的對象？

2. 為什麼小李說現在做個男人很不容易？

3. 為什麼美英說現在做女人也很難？

 王華、美英：

聽說大家都有了對象，我也想找個愛人呢！我的她必須溫柔、能幹、聽話，愛做家務，但是也能出去工作、賺錢。[1]當我出門**的時候**，她會幫我整理好要帶的東西；當我回家的時候，她已經燒好了很多我愛吃的菜，等我回來；當我需要人鼓勵的時候，她能在我身邊；當我需要考慮問題的時候，她能給我一些自由。[2]**總之**，我喜歡的對象不能太厲害，[3]**任何**事**都**應該先和我商量，[4]**等**我決定了**再**做。我不算挑剔，可是到現在還找不到女朋友。每次和女孩兒出去，我爭著付錢時，她們說我看不起人；我不付錢，她們又說我小氣。

現在做個
「男子漢」
真難！

　　　　李明

小李：

　　要是真有那麼好的對象，誰不想要一個「太太」呢？我也要人幫我洗衣、洗碗、燒飯、做家務啊！其實，做女人也不容易，既得出去賺錢，又得做家務。運氣好的，能同時做兩份工作，運氣不好的，像我媽，就得放棄⁵**好不容易才**找到的事，待在家裏照顧孩子。我並不是說職業女性比家庭主婦好，把孩子帶好也是一種很大的成就，但是母親和妻子都是沒有「收入」的工作。你願意⁶**為了**家庭幸福，放棄自己的事業，做個「家庭煮夫」嗎？哪一天男女才可能平等呢？

　　　　　　　　　　　　　　　　　　　　　　　　　美英

课文 Text

Use the following questions to guide your reading of the text.

1. 小李想要找什么样的对象？

2. 为什么小李说现在做个男人很不容易？

3. 为什么美英说现在做女人也很难？

王华、美英：

听说大家都有了对象，我也想找个爱人呢！我的她必须温柔、能干、听话，爱做家务，但是也能出去工作、赚钱。¹当我出门的时候，她会帮我整理好要带的东西；当我回家的时候，她已经烧好了很多我爱吃的菜，等我回来；当我需要人鼓励的时候，她能在我身边；当我需要考虑问题的时候，她能给我一些自由。²总之，我喜欢的对象不能太厉害，³任何事都应该先和我商量，⁴等我决定了再做。我不算挑剔，可是到现在还找不到女朋友。每次和女孩儿出去，我争着付钱时，她们说我看不起人；我不付钱，她们又说我小气。现在做个"男子汉"真难！

李明

小李：

要是真有那么好的对象，谁不想
要一个"太太"呢？我也要人帮我洗
衣、洗碗、烧饭、做家务啊！其实，
做女人也不容易，既得出去赚钱，又
得做家务。运气好的，能同时做两份
工作，运气不好的，象我妈，就得放
弃⁵**好不容易才**找到的事，待在家里

照顾孩子。我并不是说职业女性比家庭主妇好，把孩子带好也是一种
很大的成就，但是母亲和妻子都是没有"收入"的工作。你愿意⁶为
了家庭幸福，放弃自己的事业，做个"家庭煮夫"吗？哪一天男女才
可能平等呢？

美英

小對話 Mini-Dialogues

Read the supplementary dialogues for a better understanding of the text. See if you can memorize one and perform it in class.

(1) Indicating wishes

A:	我給你介紹一個對象，怎麼樣？	我给你介绍一个对象，怎么样？
Li:	好啊！	好啊！
A:	你喜歡什麼樣的姑娘？	你喜欢什么样的姑娘？
Li:	溫柔、聽話又能做家務的。	温柔、听话又能做家务的。
A:	做什麼樣的家務？	做什么样的家务？
Li:	什麼家務都做。	什么家务都做。
A:	那麼你會幫忙嗎？	那么你会帮忙吗？
Li:	我不行，我不會做飯，也沒洗過衣服。	我不行，我不会做饭，也没洗过衣服。
A:	我看你找個褓姆 bǎomǔ 好了。	我看你找个保姆好了。

A: Let me find a girlfriend for you. How about that?

Li: Great!

A: What kind of girls do you like?

Li: Those who are gentle, obedient, and can handle housework.

A: What kind of housework?

Li: All kinds of housework.

A: Will you help?

Li: No, I can't. I don't know how to cook, and I have never done the laundry.

A: I think you had better find a maid!

(2) Making concessions

Mom:	偉平，我花了好大的工夫，終於找到了一份工作。	伟平，我花了好大的工夫，终于找到了一份工作。
Dad:	你出去工作，那誰來照顧孩子啊？	你出去工作，那谁来照顾孩子啊？
Mom:	我的工作只是半天的。把孩子送去托兒所 tuō'érsuǒ，怎麼樣？	我的工作只是半天的。把孩子送去托儿所，怎么样？
Dad:	這樣不好，孩子容易生病。	这样不好，孩子容易生病。
Mom:	你能不能幫幫忙呢？	你能不能帮帮忙呢？
Dad:	我下午才下班 xiàbān，而且家不能沒有一個主婦啊！	我下午才下班，而且家里不能没有一个主妇啊！
Mom:	好吧，好吧！那我去把那份工作辭 cí 了。	好吧，好吧！那我去把那份工作辞了。

Mom: Weiping, after all of these hours I have finally found a job.

Dad: If you go to work, who will take care of the children?

Mom: I work only half days. How about sending the children to daycare?

Dad: That's not good. The children will get sick easily.

Mom: Can you help?

Dad: I won't be off from work till afternoon. Besides, it won't be a home without a housewife.

Mom: All right, all right. Then I will not take that job.

(3) Asking for and responding to help

Dad: 孩子的媽，快點兒燒飯，我餓死了。

孩子的妈，快点儿烧饭，我饿死了。

Mom: 我也餓死了！我剛下班回來，過來幫幫忙吧！

我也饿死了！我刚下班回来，过来帮帮忙吧！

Dad: 我總是越幫越忙，還是你燒飯吧！

我总是越帮越忙，还是你烧饭吧！

Mom: 你真會找藉口 jièkǒu。

你真会找借口。

Dad: 不是找藉口，你做飯做得比我好。

不是找借口，你做饭做得比我好。

Mom: 做飯也不是我的「專業」啊！我也累了一天了，我也想休息啊！

做饭也不是我的"专业"啊！我也累了一天了，我也想休息啊！

Dad: Mom, hurry up and cook. I am starving.

Mom: Me, too. I am just off from work. Come over and help.

Dad: The more I help, the worse it will be. I think it is better that you cook.

Mom: You are really good at finding excuses.

Dad: I am not finding an excuse. You do a better job cooking.

Mom: Cooking is not my "major"! I have also worked all day. I want to take a break.

(4) Summarizing opinions

Lin: 我覺得男女實在不平等！

我觉得男女实在不平等！

A: 本來就不平等嘛！男人能生孩子嗎？

本来就不平等嘛！男人能生孩子吗？

越幫越忙
more help→more work

借口
excuses

Lin:　　我說的不是那個。

A:　　　那是什麼？

Lin:　　女人做的事不比男人少，可是男人的收入多半比女人的高。

A:　　　你說得很有道理 dàolǐ。

Lin:　　而且女人在外面做事，如果做不好，別人就說 「她到底是個女人。」如果做得好，別人就說 「她根本不像個女人。」總之，女人難做！

我说的不是那个。

那是什么？

女人做的事不比男人少，可是男人的收入多半比女人的高。

你说得很有道理。

而且女人在外面做事，如果做不好，别人就说："她到底是个女人。"如果做得好，别人就说："她根本不象个女人。"总之，女人难做！

Lin: I think men and women are not equal.

A:　　They have never been equal. Can a man give birth to a child?

Lin: I don't mean that.

A:　　What do you mean then?

Lin: Women do the same jobs as men, but men, in most cases, are paid more.

A:　　What you say makes a lot of sense.

Lin: Besides, if a woman is not successful at work, others will say, "she is, after all, a woman." If she is successful, others say, "she is not a woman at all." In short, it is very difficult to be a woman!

灶神

小故事 Stories

Read the following tale for your own enjoyment and for your understanding of the highlighted expression that is relevant to the theme of the chapter.

 自知之明 zì zhī zhī míng

❀ 小李沒有自知之明，怎麼找得到對象？

戰國時候有個人叫鄒忌，長得很漂亮。一天早上，他穿了衣服，照著鏡子，問妻子說：「拿我和徐公比較，誰漂亮？」妻子回答：「你漂亮，徐公怎麼比得上你呢？」

徐公是一個有名的美男子。鄒忌不太相信，就又問他的小太太：「我和徐公，誰漂亮？」小太太也說：「當然你漂亮！」第二天，來了一個客人，鄒忌就問他：「我和徐公，誰漂亮？」客人說：「徐公不如你漂亮！」

戰國	Zhànguó	the Warring States period (475–221 B.C.)
鄒忌	Zōujì	name of a person
照鏡子	zhào jìngzi	to look in the mirror
徐公	Xúgōng	name of a person
比得上	bǐdeshàng	can compare with, compare favorably with
美男子	měinánzǐ	handsome man
小太太	xiǎotàitai	concubine
客人	kèrén	guest
不如	bùrú	not as good as

又過了一天，徐公來了。鄒忌看看他，覺得自己其實沒有徐公那麼漂亮。他想為什麼妻子、小太太、客人都說自己更漂亮呢？這是因為妻子愛我，小太太怕我，客人有事要我幫忙啊！

✎ 自知之明的意思是＿＿＿＿＿＿＿＿＿＿＿＿＿＿＿＿＿＿

自知之明 zì zhī zhī míng

✿ 小李没有自知之明，怎么找得到对象？

战国时候有个人叫邹忌，长得很漂亮。一天早上，他穿了衣服，照着镜子，问妻子说："拿我和徐公比较，谁漂亮？"妻子回答："你漂亮，徐公怎么比得上你呢？"

徐公是一个有名的美男子。邹忌不太相信，就又问他的小太太："我和徐公，谁漂亮？"小太太也说："当然你漂亮！"第二天，来了一个客人，邹忌就问他："我和徐公，谁漂亮？"客人说："徐公不如你漂亮！"

又过了一天，徐公来了。邹忌看看他，觉得自己其实没有徐公那么漂亮。他想为什么妻子、小太太、客人都说自己更漂亮呢？这是因为妻子爱我，小太太怕我，客人有事要我帮忙啊！

战国	Zhànguó	the Warring States period (475–221 B.C.)
邹忌	Zōujì	name of a person
照镜子	zhào jìngzi	to look in the mirror
徐公	Xúgōng	name of a person
比得上	bǐdeshàng	can compare with, compare favorably with
美男子	měinánzǐ	handsome man
小太太	xiǎotàitai	concubine
客人	kèrén	guest
不如	bùrú	not as good as

漢字 Characters

Study the following selected characters for further enrichment of your writing and vocabulary.

亻 rén 'person' +
壬 rén 'a carrying pole supported in the middle with one object at each end'

任

任何	rènhé	any, whatever
責任	zérèn	duty, responsibility
主任	zhǔrèn*	director, head, chair

A: 他是個很負責任的人嗎？

B: 對，他做任何事你都可以放心。

rèn 6
to serve in a position, to allow

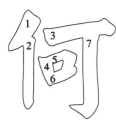

亻 rén 'person' + 可 kě phonetic

何

| 如何 | rúhé* | how, how about it |
| 無論如何 | wúlùnrúhé* | in any case, at any rate |

A: 你覺得我的想法如何？

B: 無論如何你不應該歧視別人。

Compare: 可 kě 哥 gē

hé 7
what, who, why, how

A grown up 大 man, with a 一 pin in his hair, to show that he is of age

夫

丈夫	zhàngfu*	husband
大夫	dàifu*	physician, doctor
工夫	gōngfu	time, skill, effort

A: 聽說她的丈夫是個大夫。

B: 你真有工夫，整天管別人的事。

Compare: 替 tì

fū 4
husband, man

女 nǚ a woman is holding a 帚 zhǒu broom

妇

主婦	zhǔfù	housewife
婦女	fùnǚ*	women
夫婦	fūfù*	husband and wife

A: 現在很多婦女不想做家庭主婦。

B: 所以夫婦之間容易有問題。

fù 11
woman, wife

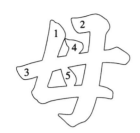

The original picture is like 女 nǚ 'woman,' plus breasts

母親	mǔqin	mother
父母	fùmǔ	parents
母校	mǔxiào*	alma mater
母雞	mǔjī*	hen

A: 你父母都在哪兒工作？

B: 父親在他的母校教書，母親在家。

Compare: 每 měi

mǔ 5
mother, female (of birds/etc.)

頁 yè 'head' + 雇 gù phonetic

| 照顧 | zhàogù | to look after, to care for |
| 顧客 | gùkè* | customer, client |

A: 那家店的顧客真多！

B: 你買東西的時候，他們還幫你照顧孩子呢！

gù 21
to turn round and look at, to attend to

广 'house' + 廷 tíng 'royal court' —court, palace hall, mansion, house family

家庭	jiātíng	family, household
大家庭	dàjiātíng*	extended family
小家庭	xiǎojiātíng*	nuclear family

A: 你喜歡大家庭還是小家庭？

B: 大或小都沒關係，只要幸福就好了。

Compare: 廳 tīng

ting 9
hall, front courtyard

矛 máo 'spear' + 攵 pū 'beat' + 力 lì 'strength' —to apply one's force

家務	jiāwù	household duties
服務	fúwù	service, to serve
服務員	fúwùyuán*	attendant, clerk
國務院	guówùyuàn*	U.S. State Department

A: 在家都是你做家務嗎？

B: 有時候我愛人也會為我服務一下。

wù 11
affair, business, must

耳 ěr 'ear' +
音 yīn 'sound' +
戈 gē
'weapon'—the
man with a lance
who commands:
profession

职

zhí 18
duty, job, post, office

| 職業 | zhíyè | occupation |
| 職員 | zhíyuán* | office worker |

B: 他現在的職業是什麼？

A: 我也不清楚，聽說他在銀行做個小職員。

A 木 mù tree
crowded with its
芔 foliage —
the moral
foliage, the
deeds of a man

业

yè 13
line of business,
industry, job

事業	shìyè	career
專業	zhuānyè	specialty, major
作業	zuòyè*	school asignment
工業	gōngyè*	industry
商業	shāngyè*	commerce, trade

A: 他的職業跟他的專業有關係嗎？

B: 沒有，可是他的事業搞得很大。

田 represents the
grain, on the top
of which the
germ is coming
up: beginning,
origin, cause

由

yóu 5
to let (sb. do sth.), via,
by

| 自由 | zìyóu | freedom, free |
| 由於 | yóuyú | owing/due/thanks to |

A: 你父母給你很多自由嗎？

B: 由於我還小，很多事都是他們決定。

Compare: 油 yóu 抽 chōu 黃 huáng

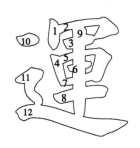

辶 chuò 'go' +
軍 jūn
phonetic

运

yùn 12
to carry, fortune, fate

運氣	yùnqi	fortune, luck
幸運	xìngyùn*	very fortunate
運動	yùndòng*	exercise, sports

A: 我很幸運，身體一直很好。

B: 那不是因為你運氣好，而是因為你常常運動。

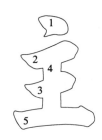

Picture of a lamp with a flame on top, symbolizing a master

主

zhǔ 5
master, to manage, main

主婦	zhǔfù	housewife
主人	zhǔrén*	master, host, owner
主義	zhǔyì	doctrine, -ism

A: 我覺得女人不應該在家當主婦。

B: 你是不是受了女性主義的影響？

Compare: 注 zhù　住 zhù　往 wǎng

卓 + 人 over 干 'trunk of a tree'—to work, occupation, ability

干

gàn 13
stem, trunk, to do

能幹	nénggàn	able, competent
樹幹	shùgàn*	tree trunk
幹活	gànhuó*	to work on a job

A: 那個小伙子很能幹嗎？

B: 對，他什麼活兒都會幹。

Compare: 午 wǔ　趕 gǎn　乾 gān

Two hands (爫 彐) struggling for possession of 丨 a stick

争

zhēng 8
to contend, to vie, to argue

| 爭著 | zhēngzhe | to fight for, to contend |
| 爭論 | zhēnglùn | to argue, to dispute |

A: 你們倆不要爭著說話。

B: 好，應該誰先說呢？

Compare: 淨 jìng　睜 zhēng　靜 jìng

頁 yè 'head' + 原 yuán phonetic

原

yuàn 19
wish, desire

願意	yuànyì	to be willing, to wish
願望	yuànwàng*	desire, wish, aspiration
自願	zìyuàn*	to act voluntarily

A: 你願意放棄一切，到中國去留學嗎？

B: 我從小就有這個願望。

而 ér 'a picture of a beard' + 雨 yǔ phonetic

需要	xūyào	to need, to want, to require
必需	bìxū*	essential, indispensable
必需品	bìxūpǐn*	necessities

A: 你需要我幫你的忙嗎？

B: 幫我買一些生活必需品吧！

xū 14
to need, to want, to require

The 彡 xū hair of the 頁 face

| 必須 | bìxū | must, have to |

A: 學中文的學生都必須做什麼？

B: 必須每天學習漢字。

Compare: 需 xu

xū 12
must, have to, beard

火 huǒ 'fire' + 堯 yáo phonetic

| 燒飯 | shāofàn | to cook |
| 發燒 | fāshāo | to have a fever |

A: 我發燒了，很不舒服。

B: 我給你燒飯，吃些好東西就好了。

shāo 16
to burn, to cook, to roast, fever

From 止 zhǐ 'foot,' with a 一 line below it

總之	zǒngzhī	in a word
之間	zhījiān	between, among
之一	zhīyī	one of

A: 你們之間到底有什麼問題？

B: 總之，我跟他談不來。

zhī 3
it, him, her, this, to go

語法和用法 Grammar and Usage

Pay attention to the function of the structure and then study the example sentences.

1. Expressing a temporal condition

（當）…（的）時（候）	(dāng)…(de) shí(hou)	by the time
（每）當…（的）時（候）	(měi)dāng…(de) shí(hou)	whenever

當我出門**的時候**，她幫我整理好要帶的東西……

1. 你昨天很晚才回家吧！　　你昨天很晚才回家吧！　　You went home late last night, right?

對，當我回去的時候，孩子已經睡了。　　对，当我回去的时候，孩子已经睡了。　　Yes. When I came home, my children were all asleep.

2. 你在這兒住了很長時間吧！　　你在这儿住了很长时间吧！　　I suppose you have lived here for a long time.

對，當我十歲的時候，我們就搬來這兒了。　　对，当我十岁的时候，我们就搬来这儿了。　　Yes. When I was ten, my family moved here.

3. 每當你想家的時候，你都會做什麼？　　每当你想家的时候，你都会做什么？　　When you feel homesick, what do you do?

我都會把家人的照片拿出來看。　　我都会把家人的照片拿出来看。　　I take out my family's pictures and look at them.

Note that 當…的時候 can mean either "at the time when" or "whenever." The context will usually make it clear which meaning is referred to. 當 can also be omitted, and it will sound more colloquial. If 每 precedes 當, it always means "whenever."

2. Expressing summation which brings closure to a series

comments 1, 2, 3, 總之…	…zǒngzhī…	to sum up; in short; anyway

總之，我喜歡的對象不能太厲害。

1.	那家店到底賣些什麼東西？	那家店到底卖些什么东西？	What does that store actually sell?
	那兒有吃的、喝的、穿的、用的，總之，什麼都賣。	那儿有吃的、喝的、穿的、用的，总之，什么都卖。	There are things to eat, drink, wear, and use. In short, they sell everything.
2.	他到底長什麼樣子？	他到底长什么样子？	What does he actually look like?
	他又高大又好看，總之，就是我一直想要找的對象。	他又高大又好看，总之，就是我一直想要找的对象。	He is big, tall, and handsome. In short, he's the guy that I've been looking for all along.
3.	你們為什麼分手了？	你们为什么分手了？	Why did you break up?
	說來話長，總之，他不願意放棄他的工作，我也不能搬到他那兒去。	说来话长，总之，他不愿意放弃他的工作，我也不能搬到他那儿去。	It's a long story. Anyway, he is not willing to give up his job, and I cannot move to his place.

總之, is a conjunction used to sum up a series of points in a discourse. Thus, there should be a list of (at least 3) sentences, clauses, verbs (example 1) preceding it.

3. Expressing the indefinite

任何O (S)都V	rènhé…dōu…	any, every

任何事都應該先和我商量……

1.	我什麼時候可以來看你們？	我什么时候可以来看你们？	When can I come to visit you?
	任何時候我們都歡迎你來。	任何时候我们都欢迎你来。	You are welcome anytime.

2.　他還需要人照顧　　他还需要人照顾　　Does he still need someone
　　嗎？　　　　　　　吗？　　　　　　　to look after him?

　　不用，他現在任何　　不用，他现在任何　　No. He can handle
　　事都能自己做。　　　事都能自己做。　　　everything by himself now.

3.　你們不怕將來生活　　你们不怕将来生活　　Aren't you afraid of
　　遇到困難嗎？　　　　遇到困难吗？　　　　running into difficulties
　　　　　　　　　　　　　　　　　　　　　in the future?

　　我覺得任何困難我　　我觉得任何困难我　　I think that we can
　　們都有辦法克服。　　们都有办法克服。　　overcome any difficulties.

The use of 任何 is straightforward. Just remember that it is coupled with the adverb
都, which precedes the verb. 任何…都 is the formal expression equivalent to the forms
QW+ 都.

4.　Expressing a sequence of upcoming events

S（等）V$_1$（了）（以後）再V$_2$　　(děng)…(le)(yǐhòu) zài…	S does V$_2$ after V$_1$

任何事都應該先和我商量，**等**我決定了**再**做。

1.　我餓死了，我們先　　我饿死了，我们先　　I am dying of hunger.
　　吃飯吧！　　　　　　吃饭吧！　　　　　　Let's eat first.

　　等大家都來了再　　　等大家都来了再　　　Wait till everyone is here.
　　吃。　　　　　　　　吃。

2.　我能不能去參加那　　我能不能去参加那　　Can I go to that dance
　　個舞會？　　　　　　个舞会？　　　　　　party?

　　等爸爸回來再說　　　等爸爸回来再说　　　We'll talk about this after
　　吧。　　　　　　　　吧。　　　　　　　　your father comes home.

3.　他的魚全死了。　　　他的鱼全死了。　　　His fish are all dead.

　　他剛跟女朋友分　　　他刚跟女朋友分　　　He just broke up with his
　　手，等他心情好一　　手，等他心情好一　　girlfriend. Let's not tell
　　點再告訴他吧。　　　点再告诉他吧。　　　him about the fish until
　　　　　　　　　　　　　　　　　　　　　he feels a little bit better.

等…再, literally 'wait until…(and) then,' is a pattern used to express a sequence of actions or events. Note that this pattern occurs in the future. If the actions occur in the past, 等…才 is used. For example, the sentence 等你來了我再走 means "I won't go until you come." The sentence 等你來了我才走 means "I didn't go until you came."

5. Expressing the difficulty of achieving something

S好(不)容易才V	…hǎo(bù)róngyì cái…	S went through great difficulty before S finally V

像我媽，就得放棄**好不容易才**找到的事，待在家裏照顧孩子。

1.	你為什麼這麼生氣？	你为什么这么生气？	Why were you so mad?
	我好不容易才做好的飛機，被妹妹搞壞了。	我好不容易才做好的飞机，被妹妹搞坏了。	My little sister broke a plane that I had spent a long time working on.
2.	今天的功課真多！	今天的功课真多！	There is so much homework today.
	可不是嗎？我好不容易才把今天的功課做完！	可不是吗？我好不容易才把今天的功课做完！	Isn't that true? I worked a long time before I finally finished my homework.
3.	我看你的辦法不太好。	我看你的办法不太好。	I don't think your idea is good.
	我好容易才想到這個辦法，你居然說不好。	我好容易才想到这个办法，你居然说不好。	It took me a long time to come up with this idea, and you say that it is lousy!

Note that the adverbs 好容易 and 好不容易 both mean 'with great difficulty.' They always precede 才 'then and only then.'

6. Expressing the reason for doing something

為了A, B	wèile…, …	In order to A, B…
B是為了A	…shì wèile…	B is for the cause of A
B為的是A	…wèideshì…	B is for the cause of A

你願意**為了**家庭幸福，放棄自己的事業……

1.	你願意為了她，放棄那份收入很高的工作嗎？	你愿意为了她，放弃那份收入很高的工作吗？	Are you willing to give up that well-paying job for her?
	我什麼都願意做。	我什么都愿意做。	I am willing to do anything.
2.	你這麼做是為了什麼？	你这么做是为了什么？	For what did you do this?
	我這麼做全是為了她。	我这么做全是为了她。	I did this all for her.
3.	為什麼很多人想移民來美國？	为什么很多人想移民来美国？	Why do many people want to immigrate to the U.S.?
	他們為的是給自己的孩子比較好的生活。	他们为的是给自己的孩子比较好的生活。	They do so in order to give their children a better life.

為了, a conjunction, always introduces the purpose or cause of an action or situation stated in the following main clause of the sentence. To express purpose or cause after the action or situation, use 是為了 or 為的是 instead. Compare this pattern with 為 (L8, G5).

文化點滴 Culture Notes

1. **Boys over girls**: In the past, Chinese people valued boys over girls, 重男輕女 zhòng nán qīng nǚ. Thus, women were often considered inferior and not encouraged to study, as illustrated in the saying, "A woman without talent is a woman of virtue" 女子無才便是德 nǚzǐ wú cái biànshì dé. Traditional women were told to follow a code of behavior, three obediences and four virtues, 三從四德 sān cóng sì dé, which say that a woman will obey her father before marriage, her husband after marriage, and her son after her husband's death. For a woman to gain status in a family she needed to give birth to sons, and those who couldn't bear an heir sought concubines for their husbands. The status and condition of Chinese women today has greatly improved. Yet in the countryside many peasants still hold the traditional concept of valuing boys over girls. Thus, orphan girls and infanticide are still a problem.

2. **Insiders vs. outsiders**: Underlying the concept of 重男輕女 is another traditional idea that distinguishes insiders from outsiders 內外有別 nèi wài yǒu bié. In general, daughters are considered "outsiders" because eventually they will marry someone out of the family and go wherever their husbands go 嫁雞隨雞、嫁狗隨狗 jià jī suí jī, jià gǒu suí gǒu. Sons, bearing the name of the lineage, are considered insiders. This concept is most evident in Chinese kinship terms. While the children of one's son is called 孫子 sūnzi, 孫女 sūnnǚ, the children of one's daughter is called 外孫 wàisūn, 外孫女 wàisūnnǚ. The same logic applies to older generations. The parents of one's mother are called 外祖父 wàizǔfù, 外祖母 wàizǔmǔ, yet the the parents of one's father are simply called 祖父 zǔfù, 祖母 zǔmǔ.

3. **Men and women**: In the past, a man was said to be in charge of work outside the home and a woman took care of work inside 男主外、女主內 nán zhǔ wài, nǚ zhǔ nèi. Today, there is much more flexibility to gender roles. There are many women, often referred to as 女強人 nǚqiángrén, who are in control of both household and career. The "liberated men" often help prepare the evening meal, do housework, look after the children, and generally put wife and family first. Nowadays, there is also a tendency for young couples to live by themselves "小家庭 xiǎojiāting," instead of living with their parents "大家庭 dàjiāting."

歌兒 Songs

快樂的男女
Happy Couple

Moderato   詞、曲：李毓真

(女)在 家　　　做 家 務，　　　一 天 到 晚 忙 東 忙　西，
Zài jiā lǐ　　　zuò jiāwù,　　　yìtiān dào wǎn máng dōng máng xī,
At home doing housework,　　　I am busy here and there all day long.

沒 有 自 由 還　被 你 看　　不 起 (男)工 作　了
měiyǒu zìyóu, hái　bèi nǐ kàn　　buqǐ.　　Gōngzuò le
I don't have freedom, and still, I'm disregarded by you.　　I can't help

一 整 天，　　心 情 難 免 會 不　　好。　　是 什 麼 道 理
yìzhěngtiān,　　xīnqíng nánmiǎn huì bù　　hǎo.　　Shì shénme dàolǐ
being in a bad mood after a whole day of work.　　What's the reason in

還 叫 我 洗　碗？　(女)女 人 希　　望 的 不 是
hái jiào wǒ　xǐwǎn?　　Nǚ rén xī　　wàng de bú shì
asking me to do the dishes?　　What a woman looks forward to is not

男 人 養，　任 何 事　　最 好 能 和 我 商 量。
nánrén yǎng,　rènhé shì　　zuìhǎo néng hé wǒ shāngliáng.
for a man to feed her.　Whatever happens, it is best that you discuss it with me.

(男) 不 管 誰　　　遇 到 困 難 都 需 要　　　鼓 勵，
Bùguǎn shéi　　　yùdào kùnnán dōu xūyào　　　gǔlì,
No matter who faces difficulty, we all need encouragement,

當 難 過 的　　　時 候，　　　才 不 會 放 棄。
dāng nánguò de　　　shíhòu,　　　cái bú huì fàngqì.
so that we won't give up when we are sad.

(男女) 快 樂 的　　　男 女 關 係　　　並 不 能 靠 運 氣。
Kuàilè de　　　nánnǚ guānxi,　　　bìng bù néng kào yùn qi,
A happy man-and-woman relationship cannot depend on luck.

總 之 兩 個 人 要 一 起 努 力，　　　你 也 能 做 到
zǒngzhī liǎng ge rén yào yìqǐ nǔlì,　　　nǐ yě néng zuòdào,
In short, both people need to strive together.　　　You, too, can make it

只　　　要 你 願　　　意。
zhǐ　　　yào nǐ yuàn　　　yì.
if you want to.

✍ **My questions:**

第十課

Theme Education and Career

Communicative Objectives
- Urging someone to do something else
- Expressing doubts
- Giving consent
- Objecting to an idea

Focus on Characters
- 即使游泳、尊敬藝術、處理成績、聯畫立功、試例鋼育

Grammar Focus
- S不但V_1O_1，連O_2也V_1
- V著玩兒（的）
- 在…看來
- 就算/即使…，S也…
- 在…的N下；在…上
- 連A都…，更別說B了

難道你想一輩子做個窮光蛋？

生詞 Vocabulary

Study the following words for their pronunciation and meaning. When an area is shaded, guess at the meaning of the word based on its constituent characters and then fill in the blank. Read the usage of words and related terms (antonyms, synonyms, compounds sharing the constituent characters, etc.) and try to answer the sample questions in Chinese. Note that proper nouns or incidental terms are not numbered.

◎By Order of Appearance

1. 難道　　nándào　　Adv　　Do you mean to say that…?　　[hard-say]
   难道

   你學了兩年的中文，難道還不懂這句話的意思嗎？

   你学了两年的中文，难道还不懂这句话的意思吗？

2. 一輩子　　yíbèizi　　N　　all one's life, a lifetime　　[one-lifetime-suffix]
   一辈子

   一輩子留在這兒，你願意嗎？

   一辈子留在这儿，你愿意吗？

3. 窮光蛋　　qióngguāng　　N　　poor wretch, pauper　　[poor-empty-egg]
   穷光蛋　　dàn

   →笨蛋 bèndàn 'dummy'、壞蛋 huàidàn 'scoundrel'

   她為什麼要嫁給那個窮光蛋？

   她为什么要嫁给那个穷光蛋？

4. 回信　　huíxìn　　VO　　　　　　　　[return-letter]

   那個學校給你回信了沒有？

   那个学校给你回信了没有？

5. 理想　　lǐxiǎng　　N/　　ideal　　[principle-think]
   　　　　　　　　Adj

   你的理想是什麼？你想你什麼時候能實現自己的理想？

   你的理想是什么？你想你什么时候能实现自己的理想？

6. 現實　　xiànshí　　N/　　reality, practical　　[present-true]
   现实　　　　　　Adj　　vs.實現

   你覺得現實和你的理想有距離嗎？

   你觉得现实和你的理想有距离吗？

7. 例外　　lìwài　　N　　exception　　[instance-outside]

   學生都怕考試，你也不例外嗎？

学生都怕考试，你也不例外吗？

| 8. | 從小 | cóngxiǎo | Adv | ████████████ | [since-small] |

从小

你從小就對什麼感興趣？

你从小就对什么感兴趣？

| 9. | 作家 | zuòjiā | N | writer | [compose-suffix] |

→畫家、藝術家、音樂家、科kē學家

你最喜歡哪一位中國作家？

你最喜欢哪一位中国作家？

| 10. | 前途 | qiántú | N | future, career, prospects | [front-road] |

你覺得學什麼比較有前途？

你觉得学什么比较有前途？

| 11. | 好處 | hǎochu | N | benefit, advantage, gain | [good-point] |

好处

你覺得什麼對身體有好處？

你觉得什么对身体有好处？

| 12. | 在…看來 | zài…kànlái | IE | in sb.'s view | |

在…看来

在你看來，什麼職業最好？為什麼？

在你看来，什么职业最好？为什么？

| 13. | 就算 | jiùsuàn | Conj | even if, granted that | [simply-count] |

就算你給我錢，我也不會幫你這個忙。

就算你给我钱，我也不会帮你这个忙。

| 14. | 即使 | jíshǐ | Conj | even, even if/though | [even if-make] |

即使你今天不睡覺，也考不好的。

即使你今天不睡觉，也考不好的。

| 15. | 目前 | mùqián | N | at present, at the moment | [eye-front] |

目前美國的經濟怎麼樣？

目前美国的经济怎么样？

| 16. | 沒關係 | méiguānxi | IE | it doesn't matter | [no-relation] |

沒關系

為什麼你覺得考不上大學也沒關係？

为什么你觉得考不上大学也没关系？

Characters with Many Strokes

輩　窮　蛋　實　例　途　處　算　即　關

17.	選擇 选择	xuǎnzé	V/N	to select, to opt	[select-choose]

你的專業是什麼？為什麼選擇這個專業？

你的专业是什么？为什么选择这个专业？

18.	熱門 热门	rèmén	Adj/ N	in great demand	[hot-opening]

↔冷門

現在學什麼最熱門？

现在学什么最热门？

19.	成績 成绩	chéngjī/jì	N	grade, achievement	[accomplish-grade]

你哪一門課的成績最好？

你哪一门课的成绩最好？

20.	公立	gōnglì	Adj	public, established and maintained by the government	[public-set up]

你覺得公立學校好，還是私立 sīlì 'private' 學校好？

你觉得公立学校好，还是私立学校好？

21.	感	gǎn	N	sense	

→成就感、幽默感、好感

什麼事讓你很有成就感？

什么事让你很有成就感？

22.	實現 实现	shíxiàn	V	to achieve	[real-appear]

你打算怎麼實現你的理想？

你打算怎么实现你的理想？

23.	理解	lǐjiě	V	to understand, to comprehend	[manage-understand]

你能理解你父母的心情嗎？

你能理解你父母的心情吗？

24.	重視 重视	zhòngshì	V	to value, to take sth. seriously	[heavy-look]

你覺得美國人重視什麼？中國人呢？

你觉得美国人重视什么？中国人呢？

25.	教育	jiàoyù	N/V	education, to educate	[teach-raise]

你覺得美國和中國的教育有什麼不同？

你觉得美国和中国的教育有什么不同？

26.	畫畫兒 画画儿	huàhuàr	VO	to draw pictures	[draw-plan]

你很會畫畫兒嗎？想當畫家嗎？

你很会画画儿吗？想当画家吗？

| 27. | 鋼琴 | gāngqín | N | piano | [steel-musical instrument] |
| | 钢琴 | | | | |

你會彈鋼琴嗎？幾歲開始學的？

你会弹钢琴吗？几岁开始学的？

| 28. | 游泳 | yóuyǒng | V | to swim | [swim-swim] |

你會游泳嗎？游得好不好？

你会游泳吗？游得好不好？

| 29. | 什麼的 | shénmede | IE | and so on, and what not | [what-suffix] |
| | 什么的 | | | | |

你想吃點兒蛋糕什麼的嗎？

你想吃点儿蛋糕什么的吗？

| 30. | 考試 | kǎoshì | N/V | examination, to test | [take test/try] |
| | 考试 | | | | |

→大考、小考、期中考、考題、考卷juàn

你昨天的考試考得怎麼樣？

你昨天的考试考得怎么样？

| 31. | 考上 | kǎoshàng | RV | to pass an entrance examination | [take test-up] |

每年有多少中國學生能考上大學？

每年有多少中国学生能考上大学？

| 32. | 名校 | míngxiào | N | famous school | [famous-school] |

美國東部有哪些名校？

美国东部有哪些名校？

| 33. | 成功 | chénggōng | Adj/ V/N | successful, to succeed, success | [accomplish-meritorious service] |

在你看來，什麼是「成功」？

在你看来，什么是"成功"？

| 34. | 別人 | biérén | N | other people | [other-people] |

你怕不怕別人笑你是個窮光蛋？

你怕不怕别人笑你是个穷光蛋？

| 35. | 尊敬 | zūnjìng | V/ Adj | to respect, honorable | [respect-respect] |

你最尊敬的人是誰？

你最尊敬的人是谁？

Characters with Many Strokes

選　擇　熱　績　解　畫　鋼　琴　游　尊

| 36. | 畫家
画家 | huàjiā | N | painter | [draw-suffix] |

在你看來，哪個畫家最偉大？

在你看来，哪个画家最伟大？

| 37. | 贊成
赞成 | zànchéng | V | to approve, to endorse | [support-all right] |

↔反對

你的父母贊成你學中文嗎？

你的父母赞成你学中文吗？

| 38. | 藝術
艺术 | yìshù | N | art, skill | [craftsmanship-technique] |

你了解中國藝術嗎？

你了解中国艺术吗？

| 39. | 道理 | dàolǐ | N | reason, sense, argument | [way-logic] |

你覺得誰說的話很有道理？

你觉得谁说的话很有道理？

| 40. | 養活
养活 | yǎnghuo | RV | to support, to feed | [raise-alive] |

在麥當勞 Màidāngláo 'McDonald' 打工能養活一家老小嗎？

在麦当劳打工能养活一家老小吗？

| 41. | 貢獻
贡献 | gòngxiàn | N/V | contribution, to contribute | [contribute-offer] |

A對B有貢獻/做出貢獻

誰對中國做出了很大的貢獻？

谁对中国做出了很大的贡献？

| 42. | 商 | shāng | N | business | |

要是我想學商，應該申請哪個學校？

要是我想学商，应该申请哪个学校？

| 43. | 開夜車
开夜车 | kāi yèchē | VO | | [drive-night-car] |

你為什麼這幾天都在開夜車？

你为什么这几天都在开夜车？

| 44. | 聯繫
联系 | liánxì | V | to contact | [join-tie] |

你跟你的好朋友多久沒聯繫了？

你跟你的好朋友多久没联系了？

Characters with Many Strokes

畫　贊　藝　術　道　養　獻　聯　繫

◎ By Grammatical Categories

Nouns/Pronouns/Measure Words

感	gǎn	sense
商	shāng	business
鋼琴	gāngqín	piano
別人	biérén	other people
作家	zuòjiā	writer
畫家	huàjiā	painter
窮光蛋	qióngguāngdàn	poor wretch, pauper
名校	míngxiào	famous school
成績	chéngjī/jì	grade, achievement
現實	xiànshí	reality, practical
理想	lǐxiǎng	ideal
考試	kǎoshì	examination, to test

教育	jiàoyù	education, to educate
道理	dàolǐ	reason, sense, argument
藝術	yìshù	art, skill
貢獻	gòngxiàn	contribution, to contribute
前途	qiántú	future, prospects
好處	hǎochu	benefit, advantage, gain
例外	lìwài	exception
目前	mùqián	at present, at the moment
一輩子	yíbèizi	all one's life, a lifetime

Verbs/Stative Verbs/Adjectives

實現	shíxiàn	to achieve
理解	lǐjiě	to understand, to comprehend
贊成	zànchéng	to approve, to endorse
重視	zhòngshì	to value, to take sth. seriously
尊敬	zūnjìng	to respect, honorable
選擇	xuǎnzé	to select, to opt
考上	kǎoshàng	to pass an entrance examination
養活	yǎnghuo	to support, to feed

聯繫	liánxì	to contact
回信	huíxìn	to write in reply
游泳	yóuyǒng	to swim
畫畫兒	huàhuàr	to draw pictures
開夜車	kāi yèchē	to burn the midnight oil
公立	gōnglì	public
熱門	rèmén	in great demand
成功	chénggōng	successful, to succeed, success

Adverbs and Others

難道	nándào	Do you mean to say that…?
從小	cóngxiǎo	from childhood
就算	jiùsuàn	even if, granted that
即使	jíshǐ	even, even though

什麼的	shénmede	and so on, and what not
沒關係	méiguānxi	it doesn't matter
在…看來	zài…kànlái	in sb.'s view

◎ By Pinyin

Entries with * indicate lexical items used in Mini-Dialogues and of possible interest for supplemental study.

biérén	别人	other people	méiguānxi	没关系	it doesn't matter
chénggōng	成功	successful	míngxiào	名校	famous school
chéngjī/jì	成绩	grade	mùqián	目前	at present
chūmíng*	出名	famous, well-known	nándào	难道	Do you mean to say that…?
cóngxiǎo	从小	from childhood	qiántú	前途	future, prospects
dàolǐ	道理	reason, sense, argument	qióngguāng dàn	穷光蛋	poor wretch
gāngqín	钢琴	piano	rèmén	热门	in great demand
gǎn	感	sense	shāng	商	business
gōnglì	公立	public	shénmede	什么的	and so on
gòngxiàn	贡献	contribution	shíjì*	实际	practical
hǎochu	好处	benefit	shíxiàn	实现	to realize
huàhuàr	画画儿	to draw pictures	tán*	弹	to play
huàjiā	画家	painter	xiànshí	现实	reality
huíxìn	回信	to write in reply	xuǎnzé	选择	to select
jiàoyù	教育	education	yǎnghuo	养活	to support
jíshǐ	即使	even, even if/though	yíbèizi	一辈子	all one's life, a lifetime
jiùsuàn	就算	even if	yīnyuèjiā*	音乐家	musician
kāi yèchē	开夜车	to burn the midnight oil	yìshù	艺术	art
kǎoshàng	考上	to pass an entrance examination	yóuyǒng	游泳	to swim
			zài…kànlái	在…看来	in sb.'s view
kǎoshì	考试	test, to test	zànchéng	赞成	to approve
liánxì	联系	to contact	zhòngshì	重视	to value
lǐjiě	理解	to understand	zūnjìng	尊敬	to respect
lìwài	例外	exception	zuòjiā	作家	writer
lǐxiǎng	理想	ideal			

課文 Text

Use the following questions to guide your reading of the text.

1. 王華為什麼說理想和現實總是有距離？

2. 小李覺得中國父母對教育的看法怎麼樣？

3. 小李為什麼決定學商？

 小李：

　　對不起，你上次的電子郵件我沒有立刻回。你心中的「她」聽起來太美了，只怕是找不到的。理想和現實總是有距離，聽說我那個「大牛」了嗎？我看[1]**不但**交朋友是這樣，**連**學習**也**不例外。

　　我從小就對文學感興趣，想當作家，但是我爸媽跟美英的父母一樣，認為那根本沒有前途、沒有「好處」。小說寫[2]**著玩兒**還行，可這種愛好不能當飯吃。[3]**在**他們**看來**，學習就是為了將來有一份好的工作，[4]**就算**目前沒有興趣**也**沒關係。就這樣，[5]**在**父母**的**「鼓勵」下我選擇了電腦這個熱門的專業。雖然我在學校的成績一直很好，上的也是最有名的公立大學，可是我一

直沒有什麼成就感，不太開心。真羨慕像小高這樣的老美，他們多半能實現自己的理想，為自己的興趣、為今天的快樂學習。

　　　　　　　　　　　　　　　　　　　　王華

王華：

　　我很能理解你的心情。我看所有的中國父母都差不多，他們雖然重視教育，從小就送孩子去學畫畫兒、學鋼琴、學游泳什麼的，可是他們最關心的還是考試和成績。他們要孩子考上名校，做個「成功」的人，受到別人的尊敬。我跟你一樣，也沒實現自己的理想。從前我想當個畫家，可是我父母不贊成我學藝術，他們問我：「難道你想一輩子做個窮光蛋嗎？」他們的話也很有道理，雖然什麼工作都好，可是如果我[6]**連**自己**都**養不活，還談什麼興趣，**更別說**要對社會有什麼貢獻了。所以我決定學商，為自己的生活、為明天的幸福努力。期末考快到了，需要開夜車、趕報告，不能再花太多時間寫信了。考試以後再聯繫吧！

                                                    李明

课文 Text

Use the following questions to guide your reading of the text.

1. 王华为什么说理想和现实总是有距离？

2. 小李觉得中国父母对教育的看法怎么样？

3. 小李为什么决定学商？

 小李：

对不起，你上次的电子邮件我没有立刻回。你心中的"她"听起来太美了，只怕是找不到的。理想和现实总是有距离，听说我那个"大牛"了吗？我看[1]**不但**交朋友是这样，**连**学习**也**不例外。

我从小就对文学感兴趣，想当作家，但是我爸妈跟美英的父母一样，认为那根本没有前途、没有"好处"。小说写[2]**著玩儿**还行，可这种爱好不能当饭吃。[3]**在**他们**看来**，学习就是为了将来有一份好的工作，[4]**就算**目前没有兴趣**也**没关系。就这样，[5]**在**父母**的**"鼓励"下我选择了电脑这个热门的专业。虽然我在学校的成绩一直很好，上的也是最有名的公立大学，可是我一直没有什么成就感，不太开心。真羡慕象小高这样的老美，他们多半能实现自己的理想，为自己的兴趣、为今天的快乐学习。

王华

王华：

我很能理解你的心情。我看所有的中国父母都差不多，他们虽然重视教育，从小就送孩子去学画画儿、学钢琴、学游泳什么的，可是他们最关心的还是考试和成绩。他们要孩子考上名

校，做个"成功"的人，受到别人的尊敬。我跟你一样，也没实现自己的理想。从前我想当个画家，可是我父母不赞成我学艺术，他们问我："难道你想一辈子做个穷光蛋吗？"他们的话也很有道理，虽然什么工作都好，可是如果我 6连自己都养不活，还谈什么兴趣，**更别说**要对社会有什么贡献了。所以我决定学商，为自己的生活、为明天的幸福努力。期末考快到了，需要开夜车、赶报告，不能再花太多时间写信了。考试以后再联系吧！

李明

小對話 Mini-Dialogues

Read the supplementary dialogues for a better understanding of the text. See if you can memorize one and perform it in class.

(1) Urging someone to do something else

Dad:	小華，你高中快畢業了，進了大學，想學什麼？
Wang:	中文吧！我正在想，還沒有決定。
Dad:	學中文有什麼用？
Wang:	我對文學有興趣啊！我想當個作家、寫寫小說。
Dad:	寫小說怎麼能養活自己呢？現在電腦最熱門，學電腦好了，將來不怕找不到工作。
Wang:	可是我對電腦沒興趣啊！
Dad:	沒關係，學學就有興趣了。

	小华，你高中快毕业了，进了大学，想学什么？
	中文吧！我正在想，还没有决定。
	学中文有什么用？
	我对文学有兴趣啊！我想当个作家、写写小说。
	写小说怎么能养活自己呢？现在电脑最热门，学电脑好了，将来不怕找不到工作。
	可是我对电脑没兴趣啊！
	没关系，学学就有兴趣了。

Dad: Xiao Hua, you are about to graduate from high school. After you enter college, what do you plan to major in?

Wang: I suppose Chinese. I am still thinking and haven't made a decision.

Dad: What is the use of studying Chinese?

Wang: I am interested in literature. I want to be a writer and write novels.

Dad: How could you support yourself by writing novels? Now computers are hot; it is better to study computers. You won't have to worry about finding a job in the future.

Wang: But I am not interested in computers.

Dad: That's not a problem. Once you start learning, you will find it interesting.

(2) Expressing doubts

Mom: 小明，將來準備學哪個專業？   小明，将来准备学哪个专业？

Li: 藝術吧！你們知道我從小就想   艺术吧！你们知道我从小就想
       做畫家。   做画家。

Mom: 有理想很好，可是當畫家怎麼   有理想很好，可是当画家怎么
       生活？   生活？

Li: 我畫得不錯，可以賣畫啊！   我画得不错，可以卖画啊！

Mom: 一張畫能賣多少錢？   一张画能卖多少钱？

Li: 等我出名 chūmíng 了，就能賣到好   等我出名了，就能卖到好价
       價錢 jiàqián。   钱。

Mom: 你不知道畫家多半都是死了以   你不知道画家多半都是死了以
       後才出名的嗎？你沒錢，靠什   后才出名的吗？你没钱，靠什
       麼生活呢？你想一輩子做個窮   么生活呢？你想一辈子做个穷
       光蛋嗎？   光蛋吗？

Mom: Xiao Ming, in what area do you plan to major?

Li: Arts. You know that I have always wanted to be a painter.

Mom: It's very good to have ideals, but how can you live by working as a painter?

Li: I paint well. I can sell my paintings.

Mom: How much can you get for one painting?

Li: After I get famous, the price will get better.

Mom: Don't you know that most painters make a name for themselves only after they die? If you don't have money, how can you live? Do you want to be poor your whole life?

👥 (3) Giving consent

Dad: 德中，你上研究所，想學什麼？學醫怎麼樣？跟你老爸一樣。

德中，你上研究所，想学什么？学医怎么样？跟你老爸一样。

Gao: 嗯，我對醫沒有興趣。我喜歡文學，我想比較中國和美國的現代文學。

嗯，我对医没有兴趣。我喜欢文学，我想比较中国和美国的现代文学。

Dad: 學文學將來會很苦。

学文学将来会很苦。

Gao: 我不怕吃苦。

我不怕吃苦。

Dad: 也好，人要活得快樂。不管做什麼，最重要的是要有興趣。沒興趣什麼都做不好。

也好，人要活得快乐。不管做什么，最重要的是要有兴趣。没兴趣什么都做不好。

Dad: Dezhong, what do you plan to study when you go to graduate school? How about medicine? Just like your dad.

Gao: Er, I am not interested in medicine. I like literature, and I want to compare modern Chinese and American literature.

Dad: If you study literature, you'll have a hard time in the future.

Gao: I don't mind working hard.

Dad: That's fine. We live to pursue happiness. No matter what you do, the key is your own interest. If you don't like something, you can't do it well.

👥 (4) Objecting to an idea

Mom: 美英，大學快畢業了，你將來到底想做什麼？

美英，大学快毕业了，你将来到底想做什么？

Lin: 拉小提琴或者彈tán鋼琴吧！

拉小提琴或者弹钢琴吧！

Mom: 當音樂家_{yīnyuèjiā}不容易。

Lin: 做什麼都不容易。只要我快樂，苦一點兒也沒關係。

Mom: 這是老美的想法！做人應該實際_{shíjì}一點兒。

Lin: 你們就是太現實了，一點兒理想也沒有。我不會做我不愛做的事。

Mom: 哎！這個孩子真不聽話。

当音乐家不容易。

做什么都不容易。只要我快乐，苦一点儿也没关系。

这是老美的想法！做人应该实际一点儿。

你们就是太现实了，一点儿理想也没有。我不会做我不爱做的事。

哎！这个孩子真不听话。

Mom: Meiying, you are about to graduate from college. What in the world are you going to do in the future?

Lin: Play violin or piano, I suppose.

Mom: It's very hard to be a musician.

Lin: It's hard no matter what you do. As long as I am happy, I don't mind it being a bit difficult.

Mom: This is the American way of thinking! To live, you got to be a bit more practical.

Lin: You are just too practical, and have no ideals at all. I won't do anything that I don't like.

Mom: Oh! This kid doesn't listen at all.

小故事 Stories

Read the following tale for your own enjoyment and for your understanding of the highlighted expression that is relevant to the theme of the chapter.

 拔苗助長/揠苗助長 bá/yà miáo zhù zhǎng

❀　太早送孩子去學鋼琴、學畫畫兒，我看是拔苗助長。

從前有個心急的農夫，他希望田裏的苗兒長得快一點兒，可是苗兒長得總是比他想的慢。

有一天，他想出了一個好辦法，就立刻跑到田裏，把每棵苗兒都往上拔了拔。他看到苗兒比原來高了不少，心裏很高興。回家以後，他對家裏的人說：「我工作了半天，真累！不過田裏的苗兒都長高了很多。」

第二天他到田裏一看，才知道苗兒都死了。

拔	bá	to pull up
苗兒	miáor	seedling, sprout
助	zhù	to help
長	zhǎng	to grow
心急	xīnjí	impatient, short-tempered
田	tián	field, farm
棵	kē	measure word for trees, vegetables, etc.
死	sǐ	to die

✎ 拔苗助長的意思是＿＿＿＿＿＿＿＿＿＿＿＿＿＿＿＿＿＿＿＿＿＿＿

拔苗助长/揠苗助长 bá/yà miáo zhù zhǎng

❀　太早送孩子去学钢琴、学画画儿 ，我看是拔苗助长。

从前有个心急的农夫，他希望田里的苗儿长得快一点儿，可是苗儿长得总是比他想的慢。

有一天，他想出了一个好办法，就立刻跑到田里，把每棵苗儿都往上拔。他看到苗儿比原来高了不少，心里很高兴。回家以后，他对家里的人说："我工作了半天，真累！不过田里的苗儿都长高了很多。"

第二天他到田里一看，才知道苗儿都死了。

拔	bá	to pull up
苗儿	miáor	seedling, sprout
助	zhù	to help
长	zhǎng	to grow
心急	xīnjí	impatient, short-tempered
田	tián	field, farm
棵	kē	measure word for trees, vegetables, etc.
死	sǐ	to die

漢字 Characters

Study the following selected characters for further enrichment of your writing and vocabulary.

艮 from 食 shí 'eat' + 卩 jié 'a person facing the food, just about to eat': immediately

即

jí 7
namely, even if

| 即使 | jíshǐ | even, even if/though |

A: 我會游泳，去那兒玩沒關係。

B: 即使你會游泳，也要小心。

Compare: 節 jié　既 jì　鄉 xiāng

亻 rén 'person' + 吏 lì phonetic

使

shǐ 8
to send, to make, if

| 大使 | dàshǐ* | ambassador |
| 使館 | shǐguǎn* | cmbassy |

A: 請問美國大使館在哪兒？

B: 就在那兒。

Compare: 史 shǐ　事 shì

The 㐆 yǎn waving motions of a 子 zǐ 'child' swimmer

游

yóu 12
to swim, to travel

游泳	yóuyǒng	to swim
下游	xiàyóu*	lower reaches (of river)
上游	shàngyóu*	upper reaches (of river)

A: 你每天都游泳嗎？在哪兒游？

B: 我都在那條河的上游游泳。

Compare: 遊 yóu

氵 shuǐ 'water' + 永 yǒng 'forever' phonetic

泳

yǒng 8
to swim

游泳池	yóuyǒngchí*	swimming pool
游泳衣	yóuyǒngyī*	swimsuit
游泳褲	yóuyǒngkù*	swimming trunks

A: 我不能跟你去游泳池游泳。

B: 怎麼？你忘了帶游泳衣嗎？

Compare: 水 shuǐ

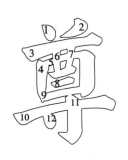

寸 'a hand' + 酉 yǒu 'a wine cup' —an offering to ancestors, in worship

| 尊敬 | zūnjìn | to respect |
| 自尊心 | zìzūnxīn* | self-respect |

A: 他的自尊心很強 qiáng，你不要笑他。
B: 我向來很尊敬他。

Compare: 遵 zūn　蹲 dūn

zūn 12
to respect

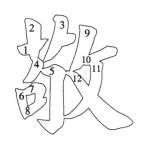

句 'to speak' + 羊 'nicely' + 攵 'to beat'

敬上	jìngshàng	respectfully
敬愛	jìng'ài*	esteemed and beloved
敬酒	jìngjiǔ*	to propose a toast

A: 他給老師的信是怎麼寫的 ？
B: 敬愛的老師，謝謝您……學生敬上。

Compare: 驚 jīng　警 jǐng

jìng 12
to respect, to offer politely

A plant 兂 on the 土 ground with a hand 丸 planting it, plus 艹 grass and 云 a cloud to water the crop

藝術	yìshù	art
藝術家	yìshùjiā*	artist
藝術片	yìshùpiàn*	art film
藝術品	yìshùpǐn*	work of art

A: 他是搞藝術的。
B: 原來他是個藝術家。

yì 19
skill, craftsmanship, art

行 xíng 'conduct' + 術 shù phonetic

技術	jìshù*	technology, skill
手術	shǒushù*	surgery
學術	xuéshù*	learning, science
美術	měishù*	fine arts, art, painting

A: 聽說他動了手術，現在怎麼樣？
B: 好多了，那個醫生的技術很好。

shù 11
art, skill, technique

Originally from 夂 zhǐ 'walk slowly' and 几 jī 'small table'—where you go and sit down

chǔ, chù 11
to handle, to get along, place

好處	hǎochu	good, benefit, gain
壞處	huàichu*	harm, disadvantage
用處	yòngchu*	use, practical application

A: 學中文對我有什麼好處？
B: 現在你不懂，將來用處可大了。

王 yù 'jade' + 里 lǐ phonetic —to polish gems according to the veins, to dispose, to rule

lǐ 11
texture, reason, to run

理想	lǐxiǎng	ideal
理解	lǐjiě	to understand
經理	jīnglǐ*	manager, to manage

A: 你覺得什麼工作最理想？
B: 當一家大公司的經理。

Compare: 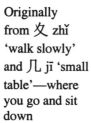里 lǐ

戊 wù is short for 茂 mào 'flourishing: succeed' + 丁 dīng phonetic

chéng 6
to accomplish, to become

成功	chénggōng	to succeed, success
成就	chéngjiù	achievement
贊成	zànchéng	to approve

A: 你覺得家庭幸福是一種成就嗎？
B: 對，那比事業上的成功還重要。

Compare: 城 chéng

糸 sī 'silk thread' + 責 zé phonetic—to twist, to spin, to achieve

jī, jì 17
to twist hempen thread, achievement

| 成績 | chéngjì | result, achievement |
| 成績單 | chéngjìdān* | report card |

A: 你的成績好不好？
B: 看看我的成績單就知道了。

耳 ěr 'ear' +
絲—get in
touch with
people by way
of their ears

聯

lián 17
to unite, to join

聯繫　　　　liánxì　　　　to get in touch with

A: 你現在跟你的中學同學還有聯繫嗎？

B: 早就沒有了。

Compare: 連 lián

聿 to draw 一
lines:
boundaries of a
田 field

画

huà 12
to draw, plan, stroke

畫畫兒	huàhuàr	to draw pictures
畫家	huàjiā	painter, artist
油畫	yóuhuà*	oil painting
國畫	guóhuà*	traditional Chinese painting

A: 你喜歡畫畫兒嗎？

B: 喜歡，可是我不會畫國畫。

Compare: 書 shū

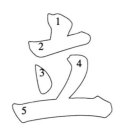

Picture of 大 a
person standing
on 一 the
ground

立

lì 5
to stand, upright,
immediate

| 公立 | gōnglì | public |
| 立刻 | lìkè* | immediately, at once |

A: 那個公立大學好嗎？

B: 好，學生一畢業立刻可以找到工作。

Compare: 位 wèi lā 音 yīn 站 zhàn

工 gōng 'work'
+ 力 lì
'strength'

功

gong 5
achievement, effect,
skill

成功	chénggōng	successful
用功	yònggōng*	hardworking, studious
功夫	gōngfu*	effort, workmanship
功課	gōngkè	homework

A: 聽說她的事業很成功？

B: 對，她是一個願意下功夫的人。

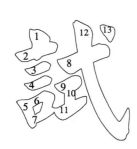

言 yán 'words'
+ 式 shì
phonetic

试

考試	kǎoshì	test
筆試	bǐshì*	written examination
口試	kǒushì*	oral examination
試試看	shìshikàn*	to have a try

A: 你明天中文課有考試嗎？

B: 有，有筆試，也有口試。

shì 13
to try, test,
examination

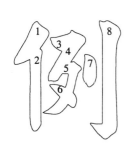

亻 rén 'person'
+ 列 liè
phonetic

例

例外	lìwài	exception
例子	lìzi	example, case, instance
例如	lìrú	for instance
例句	lìjù*	example sentence

A: 「大家都喜歡吃中國飯，只有他例
外。」

B: 這個例句很清楚。

lì 8
example, precedent,
case

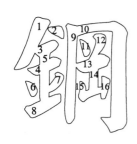

金 jīn 'metal' +
岡 gāng
phonetic

钢

| 鋼琴 | gāngqín | piano |
| 鋼筆 | gāngbǐ* | fountain pen |

A: 你會彈tán 'to play' 鋼琴嗎？

B: 會，我從小就學鋼琴。

Compare: 剛 gāng

gang 16
steel, to sharpen

厶 is 子 zǐ
'child' upside-
down + 月 ròu
'flesh' —to feed
a child so that it
becomes strong

育

| 教育 | jiàoyù | education, to teach |
| 教育家 | jiàoyùjiā* | educator |

A: 你對教育有什麼看法？

B: 我不是教育家，不懂教育。

yù 8
to give birth to, to
rear, to educate

語法和用法 Grammar and Usage

Pay attention to the function of the structure and then study the example sentences.

1. Expressing an extraordinary degree

S不但V_1O_1, 連O_2也V_1	búdàn…lián…yě…	Not only does S V_1, S even V_1O_2
不但S_1V, 連S_2也V		Not only S_1V, even S_2 V

我看**不但**交朋友如此，**連**學習也是這樣。

1. 你擔心什麼？

    你担心什么？

    What are you worrying about?

    他的健康。他不但不吃青菜，連水果也不吃。

    他的健康。他不但不吃青菜，连水果也不吃。

    His health. He not only does not eat vegetables, but he even refuses to eat fruit.

2. 我看她一點兒也不怕胖。

    我看她一点儿也不怕胖。

    I think she is not afraid of gaining weight at all.

    對，她不但愛吃巧克力糖táng，連餅乾bǐnggān、蛋糕也愛吃。

    对，她不但爱吃巧克力糖，连饼干、蛋糕也爱吃。

    Right. She not only loves chocholate candy, but even eats a lot of cookies and cakes.

3. 他結婚了嗎？我怎麼不知道？

    他结婚了吗？我怎么不知道？

    Was he married? How come I know nothing about it?

    不但他的朋友不知道，連他的父母也不知道。

    不但他的朋友不知道，连他的父母也不知道。

    Not only did his friends not know, but even his parents were kept in the dark.

不但…連…也 is a pattern expressing an extraordinary degree. O_2/S_2 should be of more extreme degree than O_1/S_1. Thus, it is odd to say "他不但會開飛機，連汽車也會開。" because one would assume that piloting a plane is harder than driving a car. Note that if the initial phrase is negative, then the degree expressed for O_2/S_2 is minimal. If the initial phrase is positive, then the degree expressed for O_2/S_2 is maximal. Compare this pattern with 不但不/沒…反而… (L5, G4).

2.　Expressing light-hearted action

V著玩兒(的)	…zhe wánr (de)	V for fun

小說寫**著玩兒**還行，可這種愛好不能當飯吃。

1.	你的畫兒畫得真好！	你的画儿画得真好！	You really paint well.
	哪裏，我只是畫著玩兒的。	哪里，我只是画着玩儿的。	No, I just paint for fun.
2.	你的專業是中文嗎？	你的专业是中文吗？	Is your major Chinese?
	不，中文我只是學著玩兒的。	不，中文我只是学着玩儿的。	No, I just study this for fun.
3.	你怎麼抽煙呢？你知道那對身體不好嗎？	你怎么抽烟呢？你知道那对身体不好吗？	Why do you smoke? Do you know that smoking is bad for your health?
	我只是抽著玩兒的，別擔心。	我只是抽着玩儿的，别担心。	I just smoke for fun. Don't worry.

V著玩兒 is a phrase used to indicate that an action was carried out for fun, not for a serious purpose or on a regular basis.

3.　Expressing one's point of view

在sb.看來	zài…kànlái	in one's view/opinion, …

在他們**看來**，學習就是為了將來有一份好的工作……

1.	你覺得學中文有前途嗎？	你觉得学中文有前途吗？	Do you think there is a future in studying Chinese?
	在我看來，學中文很有前途。	在我看来，学中文很有前途。	I think studying Chinese is promising.

2.	等我有時間再去圖書館吧！	等我有时间再去图书馆吧！	When I have the time, I'll go to the library.
	在我看來，你越早開始準備報告越好。	在我看来，你越早开始准备报告越好。	In my view, the sooner you start preparing your paper, the better.
3.	在我看來，功課越少越好。	在我看来，功课越少越好。	In my view, the less homework you give, the better.
	如果你是老師的話，你也這麼想嗎？	如果你是老师的话，你也这么想吗？	If you were the teacher, would you have the same opinion?

在…看來 is used to express one's point of view and can be paraphrased as …覺得/想．Compare this with 對 sb. 來說(L3, G1).

4. Making a concessive argument

就算S…, (S)也…	jiùsuàn…, …yě…	even if… , still...
即使S…, (S)也…	jíshǐ…, …yě…	even if …, still...

就算目前沒有興趣**也**沒關係。

1.	你幫我做功課，我給你十塊錢，好不好？	你帮我做功课，我给你十块钱，好不好？	You help me do my homework and I will give you ten dollars. All right?
	就算你給我二十塊，這個忙我也不能幫。	就算你给我二十块，这个忙我也不能帮。	Even if you gave me twenty dollars, I could not help you.
2.	你可以跟他父母談談。	你可以跟他父母谈谈。	You can talk to his parents.
	他根本不聽父母的話，就算我找他父母談也沒用。	他根本不听父母的话，就算我找他父母谈也没用。	He simply won't listen to his parents. Even if I talk with them, it's useless.

3. 你跟他結婚，將來   你跟他结婚，将来   If you marry him, you
    一定可以過好日   一定可以过好日   will certainly have a good
    子。   子。   life.

    我們不相愛，就算   我们不相爱，就算   We don't love each other.
    結婚，也不會幸福   结婚，也不会幸福   Even if we got married,
    的。   的。   we wouldn't be happy.

The movable adverb 就算 marks the first clause in a two-clause sentence. The 就算
clause states a concessive situation and the other clause, the conclusion or result. 即使
is the same as 就算 but more formal. Compare 即使 with 既然 jìrán (L14, G4).

5. Expressing an external influence or a specific aspect

在sb.的N下	zài…de…xià	under/with sb's N
在N上/方面	zài…shàng/fāngmiàn	in terms of N; in the area of N

在父母的「鼓勵」下我選擇了電腦這個熱門的專業。

1. 你因為自己努力才   你因为自己努力才   I suppose you yourself
    有這麼大的成就   有这么大的成就   have worked very hard to
    吧！   吧！   accomplish all of this!

    不，在父母的支持   不，在父母的支持   No. I wouldn't have
    zhīchí下，我才有今   下，我才有今天的   accomplished all of this
    天的成就。   成就。   without my parents' support.

2. 我覺得學習有沒有   我觉得学习有没有   I think as long as one can
    興趣沒關係，只要   兴趣没关系，只要   find a job in the future, it
    將來能找到工作就   将来能找到工作就   doesn't matter whether or
    好了。   好了。   not one has an interest in
                                                study.

    在這個問題上，我   在这个问题上，我   I don't agree with you on
    不同意你的看法。   不同意你的看法。   this issue.

3. 我想中國的生活水   我想中国的生活水   I think the living standard
    平應該沒有美國的   平应该没有美国的   of China is surely not as
    這麼高吧！   这么高吧！   high as that of the U.S.

不，這幾年來中國在經濟方面也有很大的發展fāzhǎn。	不，这几年来中国在经济方面也有很大的发展。	No, but China has made great strides in her economical development over the past few years.

The pattern 在 sb. 的 N 下 indicates an external influence and often takes abstract nouns like 鼓勵、支持、幫助、領導 lǐngdǎo 'leadership,' or 指導 zhǐdǎo 'guidance.' The pattern 在 N 上 also takes abstract nouns and it indicates a specific aspect or standpoint for the main verb phrase of the sentence. Thus, it is the same as 在 N 方面. The nouns it commonly takes are 工作、學習、生活、問題、專業、文學、音樂、經濟, etc.

6. Expressing extremity through contrast

連A都(不/沒)…，更別說B了	lián…dōu (bù/méi)…, gèngbiéshuō…le	even A is … , not to mention/let alone B

如果我**連**自己**都**養不活，還談什麼興趣，**更別說**要對社會有什麼貢獻了。

1.	她會開車嗎？	她会开车吗？	Can she drive?
	她連自行車都不會騎，更別說開車了。	她连自行车都不会骑，更别说开车了。	She can't even ride a bike, much less drive a car.
2.	咱們去看電影吧！	咱们去看电影吧！	Let's go see a movie.
	我連吃飯的時間都沒有，更別說出去看電影了。	我连吃饭的时间都没有，更别说出去看电影了。	I don't even have time to eat, much less go to a movie.
3.	他進了哪個名校？	他进了哪个名校？	Which prestigious school did he get into?
	他連一般的學校都考不上，更別說那些名校了。	他连一般的学校都考不上，更别说那些名校了。	He can't even pass the test to get into the average ones, not to mention those prestigious schools.

Similar to the pattern 不但…連…也, this pattern expresses an extreme quality by way of a contrast. One should be aware of the implied degree of difference between A and B. The inherent degree of A should be more extreme than that of B. Thus, one should not say "他連汽車都會開，更別說開飛機了。" because one would assume that piloting a plane is harder than driving a car. Very often, the first clause bears a negative meaning, with or without a negative marker.

文化點滴 Culture Notes

1. **Examination system**: China has a long tradition of selecting bureaucrats by using examinations, which were based on Confucian learning and knowledge of the Chinese classics. Only those who passed the exams could hold positions of social and political leadership. Considered the fairest of all models, exams are still deep-rooted in modern Chinese society. In order to get into a college, Chinese students have to take a joint entrance examination in July, called 高考 gāokǎo in mainland China, 聯考 liánkǎo in Taiwan, and 會考 huìkǎo in Hong Kong. The result of this single test determines a student's future. If he or she tests into a good university, the future is quite secure. Many who fail this exam will have to study and wait one more year before they can try again. Realizing that this exam cannot evaluate artistic, creative, or athletic talents, the Taiwanese government, after ten years of educational reform, abolished it in 2001 and established a multi-track entrance system.

2. **Orientation to the past or future**: It has been observed that traditional Chinese seem to orient themselves to the past. Thus, common people revere their ancestors and scholars tend to quote the oldest references they can find to validate their studies. Terms such as 前人 qiánrén 'forefathers [front-person]' or 前輩 qiánbèi 'senior person, elder [front-generation]' all seem to point to this orientation to the past. In contrast, Westerners often tend to equate the future with progress and innovation.

3. **Professions and jobs**: When talking about a career, many Chinese parents tend to encourage their children to pursue something practical and financially rewarding, sometimes at the expense of their children's interests. In most cases, parents do not encourage children to "seize the day," but instead to "work for a better tomorrow." As for the choice of professions, teaching is well-respected, but those which offer a high salary are most popular. Following is a list of common professions.

English	*Chinese Terms*		*Pinyin*
accountant	會計師	会计师	kuàijìshī
artist	藝術家	艺术家	yìshùjiā
chemist	化學家	化学家	huàxuéjiā
clerk	職員	职员	zhíyuán
computer programmer	程式設計師	程式设计师	chéngshì shèjìshī
dentist	牙醫	牙医	yáyī
doctor, physician	醫生	医生	yīshēng

engineer	工程師	工程师	gōngchéngshī
lawyer	律師	律师	lǜshī
manager	經理	经理	jīnglǐ
mathematician	數學家	数学家	shùxuéjiā
musician	音樂家	音乐家	yīnyuèjiā
nurse	護士	护士	hùshì
official	官員	官员	guānyuán
painter	畫家	画家	huàjiā
physicist	物理學家	物理学家	wùlǐxuéjiā
reporter	記者	记者	jìzhě
scientist	科學家	科学家	kēxuéjiā
secretary	秘書	秘书	mìshū
teacher	教師	教师	jiàoshī
writer	作家	作家	zuòjiā

歌兒 Songs

前途
Future

Andante   詞：劉力嘉   曲：馬定一

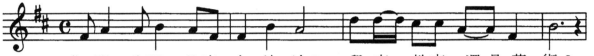

1. 你 問 我選 什麼 有 前 途？ 學 商、教育、還是 藝 術？
   Nǐ wèn wǒ xuǎn shénme yǒu qián tú? Xué shāng, jiàoyù, háishì yì shù?
   You ask me which major will give me a bright future. Should one study business, education or the arts?

2. 你 問 我做 什麼 有 好 處？ 彈 鋼琴、畫畫、或 讀 書？
   Nǐ wèn wǒ zuò shénme yǒu hǎo chù? Tán gāngqín, huàhuà, huò dú shū?
   You ask me what to do to bring me profit. Should one play piano, paint, or study?

1. 難 道 目 前 學 習 只 為 了 將 來 收 入？ 沒興
   Nán dào mùqián xuéxí zhǐ wèile jiānglái shōurù? Méi xìng
   Could it be that everything we learn today is for tomorrow's salary? Without

2. 在 我 看 來，成 功 就 是 為 別人 服 務。 沒貢
   Zài wǒ kàn lái, chénggōng jiù shì wèi biérén fúwù. Méi gòng
   In my view, success is to serve others. Without

1. 趣， 即 使 養 活了 自 己 也 不 一 定
   qù, jíshǐ yǎng huóle zì jǐ yě bù yí dìng
   enjoyment, even if one can feed oneself, one may not find

2. 獻， 就 算 實 現了 理 想 也 不 需 要
   xiàn, jiù suàn shí xiànle lǐ xiǎng yě bù xū yào
   making a contribution, even if you realize your dream, you may not receive any

1. 幸 福。 這 道 理 你 要 記 住。
   xìng fú. Zhè dào lǐ nǐ yào jì zhù.
   happiness. You need to heed this.

2. 羨 慕。 這 道 理 你 要 清 楚。
   xiàn mù. Zhè dào lǐ nǐ yào qīng chǔ.
   admiration. You should be clear about this.

Appendixes

Appendix 1. Traditional vs. Simplified Characters

Most simplified characters bear some resemblance to their traditional counterparts. Given some practice over time, you will be able to recognize both forms. The following are four basic means by which simplified characters relate to their traditional counterparts. The examples are given with the traditional characters on the top and the simplified ones below.

A. With one component (e.g., radicals) simplified

1. 學 覺
   学 觉

2. 馬 嗎 媽
   马 吗 妈

3. 這 過 還 進 邊 遠
   这 过 还 进 边 远

4. 課 誰 請 說 話 談 謝 記 該 許 語 讓
   课 谁 请 说 话 谈 谢 记 该 许 语 让

5. 見 現 視 員 貴 賽 費 贏 慣 題
   见 现 视 员 贵 赛 费 赢 惯 题

6. 給 約 紅
   给 约 红

7. 門 問 間 們
   门 问 间 们

8. 飯 館 餓

饭　館　餓

9.
長　張
长　张

10.
湯　場
汤　场

11.
錯　錢　鐘
错　钱　钟

12.
幾　機
几　机

13.
車　連　輸　輕
车　连　输　轻

14.
國　師　樣　時　對　難　歡　塊　動　腦　臉　應
国　师　样　时　对　难　欢　块　动　脑　脸　应

驗　樓　郵　幫　隊　魚　風　熱　涼　緊　報　帶
验　楼　邮　帮　队　鱼　风　热　凉　紧　报　带

掛　單　剛
挂　单　刚

B. With one component representing the whole

15.

兒 從 電 開 麵 裏 號
儿 从 电 开 面 里 号

飛 習 雖 氣 醫 離
飞 习 虽 气 医 离

C. With more than one component simplified

16.

經 練 點
经 练 点

D. With the whole character simplified

17.

兩 來 爲 書 買 實 頭 著 會 寫 聽 響
两 来 为 书 买 实 头 着 会 写 听 响

當 樂 東 專 發 變 萬 辦 總 雞 藥 擔
当 乐 东 专 发 变 万 办 总 鸡 药 担

個 麼 節 後
个 么 节 后

Appendix 2. Bibliography

Birch, Cyril, ed.
   1972   Anthology of Chinese Literature. New York: Grove Press.

Chao, Yuen Ren (趙元任)
   1968   *A Grammar of Spoken Chinese*. Berkeley: University of California Press.

Cheng, Qinhua (程欽華), ed.
   1992   *Selected Jokes from Past Chinese Dynasties* (中國歷代笑話精選). Beijing: Huayu
           Jiaoxue Chubanshe.

DeFrancis, John, ed.
   1996   *ABC Chinese-English Dictionary*. Honolulu: University of Hawai'i Press.

Gao, Shufan (高樹藩), ed.
   1984   *Zhengzhong Xing Yin Yi Zonghe Da Zidian* (正中形音義綜合大字典). Rev. 5th ed.
           Taibei: Zhengzhong Shuju.

Government Information Office, Taiwan, ROC, eds.
   2000   *The Republic of China Yearbook.* Taipei: Government Information Office.

Guojia Duiwai Hanyu Jiaoxue Lingdao Xiaozu Bangongshi (國家對外漢語教學領導小組辦公
室), eds.
   1992   *Hanyu Shuiping Cihui Yu Hanzi Dengji Dagang* (漢語水平詞匯與漢字等級大綱).
           Beijing: Beijing Yuyan Xueyuan Chubanshe.

Guojia Duiwai Hanyu Jiaoxue Lingdao Xiaozu Bangongshi (國家對外漢語教學領導小組辦公
室), eds.
   1996   *Hanyu Shuiping Dengji Biaozhun Yu Yufa Dengji Dagang* (漢語水平等級標準與語
           法等級大綱). Beijing: Gaodeng Jiaoyu Chubanshe.

Han, Jiantang (韓鑒堂), ed.
   1994   *China's Cultural Heritage* (中國文化). Beijing: Guoji Wenhua Chuban Gongsi.

Liang, Shih-chiu (梁實秋)
   1971   *A New Practical Chinese-English Dictionary* (最新實用漢英字典). Taipei: Far East Book Co.

Norman, Jerry
   1988   *Chinese.* Cambridge: Cambridge University Press.

Ramsey, S. Robert
   1987   *The Languages of China.* Princeton: Princeton University Press.

Rohsenow, John
   1991   *A Chinese-English Dictionary of Enigmatic Folk Similes.* Tucson: The University of Arizona Press.

Sinorama Magazine (光華雜誌社), eds.
   1992   *"Trademarks" of the Chinese* (中國人的「註冊商標」). Taipei: Sinorama Magazine.

Situ, Tan (司徒談), ed.
   1986   *Best Chinese Idioms.* Hong Kong: Hai Feng.

Tennenbaum, Peter, and Tom Bishop
   2002   Wenlin Software for Learning Chinese (version 3.0). Wenlin Institute.

Wang, Fang (王仿), ed.
   1990   *A Comprehensive Collection of Chinese Riddles* (中國謎語大全). Shanghai: Shanghai Wenyi Chubanshe.

Ye, Dabing (葉大兵), and Bing'an Wu (烏丙安), eds
   1990   *Zhongguo Fengsu Cidian* (中國風俗辭典). Shanghai: Shanghai Cishu Chubanshe.

Zhongguo Da Baike Quanshu Chubanshe Bianjibu (中國大百科全書出版社編輯部編), eds.
   1988   *Zhongguo Da Baike Quanshu: Yuyan Wenzi* (中國大百科全書：語言文字). Beijing: Zhongguo Da Baike Quanshu Chubanshe.

Indexes

Index 1. Vocabulary

◎ By Pinyin

Pinyin	Character	English	L
A			
ài	唉	Oh!	7.40
àihào	愛好/爱好	hobby, interest	6.10
àiqíng	愛情/爱情	romantic love	8.19
àiren	愛人/爱人	spouse	9.2
àiren*	愛人/爱人	spouse	3
àishang	愛上/爱上	to fall in love with	8.1
B			
báirén	白人	Caucasian	8.2
bàn	辦/办	to handle	1.11
bànfǎ	辦法/办法	way, means	3.20
bàntiān	半天	a long time	1.19
bǎo	飽/饱	full	5.27
bǎomǔ*	褓姆/保姆	housekeeper, nanny	9
bǎoshǒu	保守	conservative	8.27
bèijǐng	背景	background	8.14
běnlái	本來/本来	originally	6.22
biérén	別人	other people	10.34
bǐfāng shuō	比方說/比方说	for example	4.26
bìng	並/并	actually (not)	3.11
bìngrén*	病人	patient	8
bìxū	必須/必须	must	9.3
bú jiàn bú sàn*	不見不散/不见不散	won't leave without seeing each other	7
búdàn	不但	not only	5.31
bùdé bù	不得不	cannot but	5.35
bùguǎn	不管	regardless of	2.36
bùxíng	不行	to be no good	5.10
C			
càidān*	菜單/菜单	menu	5
cāidào	猜到	to figure out	7.38
cǎn	慘/惨	miserable	4.43
cāntīng	餐廳/餐厅	restaurant	4.27
cháng	嚐/尝	to taste	5.2
chángcháng	常常	often	2.10
chángtú*	長途/长途	long distance	8
chǎo	炒	to stir-fry	5.20
chǎojià	吵架	to quarrel	7.15
chénggōng	成功	successful, to succeed, success	10.33
chéngjī/jì	成績/成绩	grade	10.19
chéngjiù	成就	achievement	9.35
chī dòufu*	吃豆腐	to eat bean-curd, to flirt with	5
chīkǔ	吃苦	to bear hardship	5.42
chīsù*	吃素	to be a vegetarian	5
chúfēi	除非	only if	5.24
chūguó	出國/出国	to go abroad	1.4
chūkǒu	出口	exit	1.24
chūmíng*	出名	famous, well-known	10
chuáng	床	bed	2.20
chuánshuō	傳說/传说	it is said	3.39
chuīniú	吹牛	to brag	7.29
cí*	辭/辞	to quit (a job)	9
cōngming	聰明/聪明	intelligent	7.33
cóngxiǎo	從小/从小	from childhood	10.8
D			
dǎbàn	打扮	to dress/make up	6.28
dàfāng	大方	elegant and composed	6.42
dài	戴	to wear (glasses, etc.)	7.19
dài	帶/带	to look after, to bring	9.9
dàigōu	代溝/代沟	generation gap	8.28
dàngāo	蛋糕	cake	5.15
dàodǐ	到底	after all	7.1
dàolǐ	道理	reason, sense, argument	10.39
dàolǐ*	道理	reason, sense	9
dǎoyǎn	導演/导演	director	6.18

děngděng	等等	and so on, etc.	2.43
diǎn*	點/点	to order (dishes)	5
diǎnxīn	點心/点心	pastry	5.17
diànzǐ	電子/电子	electronic	1.33
diàoyú*	釣魚/钓鱼	to fish	6
dìfang	地方	place	2.18
dìtǎn	地毯	carpet, rug	2.28
duì…lái shuō	對…來說/ 对…来说	concerning	3.9
duìmiàn	對面/对面	opposite	7.11
duìxiàng	對象/对象	boy/girlfriend	6.40
duō(me)	多麼/多么	how, what	6.24

F

fā	發/发	to issue	1.31
fāmíng	發明/发明	invention	6.38
fǎn'ér	反而	on the contrary	5.32
fǎnduì	反對/反对	to oppose	8.33
fàngqì	放棄/放弃	to give up	9.28
fāngxiàng	方向	direction	4.12
fāpàng*	發胖/发胖	to gain weight	5
fēi…bùkě	非…不可	must	8.7
fèn(r)	份(兒)/ 份(儿)	measure word for jobs, copies, etc.	9.27
fēng	封	measure word for letters	1.32
fēnshǒu	分手	to break up	8.25
fū	夫	husband	9.42
fúqi*	福氣/福气	happy lot	3
fǒuzé	否則/否则	otherwise	5.26
fùxí	複習/复习	to review	2.15

G

gǎi	改	to change	7.25
gān	乾/干	dry	5.11
gǎn	敢	to dare	1.2
gǎn	感	sense	10.21
gǎn xìngqù	感興趣/ 感兴趣	to be interested in	1.42
gānbēi	乾杯/干杯	bottoms up	3.32
gāngqín	鋼琴/钢琴	piano	10.27
gānjìng	乾淨/干净	clean	2.26
gǎnjué	感覺/感觉	feeling	3.13

gǎnqíng	感情	feeling	7.41
gǎo	搞	to do	1.18
gāojí	高級/高级	high in rank	4.31
gè	各	each	2.2
gēnběn	根本	simply	3.24
gèng	更	even	1.41
gōnggòng*	公共	public	2
gōnglì	公立	public	10.20
gòngtóng	共同	common	6.9
gòngxiàn	貢獻/贡献	contribution	10.41
gōngyuán	公園/公园	park	4.17
gōngzuò	工作	job, to work	9.7
gūniang	姑娘	girl	7.32
guā	瓜	melon	4.34
guǎi*	拐	to turn	4
guàibude	怪不得	no wonder	5.39
guǎn xiánshì	管閑事/ 管闲事	to meddle	2.1
guǎngchǎng	廣場/广场	public square	4.11
guānniàn	觀念/观念	concept	8.26
guānxīn	關心/关心	to be concerned about	3.15
guānyú	關於/关于	about, with regard to	3.38
gǔlì	鼓勵/鼓励	encouragement	9.7
guò	過/过	to pass	1.22
guòjié	過節/过节	to celebrate a festival	3.27
guónèi	國內/国内	internal, domestic	3.28
guòqù	過去/过去	past	2.41
guōzi*	鍋子/锅子	wok, pan	5
gùshi	故事	story, tale	3.40

H

hǎiguān	海關/海关	customs	1.23
hǎochu	好處/好处	benefit	10.11
hǎogǎn	好感	favorable impression	6.21
hàoqí	好奇	curious	2.37
hǎoróngyì	好容易	with great difficulty, to have a hard time (doing sth.)	9.29
hǎozài	好在	fortunately	1.6

hútòng	胡同	lane	4.15
hòu	厚	thick	7.20
huáchuán*	划船	to row a boat	6
huàhuàr	畫畫兒/ 画画儿	to draw pictures	10.26
huàjiā	畫家/画家	painter	10.36
huānyíng*	歡迎/欢迎	to welcome	1
Huáyì	華裔/华裔	ethnic Chinese of other nationalities	8.22
huàzhuāng*	化妝/化妆	to apply makeup	6
huíxìn	回信	to write in reply	10.4
huódòng	活動/活动	activity, to exercise	2.14
huǒtuǐ*	火腿/火腿	ham	5
hùxiāng	互相	mutually	7.26
hùzhào	護照/护照	passport	1.9

J

jì…yě	既…也…	not only… but also…	3.19
jià	嫁	(of a woman) to marry	8.18
jiācháng biànfàn	家常便飯/ 家常便饭	simple meal	3.31
jiàndào	見到/见到	to see	7.2
jiǎng	講/讲	to stress, to speak	8.38
jiǎngjiu	講究/讲究	to be particular about	5.28
jiānglái	將來/将来	future	8.15
jiàngyóu*	醬油/酱油	soy sauce	5
jiànkāng	健康	health	5.4
jiànmiàn	見面/见面	to meet, to see	1.38
jiāo	交	to make (friends), to hand over	2.42
jiàocái	教材	teaching materials	2.4
jiàoshòu*	教授	professor	1
jiàoyù	教育	education	10.25
jiātíng	家庭	family	9.33
jiāwù	家務/家务	household duties	9.6
jīdàn*	雞蛋/鸡蛋	hen's egg	5
jiē	接	to pick sb. up	1.30

jiéguǒ	結果/结果	result	4.41
jièkǒu*	藉口/借口	excuse	9
jiémù	節目/节目	program	6.20
jiérì	節日/节日	festival, holiday	3.22
jiēshòu	接受	to accept	8.29
jīhū	幾乎/几乎	almost	3.34
-jíle	極了/极了	extremely	2.31
jìmò	寂寞	lonely	3.18
jīn*	斤	half a kilogram	4
jīngcǎi	精彩	brilliant	6.16
jīngguò	經過/经过	to pass	4.14
jīngjì	經濟/经济	economical	5.41
jìngrán	竟然	unexpectedly	7.9
jìngshàng	敬上	respectfully submitted	8.44
jǐnzhāng	緊張/紧张	nervous, tense	7.8
jīpiào	機票/机票	plane ticket	1.12
jíshǐ	即使	even, even if/though	10.14
jiùsuàn	就算	even if	10.13
jūrán	居然	unexpectedly	2.40
jù	句	sentence	8.6
jùlí	距離/距离	distance	6.7
jùxíng	句型	sentence pattern	2.8

K

kāfēiguǎn	咖啡館/ 咖啡馆	café	7.7
kāi yèchē	開夜車/ 开夜车	to burn the midnight oil	10.43
kāixīn	開心/开心	to feel happy	5.43
kànbuqǐ	看不起	to scorn	9.21
kànfǎ	看法	view	8.36
kào	靠	to rely on, to lean on	6.39
kǎolǜ	考慮/考虑	to consider, to think over	9.13
kǎoshàng	考上	to pass an entrance examination	10.31
kǎoshì	考試/考试	test, to test	10.30
kě	渴	thirsty	4.39
kě'ài	可愛/可爱	lovely	7.31
kèběn	課本/课本	textbook	2.5

kèfú	克服	to surmount	8.42
kèqi	客氣/客气	to be polite	3.35
kèwài	課外/课外	extra-curricular	2.13
kèwén	課文/课文	text	2.12
kěxī	可惜	It's a pity!	7.37
kěxiào	可笑	funny	4.32
kōngtiáo	空調/空调	air-conditioning	2.29
kùnnán	困難/困难	difficulty	8.43

L

lādùzi	拉肚子	to have diarrhea	4.42
láibují	來不及/来不及	can't do sth. in time	1.16
lǎo	老	tough, overdone	5.22
lǎo	老	always	7.16
lǎodà*	老大	eldest child (in a family)	3
lǎojiā*	老家	native place	3
lǎoshíshuō	老實說/老实说	to tell the truth	5.7
lǎowài	老外	foreigner	1.1
liánxì	聯繫/联系	to contact	10.44
liǎojiě	了解	to understand	3.16
lìhai	厲害/厉害	sharp	9.16
líhūn	離婚/离婚	divorce	8.16
lǐjiě	理解	to understand	10.23
lǐmào	禮貌/礼貌	polite	3.8
liú*	留	to keep	3
liúxué	留學/留学	to study abroad	1.5
lìshǐ	歷史/历史	history	2.34
liùniǎo*	遛鳥/遛鸟	to take a bird on a stroll	4
lìwài	例外	exception	10.7
lǐxiǎng	理想	ideal	10.5
luōsuo	囉嗦/罗嗦	wordy, longwinded	8.24

M

mà	罵/骂	to call names, to scold	7.18
mángbuguòlái	忙不過來/忙不过来	too busy to deal with	3.25
mǎnyì	滿意/满意	satisfied	7.5
máobing	毛病	shortcoming	7.24

měi	美	beautiful	3.37
méiguānxi	沒關係/没关系	it doesn't matter	10.16
méixiǎngdào	沒想到	unexpectedly	2.38
mí	迷	to be enchanted with	6.11
mìmì	秘密	secret	6.1
míngxiào	名校	famous school	10.32
míngxīng	明星	star	6.17
mùqián	目前	at present	10.15
mǔqin	母親/母亲	mother	9.36

N

nándào	難道/难道	Do you mean to say that…?	10.1
nánguài	難怪/难怪	no wonder	7.39
nánháir	男孩兒/男孩儿	boy	7.14
nán-nǚ-lǎo-shào	男女老少	men and women, old and young	4.18
nánzǐhàn	男子漢/男子汉	a real man	9.23
nàozhōng	鬧鐘/闹钟	alarm clock	4.4
nèiróng	內容	content	2.6
nénggàn	能幹/能干	competent	9.4
nì	膩/腻	greasy, tired of	5.16
niánjì	年紀/年纪	age	6.8
niánqīng	年輕/年轻	young	7.35
niú	牛	ox	7.13
niúròumiàn	牛肉麵/牛肉面	beef noodles	4.28
nǚháir	女孩兒/女孩儿	girl	9.19
nǚxìng	女性	woman	9.32

P

pāi	拍	to shoot film, to take a picture	6.13
páigǔ	排骨	spareribs	7.17
pàng	胖	fat, plump	5.34
pǎo	跑	to run	1.29
pǎobù	跑步	to jog	4.21
piānjiàn	偏見/偏见	bias	8.30
piānzi	片子	film	6.14

píng	瓶	bottle	4.40
píngděng	平等	equal	9.43
pīngpāngqiú*	乒乓球	ping-pong	6
píngshí	平時/平时	in ordinary times	8.5
pīnmìng	拼命	to make a do-or-die effort	5.36

Q

qí	騎/骑	to ride	4.8
qiántú	前途	future, prospects	10.10
qiānwàn	千萬/千万	by all means	6.2
qiānzhèng	簽證/签证	visa	1.10
qǐchuáng	起床	to get up (from bed)	4.6
qìgōng	氣功/气功	deep breathing exercises	4.20
qīngchu	清楚	clear	6.31
qíngkuàng	情況/情况	situation, circumstances	1.39
qìngzhù	慶祝/庆祝	to celebrate	3.21
qīnqiè	親切/亲切	cordial	3.7
qióngguāngdàn	窮光蛋/穷光蛋	poor wretch	10.3
qíshì	歧視/歧视	discrimination	8.11
qīzi	妻子	wife	9.37
quàn	勸/劝	to advise	8.20
què	卻/却	however, yet	2.30

R

rèmén	熱門/热门	in great demand	10.18
rèn	認/认	to recognize	7.23
rènhé	任何	any	9.17
rènwéi	認爲/认为	to think that	6.25
rèqíng	熱情/热情	enthusiastic, warm	3.6
rìzi	日子	day, days	5.30
ruǎn*	軟/软	soft	2

S

shāfā	沙發/沙发	sofa	2.25
shāng	商	business	10.42
shàng	上	to submit (a letter)	1.35
shàngcì	上次	last time	3.3
shàngdàng	上當/上当	to be taken in	4.38
shāngdiàn	商店	shop	4.25

shāngliang	商量	to consult	9.18
shāo	燒/烧	to cook, to roast, to burn	9.10
shēng	生	raw, green	5.21
shēngcí	生詞/生词	new word	2.7
shēngyīn	聲音/声音	sound	1.27
shénmede	什麼的/什么的	and so on	10.29
shēnqǐng	申請/申请	to apply for	1.8
shènzhì	甚至	so much so that	2.23
shīfu*	師傅/师傅	master worker	1
shìjì	世紀/世纪	century	6.36
shíjì*	實際/实际	practical	10
shímáo	時髦/时髦	fashionable	6.41
shìqing	事情	affair, matter	1.44
shīwàng	失望	to become disappointed	6.33
shíwù	食物	food	5.9
shíxiàn	實現/实现	to realize	10.22
shìyè	事業/事业	career	9.40
shìyìng	適應/适应	to get used to	2.3
shízài	實在/实在	indeed, really	3.17
shūdāizi	書呆子/书呆子	bookworm	7.28
shòu	瘦	thin, lean	5.33
shòudào	受到	to receive	8.31
shōurù	收入	income	8.35
shúxī	熟悉	familiar	1.26
shuài	帥/帅	handsome	7.3
shuǐguǒ	水果	fruit	4.35
shùnlì	順利/顺利	smooth	1.14
shùnzhe	順著/顺着	to go along	4.10
shuōbudìng	說不定/说不定	perhaps	6.32
shuōlái huà cháng	說來話長/说来话长	it's a long story	7.6
shǔtiáor	薯條兒/薯条儿	french fries	5.13
sìhéyuàn	四合院	compound with houses around a courtyard	4.16
suàn	算	to regard as	8.32
suān-tián-	酸甜苦辣	all flavors	5.1

kǔ-là suǒwèi	所謂/所谓	so-called	5.19

T

tàijíquán	太極拳/太极拳	a kind of shadow-boxing	4.19
tàikōngrén	太空人	astronaut	3.41
tàitai	太太	wife, Mrs.	9.1
tán liàn'ài	談戀愛/谈恋爱	to court	6.35
tán*	彈/弹	to play	10
tào	套	set	2.24
tǎojià-huánjià	討價還價/讨价还价	to bargain	4.36
tǎolùn	討論/讨论	to discuss, discussion	2.11
tǎoyàn	討厭/讨厌	to be disgusted with	6.19
tī*	踢	to kick	6
tiānliàng	天亮	daybreak	4.3
tiáojiàn	條件/条件	condition	9.39
tiāotì	挑剔	nitpicky, to nitpick	5.8
tiàowǔ	跳舞	to dance	4.22
tídào	提到	to mention	3.4
tīngdào	聽到/听到	to hear	1.36
tīnghuà	聽話/听话	obedient	9.5
tíxǐng	提醒	to remind	8.8
tóngshí	同時/同时	(at) the same time	9.26
tóngyì	同意	to agree	8.37
tūrán	突然	suddenly	1.25
tóuténg	頭疼/头疼	headache	2.33
tǔbāozi	土包子	rube, hick	6.26
tuō'érsuǒ*	托兒所/托儿所	child-care center	9

W

wàihào	外號/外号	nickname	7.12
wǎndiǎn	晚點/晚点	late	1.20
wǎng	網/网	net	6.3
wǎngyǒu	網友/网友	net pal	6.4
wánquán	完全	completely	6.6
wěidà	偉大/伟大	great	6.37
wèile	爲了/为了	for	9.39

wéiyī	唯一	only, sole	2.32
wènhǎo	問好/问好	to say hello to	4.44
wénhuà	文化	culture	8.13
wēnróu	溫柔	gentle and soft	7.30
wénxué	文學/文学	literature	8.3
wúlùn	無論/无论	no matter what/how, regardless of	2.17
wùhuì	誤會/误会	to mis-understand	3.5

X

xì	系	department (in a college)	2.35
xiàbān*	下班	to get off work	9
xián	鹹/咸	salty	5.23
xián	嫌	to dislike the fact that	8.23
xiāng	香	fragrant	5.6
xiǎng	響/响	to ring	4.5
xiāng'ài	相愛/相爱	to love each other	8.41
xiāngfǎn	相反	opposite	3.14
xiǎngjiā	想家	to be homesick	3.29
xiànglái	向來/向来	always, all along	6.27
xiǎngniàn	想念	to miss	5.5
xiǎngshòu	享受	to enjoy, enjoyment	5.40
xiǎngxiàng	想像/想象	to imagine, to fancy	2.19
xiāngxìn	相信	to believe	1.3
xiànmù	羨慕/羡慕	to envy	5.38
xiànshí	現實/现实	reality	10.6
xiǎofàn	小販/小贩	peddler	4.33
xiǎohuǒzi	小伙子	young fellow	7.36
xiǎoqi	小氣/小气	stingy	9.22
xiāoxi	消息	news	1.37
xiǎoyìsi*	小意思	small token of kindly feelings	3
xiàoyuán	校園/校园	campus	4.2
xiàqí	下棋	to play chess	4.23
xiézi	鞋子	shoes	6.30
xìngfú	幸福	happiness	8.40
xíngli	行李	luggage	1.21
xīnqíng	心情	mood	3.26
xīnshì	心事	weight on	6.34

		one's mind, worry	
xǐwǎn	洗碗	to do dishes	9.24
xūyào	需要	to need	9.11
xuǎnzé	選擇/选择	to select	10.17
xuéxí	學習/学习	to study, to learn	1.43

Y

yán*	鹽/盐	salt	5
yǎnghuo	養活/养活	to support	10.40
yángrén	洋人	foreigner	8.9
yǎnjìng	眼鏡/眼镜	glasses	7.21
yánjiūshēng	研究生	graduate student	7.27
yǎnxì	演戲/演戏	to act in a play	6.15
yào	藥/药	medicine	5.3
(yào)burán	(要)不然	otherwise	1.7
yàobushì	要不是	if it were not for, but for	1.15
yàomìng	要命	extremely	3.23
yī	醫/医	medical science	8.21
yìbān	一般	ordinary	5.18
yíbèizi	一輩子/一辈子	all one's life	10.2
yīfu	衣服	clothing	6.29
-yǐlái	以來/以来	since	2.39
yímín	移民	emigrant/immigrant	5.29
yìng*	硬	hard	2
yǐngxiǎng	影響/影响	influence, to influence	8.12
yíngyǎng*	營養/营养	nutrition	5
yìnxiàng	印象	impression	7.4
yīnyuèhuì*	音樂會/音乐会	concert	7
yīnyuèjiā*	音樂家/音乐家	musician	10
yìqǐ	一起	together, in the same place	8.10
yíqiè	一切	all, everything	1.13
yìshù	藝術/艺术	art	10.38
yìsi	意思	meaning	3.12
yíxiàzi	一下子	at once	7.22
yǐzi	椅子	chair	2.22
yúkuài	愉快	happy	3.30

yóu	油	oily, oil	5.14
yǒudeshì	有的是	to have plenty of	5.37
yóujiàn	郵件/邮件	postal matter, mail	1.34
yǒumíng	有名	famous	4.29
yōumò	幽默	humorous	7.34
yǒuqù	有趣	interesting	1.40
yóuyǒng	游泳	to swim	10.28
yǒuyòng	有用	useful	2.9
yuán	圓/圆	round	3.2
yuánlái	原來/原来	as it turns out	1.28
yuànyi	願意/愿意	to be willing	9.38
yuányīn	原因	reason	8.34
yùdào	遇到	to run into	7.10
yuèbǐng	月餅/月饼	moon cake	3.36
yuēhuì	約會/约会	to date	6.23
yuèliang	月亮	moon	3.1
yuèqiú	月球	moon	3.42
yùnqi	運氣/运气	fortune, luck	9.25
yùshì*	浴室	bathroom, shower room	2
yùxí	預習/预习	to prepare lessons before class	2.16

Z

zài…kànlái	在…看來/在…看来	in sb.'s view	10.12
zàishuō	再說/再说	besides	8.17
zànchéng	贊成/赞成	to approve	10.37
zǎodiǎn	早點/早点	breakfast	4.7
zhá	炸	to deep-fry	5.12
zhǎngdà	長大/长大	to grow up	8.4
zhàogù	照顧/照顾	to look after	9.30
zhēng	爭/争	to fight for	9.20
zhěnglǐ	整理	to put in order	9.8
zhěngqí	整齊/整齐	neat, tidy	2.27
zhī jiān	之間/之间	between	6.5
zhǐyào	只要	so long as	4.30
zhíyè	職業/职业	occupation	9.31
Zhōngguóchéng	中國城/中国城	Chinatown	5.25
zhōngjiān	中間/中间	center, middle	4.13

zhòngshì	重視/重视	to value	10.24
zhǔ	煮	to cook, to boil	9.41
zhù*	祝	to wish	3
zhuǎnjī	轉機/转机	to change planes	1.17
zhǔfù	主婦/主妇	housewife	9.34
zhuōzi	桌子	table, desk	2.21
zhùyì	注意	to pay attention to	4.24
zìcóng	自從/自从	since	4.1
zìrán	自然	natural, naturally, nature	3.10

zìxíngchē	自行車/自行车	bicycle	4.9
zìyóu	自由	freedom, free	9.14
zǒngzhī	總之/总之	in a word	9.15
zūnjìng	尊敬	to respect	10.35
zúqiú	足球	soccer	6.12
zuì	醉	drunk	3.33
zuìhòu	最後/最后	final	4.37
zuòjiā	作家	writer	10.9

◎ By English

English	Pinyin	Character	L
A			
about	guānyú	關於/关于	3.38
accept, to	jiēshòu	接受	8.29
achievement	chéngjiù	成就	9.35
act in a play, to	yǎnxì	演戲/演戏	6.15
activity	huódòng	活動/活动	2.14
actually (not)	bìng	並/并	3.11
advise, to	quàn	勸/劝	8.20
affair	shìqing	事情	1.44
after all	dàodǐ	到底	7.1
age	niánjì	年紀/年纪	6.8
agree, to	tóngyì	同意	8.37
air-condition-ing	kōngtiáo	空調/空调	2.29
alarm clock	nàozhōng	鬧鐘/闹钟	4.4
all	yíqiè	一切	1.13
all along	xiànglái	向來/向来	6.27
all flavors	suān-tián-kǔ-là	酸甜苦辣	5.1
all one's life	yíbèizi	一輩子/一辈子	10.2
almost	jīhū	幾乎/几乎	3.34
always	lǎo	老	7.16
always	xiànglái	向來/向来	6.27
and so on	děngděng	等等	2.43
and so on	shénmede	什麼的/什么的	10.29

English	Pinyin	Character	L
any	rènhé	任何	9.17
apply for, to	shēnqǐng	申請/申请	1.8
apply make-up, to	huàzhuāng*	化妝/化妆	6
approve, to	zànchéng	贊成/赞成	10.37
argument	dàolǐ	道理	10.39
art	yìshù	藝術/艺术	10.38
as it turns out	yuánlái	原來/原来	1.28
astronaut	tàikōngrén	太空人	3.41
at once	yíxiàzi	一下子	7.22
at present	mùqián	目前	10.15
B			
background	bèijǐng	背景	8.14
bargain, to	tǎojià-huánjià	討價還價/讨价还价	4.36
bathroom	yùshì*	浴室	2
bear hardship, to	chīkǔ	吃苦	5.42
beautiful	měi	美	3.37
bed	chuáng	床	2.20
beef noodles	niúròumiàn	牛肉麵/牛肉面	4.28
believe, to	xiāngxìn	相信	1.3
benefit	hǎochu	好處/好处	10.11
besides	zàishuō	再說/再说	8.17
between	zhī jiān	之間/之间	6.5
bias	piānjiàn	偏見/偏见	8.30
bicycle	zìxíngchē	自行車/	4.9

		自行车	
boil, to	zhǔ	煮	9.41
bookworm	shūdāizi	書呆子/	7.28
		书呆子	
bottle	píng	瓶	4.40
bottoms up	gānbēi	乾杯/干杯	3.32
boy	nánháir	男孩兒/	7.14
		男孩儿	
boyfriend	duìxiàng	對象/对象	6.40
brag, to	chuīniú	吹牛	7.29
break up, to	fēnshǒu	分手	8.25
breakfast	zǎodiǎn	早點/早点	4.7
brilliant	jīngcǎi	精彩	6.16
bring, to	dài	帶/带	9.9
burn the midnight oil, to	kāi yèchē	開夜車/ 开夜车	10.43
burn, to	shāo	燒/烧	9.10
business	shāng	商	10.42
but for	yàobushì	要不是	1.15
by all means	qiānwàn	千萬/千万	6.2

C

café	kāfēiguǎn	咖啡館/ 咖啡馆	7.7
cake	dàngāo	蛋糕	5.15
call names, to	mà	罵/骂	7.18
campus	xiàoyuán	校園/校园	4.2
can't do sth. in time	láibují	來不及/ 来不及	1.16
cannot but	bùdé bù	不得不	5.35
career	shìyè	事業/事业	9.40
carpet	dìtǎn	地毯	2.28
Caucasian	báirén	白人	8.2
celebrate a festival, to	guòjié	過節/过节	3.27
celebrate, to	qìngzhù	慶祝/庆祝	3.21
center	zhōngjiān	中間/中间	4.13
century	shìjì	世紀/世纪	6.36
chair	yǐzi	椅子	2.22
change planes, to	zhuǎnjī	轉機/转机	1.17
change, to	gǎi	改	7.25
child-care	tuō'érsuǒ*	托兒所	9

center		托兒所	
Chinatown	Zhōngguó chéng	中國城/ 中国城	5.25
circumstances	qíngkuàng	情況/情况	1.39
clean	gānjìng	乾淨/干净	2.26
clear	qīngchu	清楚	6.31
clothing	yīfu	衣服	6.29
common	gòngtóng	共同	6.9
competent	nénggàn	能幹/能干	9.4
completely	wánquán	完全	6.6
compound with houses around a courtyard	sìhéyuàn	四合院	4.16
concept	guānniàn	觀念/观念	8.26
concerned about, to be	guānxīn	關心/关心	3.15
concerning	duì…lái shuō	對…來說/ 对…来说	3.9
concert	yīnyuèhuì*	音樂會/ 音乐会	7
condition	tiáojiàn	條件/条件	8.39
conservative	bǎoshǒu	保守	8.27
consider, to	kǎolǜ	考慮/考虑	9.13
consult, to	shāngliang	商量	9.18
contact, to	liánxì	聯繫/联系	10.44
content	nèiróng	內容	2.6
contribution	gòngxiàn	貢獻/贡献	10.41
cook, to	shāo	燒/烧	9.10
cook, to	zhǔ	煮	9.41
cordial	qīnqiè	親切/亲切	3.7
court, to	tán liàn'ài	談戀愛/ 谈恋爱	6.35
culture	wénhuà	文化	8.13
curious	hàoqí	好奇	2.37
customs	hǎiguān	海關/海关	1.23

D

dance, to	tiàowǔ	跳舞	4.22
dare, to	gǎn	敢	1.2
date, to	yuēhuì	約會/约会	6.23
day(s)	rìzi	日子	5.30
daybreak	tiānliàng	天亮	4.3

deep breathing exercises	qìgōng	氣功/气功	4.20
deep-fry, to	zhá	炸	5.12
department (in a college)	xì	系	2.35
desk	zhuōzi	桌子	2.21
difficulty	kùnnán	困難/困难	8.43
direction	fāngxiàng	方向	4.12
director	dǎoyǎn	導演/导演	6.18
disappointed, to become	shīwàng	失望	6.33
discrimination	qíshì	歧視/歧视	8.11
discuss, to	tǎolùn	討論/讨论	2.11
discussion	tǎolùn	討論/讨论	2.11
disgusted with, to be	tǎoyàn	討厭/讨厌	6.19
dislike the fact that, to	xián	嫌	8.23
distance	jùlí	距離/距离	6.7
divorce	líhūn	離婚/离婚	8.16
do dishes, to	xǐwǎn	洗碗	9.24
Do you mean to say that …?	nándào	難道/难道	10.1
do, to	gǎo	搞	1.18
domestic	guónèi	國內/国内	3.28
draw pictures, to	huàhuàr	畫畫兒/画画儿	10.26
dress/make up, to	dǎbàn	打扮	6.28
drunk	zuì	醉	3.33
dry	gān	乾/干	5.11

E

each	gè	各	2.2
eat beancurd, to	chī dòufu*	吃豆腐	5
economical	jīngjì	經濟/经济	5.41
education	jiàoyù	教育	10.25
eldest child (in a family)	lǎodà*	老大	3
electronic	diànzǐ	電子/电子	1.33
elegant and composed	dàfāng	大方	6.42
emigrant	yímín	移民	5.29
enchanted	mí	迷	6.11

with, to be encouragement	gǔlì	鼓勵/鼓励	9.7
enjoy, to	xiǎngshòu	享受	5.40
enthusiastic	rèqíng	熱情/热情	3.6
envy, to	xiànmù	羨慕/羡慕	5.38
equal	píngděng	平等	9.43
etc.	děngděng	等等	2.43
ethnic Chinese of other nationalities	Huáyì	華裔/华裔	8.22
even	gèng	更	1.41
even	jíshǐ	即使	10.14
even if	jiùsuàn	就算	10.13
even if/though	jíshǐ	即使	10.14
everything	yíqiè	一切	1.13
exception	lìwài	例外	10.7
excuse	jièkǒu*	藉口/借口	9
exercise, to	huódòng	活動/活动	2.14
exit	chūkǒu	出口	1.24
extra-curricular	kèwài	課外/课外	2.13
extremely	-jíle	極了/极了	2.31
extremely	yàomìng	要命	3.23

F

fall in love with, to	àishang	愛上/爱上	8.1
familiar	shúxī	熟悉	1.26
family	jiātíng	家庭	9.33
famous	chūmíng*	出名	10
famous	yǒumíng	有名	4.29
famous school	míngxiào	名校	10.32
fancy, to	xiǎngxiàng	想像/想象	2.19
fashionable	shímáo	時髦/时髦	6.41
fat	pàng	胖	5.34
favorable impression	hǎogǎn	好感	6.21
feel happy, to	kāixīn	開心/开心	5.43
feeling	gǎnjué	感覺/感觉	3.13
feeling	gǎnqíng	感情	7.41
festival	jiérì	節日/节日	3.22
fight for, to	zhēng	爭/争	9.20
figure out, to	cāidào	猜到	7.38

film	piānzi	片子	6.14
final	zuìhòu	最後/最后	4.37
fish, to	diàoyú*	釣魚/钓鱼	6
food	shíwù	食物	5.9
for	wèile	爲了/为了	9.39
for example	bǐfāng shuō	比方說/比方说	4.26
foreigner	lǎowài	老外	1.1
foreigner	yángrén	洋人	8.9
fortunately	hǎozài	好在	1.6
fortune	yùnqi	運氣/运气	9.25
fragrant	xiāng	香	5.6
free	zìyóu	自由	9.14
freedom	zìyóu	自由	9.14
french fries	shǔtiáor	薯條兒/薯条儿	5.13
from childhood	cóngxiǎo	從小/从小	10.8
fruit	shuǐguǒ	水果	4.35
full	bǎo	飽/饱	5.27
funny	kěxiào	可笑	4.32
future	jiānglái	將來/将来	8.15
future	qiántú	前途	10.10

G

gain weight, to	fāpàng*	發胖/发胖	5
generation gap	dàigōu	代溝/代沟	8.28
gentle and soft	wēnróu	溫柔	7.30
get off work, to	xiàbān*	下班	9
get up (from bed), to	qǐchuáng	起床	4.6
get used to, to	shìyìng	適應/适应	2.3
girl	gūniang	姑娘	7.32
girl	nǚháir	女孩兒/女孩儿	9.19
girlfriend	duìxiàng	對象/对象	6.40
give up, to	fàngqì	放棄/放弃	9.28
glasses	yǎnjìng	眼鏡/眼镜	7.21
go abroad, to	chūguó	出國/出国	1.4
go along, to	shùnzhe	順著/顺着	4.10
grade	chéngjī/jì	成績/成绩	10.19
graduate student	yánjiūshēng	研究生	7.27

greasy	nì	膩/腻	5.16
great	wěidà	偉大/伟大	6.37
great demand, in	rèmén	熱門/热门	10.18
green	shēng	生	5.21
grow up, to	zhǎngdà	長大/长大	8.4

H

half a kilogram	jīn*	斤	4
ham	huǒtuǐ*	火腿/火腿	5
hand over, to	jiāo	交	2.42
handle, to	bàn	辦/办	1.11
handsome	shuài	帥/帅	7.3
happiness	xìngfú	幸福	8.40
happy	yúkuài	愉快	3.30
happy lot	fúqi*	福氣/福气	3
hard	yìng*	硬	2
have a hard time (doing sth.), to	hǎoróngyì	好容易	9.29
have diarrhea, to	lādùzi	拉肚子	4.42
have plenty of, to	yǒudeshì	有的是	5.37
headache	tóuténg	頭疼/头疼	2.33
health	jiànkāng	健康	5.4
hear, to	tīngdào	聽到/听到	1.36
hen's egg	jīdàn*	雞蛋/鸡蛋	5
hick	tǔbāozi	土包子	6.26
high in rank	gāojí	高級/高级	4.31
history	lìshǐ	歷史/历史	2.34
hobby	àihào	愛好/爱好	6.10
holiday	jiérì	節日/节日	3.22
homesick, to be	xiǎngjiā	想家	3.29
household duties	jiāwù	家務/家务	9.6
housekeeper	bǎomǔ*	褓姆/保姆	9
housewife	zhǔfù	主婦/主妇	9.34
how	duō(me)	多(麼)/多(么)	6.24
however	què	卻/却	2.30
humorous	yōumò	幽默	7.34
husband	fū	夫	9.42

I

stand , to			
mood	xīnqíng	心情	3.26
moon	yuèliang	月亮	3.1
moon	yuèqiú	月球	3.42
moon cake	yuèbǐng	月餅/月饼	3.36
mother	mǔqin	母親/母亲	9.36
Mrs.	tàitai	太太	9.1
musician	yīnyuèjiā*	音樂家/音乐家	10
must	bìxū	必須/必须	9.3
must	fēi...bùkě	非…不可	8.7
mutually	hùxiāng	互相	7.26

N

nanny	bǎomǔ*	褓姆/保姆	9
native place	lǎojiā*	老家	3
natural(ly)	zìrán	自然	3.10
nature	zìrán	自然	3.10
neat	zhěngqí	整齊/整齐	2.27
need, to	xūyào	需要	9.11
nervous	jǐnzhāng	緊張/紧张	7.8
net	wǎng	網/网	6.3
net pal	wǎngyǒu	網友/网友	6.4
new word	shēngcí	生詞/生词	2.7
news	xiāoxi	消息	1.37
nickname	wàihào	外號/外号	7.12
nitpick, to	tiāotì	挑剔	5.8
nitpicky	tiāotì	挑剔	5.8
no good, to be	bùxíng	不行	5.10
no matter what/how	wúlùn	無論/无论	2.17
no wonder	guàibude	怪不得	5.39
no wonder	nánguài	難怪/难怪	7.39
not only	búdàn	不但	5.31
not only... but also...	jì...yě	既…也	3.19
nutrition	yíngyǎng*	營養/营养	5

O

obedient	tīnghuà	聽話/听话	9.5
occupation	zhíyè	職業/职业	9.31
often	chángcháng	常常	2.10
Oh!	ài	唉	7.40
oil	yóu	油	5.14

oily	yóu	油	5.14
on the contrary	fǎn'ér	反而	5.32
only	wéiyī	唯一	2.32
only if	chúfēi	除非	5.24
oppose, to	fǎnduì	反對/反对	8.33
opposite	duìmiàn	對面/对面	7.11
opposite	xiāngfǎn	相反	3.14
order (dishes), to	diǎn*	點/点	5
ordinary	yìbān	一般	5.18
ordinary times, in	píngshí	平時/平时	8.5
originally	běnlái	本來/本来	6.22
other people	biérén	別人	10.34
otherwise	(yào)burán	(要)不然	1.7
otherwise	fǒuzé	否則/否则	5.26
overdone	lǎo	老	5.22
ox	niú	牛	7.13

P

painter	huàjiā	畫家/画家	10.36
pan	guōzi*	鍋子/锅子	5
park	gōngyuán	公園/公园	4.17
particular about, to be	jiǎngjiu	講究/讲究	5.28
pass an entrance examination, to	kǎoshàng	考上	10.31
pass, to	guò	過/过	1.22
pass, to	jīngguò	經過/经过	4.14
passport	hùzhào	護照/护照	1.9
past	guòqù	過去/过去	2.41
pastry	diǎnxīn	點心/点心	5.17
patient	bìngrén*	病人	8
pay attention to, to	zhùyì	注意	4.24
peddler	xiǎofàn	小販/小贩	4.33
perhaps	shuōbudìng	說不定/说不定	6.32
piano	gāngqín	鋼琴/钢琴	10.27
pick sb. up, to	jiē	接	1.30
ping-pong	pīngpāng qiú*	乒乓球	6
place	dìfang	地方	2.18

plane ticket	jīpiào	機票/机票	1.12
play chess, to	xiàqí	下棋	4.23
play, to	tán*	彈/弹	10
plump	pàng	胖	5.34
polite	lǐmào	禮貌/礼貌	3.8
polite, to be	kèqi	客氣/客气	3.35
poor wretch	qióngguāngdàn	窮光蛋/穷光蛋	10.3
postal matter	yóujiàn	郵件/邮件	1.34
practical	shíjì*	實際/实际	10
prepare lessons before class, to	yùxí	預習/预习	2.16
professor	jiàoshòu*	教授	1
program	jiémù	節目/节目	6.20
prospects	qiántú	前途	10.10
public	gōnggòng*	公共	2
public	gōnglì	公立	10.20
public square	guǎngchǎng	廣場/广场	4.11
put in order, to	zhěnglǐ	整理	9.8

Q

quarrel, to	chǎojià	吵架	7.15
quit (a job), to	cí*	辭/辞	9

R

raw	shēng	生	5.21
real man, a	nánzǐhàn	男子漢/男子汉	9.23
reality	xiànshí	現實/现实	10.6
realize, to	shíxiàn	實現/实现	10.22
really	shízài	實在/实在	3.17
reason	dàolǐ	道理	10.39
reason	yuányīn	原因	8.34
receive, to	shòudào	受到	8.31
recognize, to	rèn	認/认	7.23
regard as, to	suàn	算	8.32
regardless of	bùguǎn	不管	2.36
regardless of	wúlùn	無論/无论	2.17
rely on, to	kào	靠	6.39
remind, to	tíxǐng	提醒	8.8
respect, to	zūnjìng	尊敬	10.35

respectfully submitted	jìngshàng	敬上	8.44
restaurant	cāntīng	餐廳/餐厅	4.27
result	jiéguǒ	結果/结果	4.41
review, to	fùxí	複習/复习	2.15
ride, to	qí	騎/骑	4.8
ring, to	xiǎng	響/响	4.5
roast, to	shāo	燒/烧	9.10
romantic love	àiqíng	愛情/爱情	8.19
round	yuán	圓/圆	3.2
row boat, to	huáchuán*	划船	6
rube	tǔbāozi	土包子	6.26
rug	dìtǎn	地毯	2.28
run into, to	yùdào	遇到	7.10
run, to	pǎo	跑	1.29

S

salt	yán*	鹽/盐	5
salty	xián	鹹/咸	5.23
same place, in the	yìqǐ	一起	8.10
same time, (at) the	tóngshí	同時/同时	9.26
satisfied	mǎnyì	滿意/满意	7.5
say hello to, to	wènhǎo	問好/问好	4.44
scold, to	mà	罵/骂	7.18
scorn, to	kànbuqǐ	看不起	9.21
secret	mìmì	秘密	6.1
see, to	jiàndào	見到/见到	7.2
see, to	jiànmiàn	見面/见面	1.38
select, to	xuǎnzé	選擇/选择	10.17
sense	dàolǐ	道理	10.39
sense	gǎn	感	10.21
sentence	jù	句	8.6
sentence pattern	jùxíng	句型	2.8
set	tào	套	2.24
shadow-boxing, a kind of	tàijíquán	太極拳/太极拳	4.19
sharp	lìhai	厲害/厉害	9.16
shoes	xiézi	鞋子	6.30
shoot film, to	pāi	拍	6.13
shop	shāngdiàn	商店	4.25
shortcoming	máobing	毛病	7.24

shower room	yùshì*	浴室	2
simple meal	jiācháng biànfàn	家常便飯/家常便饭	3.31
simply	gēnběn	根本	3.24
since	-yǐlái	以來/以来	2.39
since	zìcóng	自從/自从	4.1
situation	qíngkuàng	情況/情况	1.39
small token of kindly feelings	xiǎoyìsi*	小意思	3
smooth	shùnlì	順利/顺利	1.14
so long as	zhǐyào	只要	4.30
so much so that	shènzhì	甚至	2.23
so-called	suǒwèi	所謂/所谓	5.19
soccer	zúqiú	足球	6.12
sofa	shāfā	沙發/沙发	2.25
soft	ruǎn*	軟/软	2
sole	wéiyī	唯一	2.32
sound	shēngyīn	聲音/声音	1.27
soy sauce	jiàngyóu*	醬油/酱油	5
spareribs	páigǔ	排骨	7.17
speak, to	jiǎng	講/讲	8.38
spouse	àiren	愛人/爱人	9.2
spouse	àiren*	愛人/爱人	3
star	míngxīng	明星	6.17
stingy	xiǎoqi	小氣/小气	9.22
stir-fry, to	chǎo	炒	5.20
story	gùshi	故事	3.40
stress, to	jiǎng	講/讲	8.38
study abroad, to	liúxué	留學/留学	1.5
study, to	xuéxí	學習/学习	1.43
submit (a letter), to	shàng	上	1.35
succeed, to	chénggōng	成功	10.33
success	chénggōng	成功	10.33
successful	chénggōng	成功	10.33
suddenly	tūrán	突然	1.25
support, to	yǎnghuo	養活/养活	10.40
surmount, to	kèfú	克服	8.42
swim, to	yóuyǒng	游泳	10.28

T

table	zhuōzi	桌子	2.21
take a bird on a stroll, to	liùniǎo*	遛鳥/遛鸟	4
take a picture, to	pāi	拍	6.13
taken in, to be	shàngdàng	上當/上当	4.38
tale	gùshi	故事	3.40
taste, to	cháng	嚐/尝	5.2
teaching materials	jiàocái	教材	2.4
tell the truth, to	lǎoshíshuō	老實說/老实说	5.7
tense	jǐnzhāng	緊張/紧张	7.8
test	kǎoshì	考試/考试	10.30
test, to	kǎoshì	考試/考试	10.30
text	kèwén	課文/课文	2.12
textbook	kèběn	課本/课本	2.5
thick	hòu	厚	7.20
thin	shòu	瘦	5.33
think over, to	kǎolǜ	考慮/考虑	9.13
think that, to	rènwéi	認爲/认为	6.25
thirsty	kě	渴	4.39
tidy	zhěngqí	整齊/整齐	2.27
tired of	nì	膩/腻	5.16
together	yìqǐ	一起	8.10
too busy to deal with	mángbuguòlái	忙不過來/忙不过来	3.25
tough	lǎo	老	5.22
turn, to	guǎi*	拐	4

U

understand, to	liǎojiě	了解	3.16
understand, to	lǐjiě	理解	10.23
unexpectedly	jìngrán	竟然	7.9
unexpectedly	jūrán	居然	2.40
unexpectedly	méixiǎngdào	沒想到	2.38
useful	yǒuyòng	有用	2.9

V

value, to	zhòngshì	重視/重视	10.24
vegetarian, to be a	chīsù*	吃素	5
view	kànfǎ	看法	8.36
visa	qiānzhèng	簽證/签证	1.10

W

warm	rèqíng	熱情/热情	3.6
way	bànfǎ	辦法/办法	3.20
wear (glasses, etc), to	dài	戴	7.19
weight on one's mind	xīnshì	心事	6.34
welcome, to	huānyíng*	歡迎/欢迎	1
well-known	chūmíng*	出名	10
what	duō(me)	多(麼)/多(么)	6.24
wife	qīzi	妻子	9.37
wife	tàitai	太太	9.1
willing, to be	yuànyi	願意/愿意	9.38
wish, to	zhù*	祝	3
with great difficulty	hǎoróngyì	好容易	9.29

with regard to	guānyú	關於/关于	3.38
wok	guōzi*	鍋子/锅子	5
woman	nǚxìng	女性	9.32
won't leave without seeing each other	bú jiàn bú sàn*	不見不散/不见不散	7
wordy	luōsuo	囉嗦/罗嗦	8.24
work, to	gōngzuò	工作	9.7
worry	xīnshì	心事	6.34
write in reply, to	huíxìn	回信	10.4
writer	zuòjiā	作家	10.9

Y

yet	què	卻/却	2.30
young	niánqīng	年輕/年轻	7.35
young fellow	xiǎohuǒzi	小伙子	7.36

Index 2. Characters

◎ By Pinyin

Pinyin	Character	S #	L. C #
A			
ài	愛/爱	13	6.4
B			
bái	白	5	8.10
bān	般	10	5.20
bān	班	10	7.20
bǎo	飽/饱	13	5.12
bǎo	保	9	8.7
bēi	杯	8	3.4
bèi	背	9	8.3
biàn	便	9	3.11
bìng	並/并	8	3.17
bù	步	7	4.14
C			
cāi	猜	11	7.17
cǎi	彩	11	6.12
cān	餐	16	4.12
chéng	城	9	5.14
chéng	成	6	10.11
chǔ	楚	13	6.10
chǔ	處/处	11	10.9
chuáng	床	7	2.8
cōng	聰/聪	17	7.8
D			
dāi	呆	7	7.7
dài	戴	17	7.10
dài	代	5	8.19
dàn	蛋	11	5.9
dǎo	導/导	15	6.5
dì	地	6	2.14
dù	肚	7	4.17
F			
fǎn	反	4	3.20
fēi	啡	11	7.16
fū	夫	4	9.3
fú	福	13	8.6
fǒu	否	7	5.17
fù	婦/妇	11	9.4
G			
gān	乾/干	11	3.1
gǎn	感	13	1.1
gǎn	敢	12	1.5
gàn	幹/干	13	9.14
gāng	鋼/钢	16	10.19
gǎo	搞	13	1.16
gè	各	6	2.13
gēn	根	10	3.16
gū	姑	8	7.3
gōng	公	4	4.5
gōng	功	5	10.16
gù	故	9	3.12
gù	顧/顾	21	9.6
guā	瓜	5	4.11
guài	怪	8	5.13
guān	關/关	19	1.12
guān	觀/观	25	8.14
guǎng	廣/广	14	4.20
H			
hǎi	海	10	1.11
hé	合	6	4.10
hé	何	7	9.2
hù	互	4	7.5
huà	化	4	8.2
huà	畫/画	12	10.14
huó	活	9	3.14
huǒ	伙	6	7.18
J			
jí	極/极	12	2.15
jí	級/级	9	4.4
jí	即	7	10.1
jī	績/绩	17	10.12
jì	既	9	3.18
jì	濟/济	17	5.15
jì	紀/纪	9	6.2
jià	架	9	7.12

◎ **By Stroke Number**

S #	Pinyin	Character	L. C #
3			
3	tǔ	土	6.19
3	zhī	之	9.20
4			
4	fǎn	反	3.20
4	fū	夫	9.3
4	gōng	公	4.5
4	hù	互	7.5
4	huà	化	8.2
4	piàn	片	6.8
4	qiè	切	1.15
5			
5	bái	白	8.10
5	dài	代	8.19
5	gōng	功	10.16
5	guā	瓜	4.11
5	lì	立	10.15
5	mín	民	5.16
5	mù	目	6.20
5	mǔ	母	9.5
5	shī	失	6.13
5	shǐ	史	2.12
5	shì	世	6.1
5	yìn	印	7.13
5	yóu	由	9.11

S #	Pinyin	Character	L. C #
5	zhǔ	主	9.13
6			
6	chéng	成	10.11
6	dì	地	2.14
6	gè	各	2.13
6	hé	合	4.10
6	huǒ	伙	7.18
6	jiàn	件	8.20
6	jiāo	交	2.19
6	rèn	任	9.1
6	shǒu	守	8.8
6	zhì	至	2.6
7			
7	bù	步	4.14
7	chuáng	床	2.8
7	dāi	呆	7.7
7	dù	肚	4.17
7	fǒu	否	5.17
7	hé	何	9.2
7	jí	即	10.1
7	kè	克	8.17
7	kùn	困	8.18
7	lì	利	1.17
7	yíng	迎	1.8
7	zú	足	6.18
8			

S #	Pinyin	Character	L. C #
8	bēi	杯	3.4
8	bìng	並/并	3.17
8	gū	姑	7.3
8	guài	怪	5.13
8	jū	居	2.18
8	kā	咖	7.15
8	lì	例	10.18
8	mìng	命	3.15
8	pāi	拍	6.7
8	shǐ	使	10.2
8	wù	物	5.8
8	xìng	幸	8.5
8	yú	於/于	3.19
8	yǒng	泳	10.4
8	yù	育	10.20
8	zhēng	爭/争	9.15
8	zhù	注	4.16
9			
9	bǎo	保	8.7
9	bèi	背	8.3
9	biàn	便	3.11
9	chéng	城	5.14
9	gù	故	3.12
9	huó	活	3.14
9	jí	級/级	4.4

13	chǔ	楚	6.10	14	wǔ	舞	4.8	17	jī	績/绩	10.12
13	fú	福	8.6	14	xū	需	9.17	17	jì	濟/济	5.15
13	gǎn	感	1.1	14	yǎn	演	6.6	17	jiǎng	講/讲	5.19
13	gàn	幹/干	9.14	**15**				17	lǐ	禮/礼	3.3
13	gǎo	搞	1.16	15	dǎo	導/导	6.5	17	lián	聯/联	10.13
13	jiě	解	3.10	15	kào	靠	6.16	17	shēng	聲/声	1.18
13	shì	試/试	10.17	15	lùn	論/论	2.10	**18**			
13	tiào	跳	4.7	15	qù	趣	1.4	18	qí	騎/骑	4.15
13	xián	嫌	8.16	15	shú	熟	1.9	18	qí	歧	8.13
13	yè	業/业	9.10	**16**				18	zhí	職/职	9.9
13	yuán	圓/圆	3.13	16	cān	餐	4.12	**19**			
13	yuán	園/园	4.6	16	gāng	鋼/钢	10.19	19	guān	關/关	1.12
14				16	lì	歷/历	2.11	19	jìng	鏡/镜	7.11
14	guǎng	廣/广	4.20	16	mà	罵/骂	7.6	19	quàn	勸/劝	8.11
14	jīng	精	6.11	16	qīn	親/亲	3.6	19	yì	藝/艺	10.7
14	là	辣	5.4	16	shāo	燒/烧	9.19	19	yuàn	願/愿	9.16
14	mǎn	滿/满	7.14	16	xǐng	醒	8.12	**21**			
14	qí	齊/齐	2.4	16	xìng	興/兴	1.3	21	gù	顧/顾	9.6
14	rèn	認/认	6.15	16	zhěng	整	2.3	**25**			
14	suān	酸	5.1	**17**				25	guān	觀/观	8.14
14	wù	誤/误	3.9	17	cōng	聰/聪	7.8				
				17	dài	戴	7.10				

Index 3. Sentence Patterns

◎ By Pinyin

Pinyin	Character	English	Lesson. Grammar #
B			
běnlái/yuánlái…xiànzài/ hòulái…	本來/原來…現在/後來…	formerly/originally…now/later on	6.2
bìng/bìngméi(yǒu)…	S 並不/並沒（有）V	don't (emphatic); actually not	3.2
búdàn…lián…yě…	S不但V$_1$O$_1$，連O$_2$也V$_1$ 不但S$_1$V，連S$_2$也V	Not only does S V$_1$, S even V$_1$O$_2$ Not only S$_1$V, even S$_2$ V	10.1
búdànméi/bù…fǎn'ér…	不但沒/不…反而…	not only not…, on the contrary…	5.4
bùdébù…	不得不V	cannot not V; must	5.5
bùguǎn …dōu (bù/ méi)	不管…，S都（不/沒）	No matter how/what/why/when…,	2.1
bùhuìbù…	不會不V	will certainly V	5.5
bùnéngbù…	不能不V	can't help but; must	5.5
C			
cái…jiù… gāng…jiù…	S才V$_1$(Time Span)(S)就V$_2$ S剛V$_1$(Time Span)(S)就V$_2$	It's only …, S already…	5.6
chū…lái	S V（不）出(O)來 S （沒）V出(O)來	S cannot V out (O) S didn't V out (O)	7.4
chúfēi…fǒuzé	除非…否則…	Unless…, otherwise…	5.2
chúfēi…(yào)bùrán …, chúfēi	除非…要不然… …，除非	S will (not) do sth. unless…	
cónglái bù… cónglái méi…guò…	S 從來不V S 從來沒V過 (O)	S never V S has never V-ed	6.5
D			
(dāng)…(de) shí(hou)	（當）…（的）時（候）	by the time	9.1
dàodǐ…(ne)	S到底QW（呢）	actually…?	7.1
de(rén)…, …de(rén)…	V$_1$ (O$_1$) 的（人）V$_1$ (O$_1$)， V$_2$ (O$_2$) 的（人）V$_2$ (O$_2$)	some do…, others do…	4.4
(děng)…(le) (yǐhòu) zài…	S （等）V$_1$（了）（以後）再V$_2$	S does V$_2$ after V$_1$	9.4
duì… de yìnxiàng…	A對B的印象Adj	A's impression of B is…	7.2
duì …yǒu…de yìnxiàng	A對B有Adj的印象	A has a …impression of B	
gěi …liúxiàle…de yìnxiàng	B給A留下了Adj的印象	B leaves A with a…impression	
duì…gǎn xìngqù	A對B(Adv)感興趣	A is interested in B	1.6
duì…láishuō	對 sb. 來說	as for, as to…	3.1
duō (me) …a	多（麼）Adj 啊	How…! So...!	6.4
F			
fēi (yào/děi)…bùkě	S非（要/得）VO不可	S absolutely must VO	8.2

G

gēn...(méi)yǒu guānxi	A跟B（沒）有關係	A is (not) related to B	2.6
	A跟B有一點關係	A is somewhat related to B	
	A跟B沒有什麼關係	A is not really related to B	
	A跟B一點關係也沒有	A is not related to B at all	
gēnběn (jiù) bù/méi...	根本（就）不/沒…	simply not...; not at all	3.4
guānyú	S V 關於…的N	...about N	3.6
	S是關於…的	Concerning, in regard to...	
	關於…,S…	Regarding..., S	

H

hǎo(bù)róngyì cái...	S 好（不）容易才V	S went through great difficulty before S finally V	9.5
hǎozài...(yàoburán)...	好在(S)…（要不然）…	fortunately...(otherwise)	1.1

J

jì...yě	S 既…也…	not only...but also...; both...and...	3.3
jì...yòu...	S 既…又…		
jìngrán (bù/méi)...	S竟然（不/沒）V	unexpectedly; surprisingly	7.3
jíshǐ..., ...yě...	即使S…,(S)也…	Even if..., still...	10.4
jiù hǎole/jiù xíngle/jiù kěyǐle	（只要）…就好了	... then it will be all right	6.6
	（只要）…就行了	... then it should be fine	
	（只要）…就可以了		
jiùshì	A就是B	A is B	1.5
jiùshì...de yìsi	A就是B的意思	A means/refers to B	1.5
jiùsuàn..., ...yě...	就算S…,(S)也…	Even if..., still...	10.4
jūrán	S$_1$（沒想到）S$_2$居然V	Surprisingly S$_2$...	2.5

L

lái	這 time span （以）來	over the past (days/months, etc.)	2.4
lián...dōu (bù/méi)..., gèngbiéshuō...le	連A都（不/沒）…,更別說B了	even A is..., not to mention/let alone B	10.6

M

mángzhe	S 忙著V (O)	S is busy V-ing	4.2
(měi)dāng...(de) shí(hou)	（每）當…（的）時（候）	whenever	9.1

N

nánguài/guàibùdé...	難怪/怪不得 S...	No wonder...	7.6
nǎr/nǎli...(ne)?	(S) 哪兒/哪裏…（呢）？	How can it be the case that...? S surely doesn't...	3.5
néng...jiù...	能V…就V	If one can possibly V...then V...	8.1
néng shǎo..., jiù shǎo...	能少…,就少	If one can avoid...then don't...	
néng bù..., jiù bù...	能不…,就不		

Q

qiānwàn bié/yào/děi...	S千萬別/要/得V	by all means; must (not) V	6.1
qǐlái...	V起來 Adj	when, in the doing of V	1.3

R

reduplication	N: A→AA;AB→AABB	pluralizer	4.3
	Adj: A→AA;AB→AABB	intensifier	
	V: A→AA;AB→ABAB	to do sth. briefly or casually	
rènhé…dōu…	任何O(S)都V	any, every	9.3

S

shènzhì hái yǒu…	…甚至還有N	…even has N…	2.2
shènzhì hái yào…	…甚至還要V	…even needs to V…	
shènzhì (lián)…dōu…	…甚至(連)NP都V	…even …	
shòudào (…de) qíshì	A受到(B的)歧視	A is discriminated against by B	8.5
shòudào (…de) yǐngxiǎng	A受到(B的)影響	A is influenced by B	
shòudào (…de) huānyíng	A受到(B的)歡迎	A is welcomed by B	
suīrán…(dànshì/kěshì)…què	雖然S…(但是/可是)(S)卻	although…., …yet	2.3

W

wèi…	A為B Adj/VO	A Adj/VO for the sake of B	8.6
wèile	為了A, B	In order to A, B…	9.6
shì wèile…	B是為了A	B is for the cause of A	
wèideshì…	B為的是A	B is for the cause of A	
wúlùn… dōu (bù/ méi)	無論…, S都(不/沒)	no matter how/what/why/when…,	2.1

X

xián…	A嫌B sth. negative	A dislikes/minds/complains of B…	8.4
xiàng…zhèyàng/nàyang…de	像…這樣/那樣Adj的N	(Adj) somebody/something like this/that…	5.3
xiàng…zhème/nàme…de…	像…這麼/那麼Adj的N		
xiànglái (bù)…	S 向來(不)V	S always V/never V	6.5

Y

yàobùrán…yě/jiù	…, 要不然S也/就…	If it were not for a regrettable condition, one would otherwise do something else.	7.5
yàobù…yě/jiù	…, 要不S也/就…		
bùrán…yě/jiù	…, 不然S也/就…		
(yào)bushì…jiùshì…(zài)bùrán jiù…	(要)不是…就是…(再)不然就…	If it isn't…then it's…or else it's…	5.1
yàobushì… (zǎo)jiù	要不是S₁…, S₂(早)就	If it had not been for…, then…	1.2
yě/dōu bù…jiù…	S(O)V也/都不V就	S…without V-ing	4.6
yě/dōu méi…jiù…	S(O)V也/都沒V就		
yīlái…èrlái…(sānlái…)	一來…二來… (三來…)	First…, second …, third…	6.3
yǐwéi…nǎzhīdào	(以為)…哪知道…	(thought)…who knew that…	1.4
yǐwéi…qíshí	(以為)…其實…	(thought)…actually…	1.4
yǐwéi…yuánlái	(以為)…原來…	(thought)…it turns out that…	1.4

Z

zài…de…xià	在sb.的N下	under /with sb's N	10.5
zài…kànlái	在 sb. 看來	in one's view/opinion, …	10.3
zài…shàng/fāngmiàn	在N上/方面	in terms of N; in the area of N	10.5

zàishuō…	···，再說···	moreover; furthermore	8.3
zhe	S V$_2$著O$_2$ V$_1$O$_1$	S does V$_1$ O$_1$ while doing V$_2$ O$_2$ (as accompanying action)	4.2
zhe wánr (de)	V著玩兒(的)	V for fun	10.2
zhǐyào…, …jiù…	只要S···，(S) 就··· S只要···，(S) 就···	as long as…, then; provided that…	4.5
zìcóng…yǐhòu,…jiù	自從 S$_1$ VO 以後，(S$_1$)/S$_2$ 就	ever since…, (S$_1$)/S$_2$…	4.1
zǒngzhī…	···，總之···	to sum up; in short	9.2

◎ By Function

Function	Pinyin	Character	English	Lesson. Grammar #
A				
actual reality behind a false assumption, expressing the	yǐwéi…nǎzhīdào	(以爲)···哪知道···	(thought)…who knew that…	1.4
actual reality behind a false assumption, expressing the	yǐwéi…qíshí	(以爲)···其實···	(thought)…actually…	1.4
actual reality behind a false assumption, expressing the	yǐwéi…yuánlái	(以爲)···原來···	(thought)…it turns out that…	1.4
additional reason, introducing an	zàishuō…	···，再說···	moreover; furthermore	8.3
argument with a concessive clause, making an	suīrán…(dànshì/kěshì) …què	雖然S···(但是/可是)(S) 卻	although…. , …yet	2.3
C				
capacity to act, expressing the	néng…jiù… néng shǎo…, jiù shǎo néng bù…, jiù bù	能V···就V 能少···，就少 能不···，就不	If one can possibly V…then V… If one can avoid…then don't…	8.1
change of state, expressing a	chū…lái	S V(不)出(O)來 S (沒)V出(O)來	S cannot V out (O) S didn't V out (O)	7.4
changed circumstances, expressing	běnlái/yuánlái… xiànzài/hòulái…	本來/原來…現在/後來…	formerly/originally…now/later on	6.2
concessive argument, making a	jíshǐ…, …yě…	即使S···，(S)也···	Even if…, still…	10.4
concessive argument, making a	jiùsuàn…, …yě…	就算S···，(S)也···	Even if…, still…	10.4
concurrent actions, expressing	mángzhe	S 忙著V (O)	S is busy V-ing	4.2

expressing a

G

general status through a range of alternatives, describing a	(yào)bushì…jiùshì… (zài)bùrán jiù…	（要)不是…就是…(再) 不然就…	If it isn't…then it's…or else it's…	5.1

H

| habitual action or untried experience, expressing | cónglái bù… cónglái méi…guò… | S 從來不V S 從來沒V過 (O) | S never V S has never V-ed | 6.5 |
| habitual action, expressing | xiànglái (bù)… | S 向來(不)V | S always V/never V | 6.5 |

I

impact of something, expressing the	shòudào (…de) qíshì shòudào (..de) yǐngxiǎng shòudào (de) huānyíng	A受到(B的)歧視 A受到(B的)影響 A受到(B的)歡迎	A is discriminated against by B A is influenced by B A is welcomed by B	8.5
impression, expressing one's	duì… de yìnxiàng duì…yǒu…de yìnxiàng gěi…liúxiàle..deyìnxiàng	A對B的印象Adj A對B有Adj的印象 B給A留下了Adj的印象	A's impression of B is… A has a…impression of B B leaves A with a… impression	7.2
indefinite, expressing the	rènhé…dōu…	任何O(S)都V	any, every	9.3
indispensable condition, expressing an	chúfēi…fǒuzé chúfēi…(yào)bùrán …, chúfēi	除非…否則… 除非…要不然… …，除非	Unless…, otherwise… S will (not) do sth. unless…	5.2
inevitability with double negation, expressing	bùhuìbù…	不會不V	will certainly V	5.5
interest in sth., expressing	duì…gǎn xìngqù	A對B(Adv)感興趣	A is interested in B	1.6
invariability, expressing	bùguǎn …dōu (bù/ méi)	不管…，S都(不/沒)	No matter how/what/why/when…,	2.1
invariability, expressing	wúlùn… dōu (bù/ méi)	無論…，S都(不/沒)	no matter how/what/why/when…,	2.1

L

| light-hearted action, expressing | zhe wánr (de) | V著玩兒(的) | V for fun | 10.2 |

M

| minimal requirement, expressing a | jiù hǎole/jiù xíngle/jiù kěyǐle | （只要)…就好了 （只要)…就行了 （只要)…就可以了 | … then it will be all right … then it should be fine | 6.6 |

N

| necessary condition, expressing a | zhǐyào…, …jiù… | 只要S…，(S)就… S只要…，(S)就… | As long as…, then; provided that… | 4.5 |
| necessity or obligation with | fēi (yào/děi)…bùkě | S非(要/得)VO不可 | S absolutely must VO | 8.2 |

Index 4. Idioms

Pinyin	Character	English	Lesson #
bá miáo zhù zhǎng yà miáo zhù zhǎng	拔苗助長/拔苗助长 揠苗助長/揠苗助长	to try to help the shoots grow by pulling them upward—to spoil things by excessive enthusiasm; nothing before its time	10
Dōngshī xiào pín	東施效顰/东施效颦	Dong Shi, an ugly woman, knitting her brows in imitation of the famous beauty Xi Shi, only to make herself uglier—blind imitation with ludicrous effect	6
duōduō yì shàn	多多益善	the more, the better	3
húlún tūn zǎo	囫圇吞棗/囫囵吞枣	to swallow dates whole—lap up information without digesting it; read without understanding	5
jǐng dǐ zhī wā	井底之蛙	a frog in a well—a person with a very limited outlook	1
qí mào bù yáng	其貌不揚/其貌不扬	undistinguished in appearance—said of someone ugly in appearance	7
xiāzi mō xiàng	瞎子摸象	blind people groping for the shape of an elephant—can't get the whole picture of sth.	4
yúgōng yí shān	愚公移山	The Foolish Old Man removed the mountains—if there is a will, there is a way.	2
yuèxià lǎorén	月下老人	the old man under the moon—the god who unites persons in marriage; matchmaker	8
zì zhī zhī míng	自知之明	the wisdom of knowing oneself—said of a person who has an accurate appraisal of himself	9